**Dan Kieran** has written for the *Guardian*, the *Observer*, the *Telegraph* and the *Sunday Times* and edited the *Sunday Times*'s bestselling *Crap* trilogy: *Crap Towns*, *Crap Jobs* and *Crap Holidays*. He appears regularly on BBC Radio's *Five Live*, *Newsnight* and the *Daily Politics* programme and is deputy Editor of *The Idler*. He lives in London in a small flat with his small family and loves big adventures.

www.**booksattransworld**.co.uk

*Also by Dan Kieran*

The Idler Book of Crap Holidays
The Idler Book of Crap Jobs

The Idler Book of Crap Towns (co-author)
The Idler Book of Crap Towns II (co-author)
The Myway Code (co-author)
How Very Interesting!: Peter Cook's Universe and
All That Surrounds It (co-author)

# I FOUGHT THE LAW

### Dan Kieran

## BANTAM PRESS

LONDON  ·  TORONTO  ·  SYDNEY  ·  AUCKLAND  ·  JOHANNESBURG

TRANSWORLD PUBLISHERS
61–63 Uxbridge Road, London W5 5SA
a division of The Random House Group Ltd
www.booksattransworld.co.uk

First published in Great Britain
in 2007 by Bantam Press
a division of Transworld Publishers

This book is substantially a work of non-fiction based on the life, experiences and
recollections of the author. In some limited cases names of people, places, dates,
sequences or the detail of events have been changed solely to protect the privacy of
others. The author has stated to the publishers that, except in such minor respects not
affecting the substantial accuracy of the work, the contents of this book are true.

A CIP catalogue record for this book
is available from the British Library.

ISBN 9780593058084

Addresses for Random House Group Ltd companies outside the UK
can be found at: www.randomhouse.co.uk
The Random House Group Ltd Reg. No. 954009

The Random House Group Ltd makes every effort to ensure that the papers used in its
books are made from trees that have been legally sourced from well-managed and credibly
certified forests. Our paper procurement policy can be found at:
www.randomhouse.co.uk/paper.htm

Typeset in12.5/15.5 Ehrhardt by
Falcon Oast Graphic Art Ltd.

Printed and bound in Great Britain by
Clays Ltd, Bungay, Suffolk

2 4 6 8 10 9 7 5 3 1

For Rachel and Wilf

'Albion: Britain or England, unrecorded'

*Concise Oxford English Dictionary*

# Contents

# Introduction

Voltaire once quipped, 'I do not agree with what you have to say, but I'll defend to the death your right to say it.' The use of a quotation from a Frenchman to define what it means to be British may offend some, but then that neatly sums up the contradictory nature of the British people. Sadly, today no-one can claim that Voltaire's words speak for this country any more. On 1 August 2005, to the widespread shrugging of shoulders across the land, it became illegal to hold a spontaneous political demonstration outside the House of Commons. The nation's apathy towards losing the right to free speech at the seat of its government, something supposedly as intrinsic to this 'green and pleasant land' as warm beer and Freddie Flintoff, posed the question what, if anything, does Britain actually stand for today?

Twenty miles from London, along the Thames, you will find a field opposite an island in the river. The field contains a monument erected by the American Bar Association. In the field next to it there is a memorial garden to John F. Kennedy to commemorate his role in the Civil Rights movement. Why on earth, you may imagine, are there American monuments in fields by the Thames? There are no other monuments. There is nothing to commemorate anything British. Perhaps an important figure in American history was born there? Nope. The site is far more important to the American people than that. On that unmarked island, in 1215, something was written down that over five hundred years later became the Fifth Amendment of the American Bill of Rights. 'No freeman shall be taken, imprisoned ... or in any other way destroyed ... except by the lawful judgment of his peers, or by the law of the land. To no-one will we sell, to none will we deny or delay, right or justice.' For Americans, this became, 'No person shall ... be deprived of life, liberty, or property, without due process of law.' The original document was, of course, the Magna Carta.

Nearly eight hundred years ago King John was held to account by a group of rebel barons who demanded a charter of liberties to protect England from his unfair and erratic behaviour. That was when the principle of a power higher than the sovereign was established. That higher power was the rule of law. The Magna Carta has since been described as the most potent symbol of freedom under law in western civilization. It is something, you would imagine, that even our embarrassed nation would manage to be proud of. At the very least you'd think we might have one of those blue plaques down there some-where. 'Liberty under law started here' perhaps, nailed to a nearby tree. It would be nice to have something to commemorate the birth of British freedom, but there is nothing.

Today, Britain, and the western world, hosts another dominant power that behaves pretty much as it likes and there seems little chance that it will be forced to adhere to a higher law. This dominant power is not even bound by any laws of basic morality. In fact, according to the American Bar Association[1] and the late Milton Friedman, one of the most influential economists of all time, it is actually illegal for a corporation to act altruistically or for the good of their community, country or, heaven forbid, the world.[2] A CEO who puts the interests of the community ahead of the company's shareholders could actually be sent to prison. You see King John had nothing on the modern-day corporation.

If we all lived in a corporation rather than a country, then at least we would reap the benefits of this immoral logic. But unlike corporations, most societies consider basic morality to be something of value. The government, meanwhile, is doing all it can to help corporations turn us into consumers of Britain rather than citizens of it. So I thought I'd better go out and find the Britain of our dreams, sometimes known as Albion, so we can all go and live there instead.

The original idea for this book was nothing like the one you now hold in your hands. It was supposed to be a guide to some of the most absurd ancient legislation still on the statute book. I'd had this great idea to go round the country on a crime spree, breaking as many silly old laws as I could find, for your amusement. There are hundreds of these ridiculous laws still in force in Britain. For example, to this day it is illegal to flag down a London taxi if you have the plague. In Chester you can't shoot a Welshman with a bow and arrow before midnight, but you can after midnight. It's also against the law to beat a carpet in the Metropolitan Police District. Neither can you carry a sack of soot along a path in a place called Congleton, and it is still unlawful to get within a few hundred yards of the Queen without wearing socks. The list goes on and on. However, in the process of researching these laws I couldn't help noticing another glut of legislation that seemed even more ludicrous. Great, you may think, but no. You see, there was one problem. Most of our silly laws have trickled onto the statute book over centuries, but this particular set had all come from our current government. And when you meet a man who got arrested after eating a cake with 'Freedom of Speech' written on it in icing, and someone else who has a criminal record for holding a banner made of fridge packing in Parliament Square that had 'Freedom of Speech' written on it in biro, the idea of breaking the Adulteration of Tea Act of 1776 starts to seem a little frivolous. Of course, once I started lifting up this legal concrete slab in the garden of England all sorts of other creepy crawlies emerged that cast doubt on the health of the nation. So this book became, quite by co-incidence, a very different thing entirely.

Of course, on paper Britain is doing rather well for itself. We have enjoyed unparalleled economic prosperity since Labour came to power. There are more billionaires in the UK today than ever before, there are more shiny things to spend our money on than you could possibly imagine, and, despite widely being portrayed as America's lapdog, we do appear to have some standing in the world at large. But who else lives in Britain apart from all the high-flyers, over-achievers and entrepreneurs who have helped this great land to secure membership of the G8, the club for the most economically powerful nations on earth? How does Britain seem to everybody else who lives here? You know, the other ones. You and me. Those of us floundering in the highest levels of debt in Europe; the ones afraid of poverty in retirement; the ones being forced to work forty-plus hours a week with only four weeks off a year; the ones terrified of violent crime, of their children being adversely affected by the MMR jab; the ones suffering from depression because they can't handle the stress of their jobs; the ones Carol Vorderman is hoping will consolidate their debt so she can keep her no doubt lucrative advertising contract; even those who aren't born yet, hoping to live here one day too, the future generations who will be around when the icecaps start to melt and vast swathes of this country vanish under the ocean.

To find out, I went on a journey around Britain to meet some of the people still fighting for Albion among the uniform high streets, no-go estates, monochrome offices and shopping malls of corporate Britain. I found an unlikely selection of eccentrics to guide me on my journey who, incidentally, weren't fighting against the government or the corporations profiting from this land; they were fighting *for* something instead, which is a much more powerful incentive. On one level they were simply fighting for themselves and their communities; on another they were fighting for every one of us hoping to enjoy Britain's future. People like the pensioners who let off stink bombs to force an extension to a public inquiry. The hairy history expert who got paid to have custard pies thrown at his beard by Ant and Dec. The man who dresses like Chaplin's tramp and keeps getting arrested outside Downing Street because we no longer have the right to remain silent either. The world-famous fisherman with a penchant for firing home-made rockets into space. The man who enjoys howling like a wolf in his back garden. The Robin Hood of the squatting world who gets into empty buildings and hands the keys over to homeless people who can't afford anywhere to live. The woman living on the roof of a bus station in Derby. An activist who organizes picketing campaigns outside the homes of drug dealers. The ex-MI5 agent now reduced to peddling conspiracy theories to complete strangers about 9/11. Along with encouragement from Billy Childish (one of Kurt Cobain's favourite musicians), Gavin Hills, Arthur Pendragon, George Orwell and William Blake. Britain needs these people.

It needs them all because things are getting a bit Monty Python down in Albion. From the towns we live in to the countryside itself, the cult of overwork and over-consumption is spreading like a disease, bringing with it a greater dependence on anti-depressants and huge numbers of stress-related health problems and tightening us all in an ever-growing grip of fear. Fear of violent crime, fear of poverty in retirement, fear of global warming and, of course, the greatest of them all: the fear of terrorism. Today, the wonder of Albion, if it ever existed, certainly seems to have been obliterated by Britain plc.

And it's not just an ideological shift being discussed over cigars and whisky by the political fraternity, it's a reality that's changing every aspect of our daily lives. As you'll soon discover, anyone who actually wants to behave like a citizen of this country, rather than just a consumer of it, quickly finds themselves on the wrong side of the law.

Dan Kieran
Brockley
Autumn 2006

# CHAPTER 1

My descent into Britain's shady, criminal underworld began at the Young Men's Christian Association on Fitzroy Square in London, where I attended a meeting with a group of protesters, five of whom had been arrested for eating a picnic in Parliament Square.

Now, picnicking in Parliament Square may not strike you as much of a crime. Back in 1992 when Tony Blair was a lowly member of the opposition he pledged that Labour would be 'tough on crime and tough on the causes of crime'; few could have guessed that picnicking was what he had in mind. After all, even Marie Antoinette was prepared to let the peasants eat cake. But this was no ordinary picnic. The picnickers were eating cakes with the words 'Freedom of Speech', 'Freedom to Protest' and 'Save our Speech' written on them in icing.

According to Section 132 of the Serious and Organised Crime and Police Act (SOCPA), it is illegal for anyone to protest within a thousand metres of Parliament without the prior consent of the police. This designated area encompasses parts of the South Bank, Trafalgar Square, Downing Street and Parliament Square itself. The law doesn't do a very good job of defining what it means by a 'demonstration', so a single person wearing a T-shirt with 'Freedom' written on it who wanders within a kilometre of the seat of government could be arrested for holding an illegal protest. Neither does the Act specify in which directions the thousand-metre zone applies, so if you find yourself on the Jubilee Line below Westminster having a heated political debate, passing overhead in a light aircraft talking about the pensions crisis, or even on the London Eye pointing out all the rubbish on the streets below, make sure there aren't any police around or you may end up spending the night at Charing Cross police station.

Now you may think that it doesn't matter if the law is a bit weak when it comes to defining what is or isn't a protest or a demonstration. You may trust the courts never actually to convict anyone for something as innocuous as wearing a T-shirt, or pinning a slogan on their jumper, because that would be ridiculous. Maybe you trust the government's motives despite the authoritarian nature of this law. But how would you feel if the courts *did* convict someone for standing in Parliament Square with a banner that read 'Freedom of Speech'? What if someone *was* convicted for reading out the names of dead British soldiers by the Cenotaph outside Downing Street? Would that be something to worry about? Ask Maya Evans. She got convicted at Bow Street Magistrates Court for that last one. She's now got a criminal record, for remembering Britain's war dead.

In Parliament's defence, not all MPs were convinced that making a spontaneous act of protest within a kilo-metre of the House of Commons illegal was a very well-thought-out proposal. During the Second Standing Committee for SOCPA on 12 October 2005 the Conservative MP Edward Garnier commented that the terms of Section 132 were so vague that a single person walking across Westminster Bridge wearing a badge with 'Bollocks to Blair'[3] written on it could be deemed to be holding a political demonstration and would therefore be breaking the law.

So why would the government want to remove the right to protest near Parliament? Withholding basic rights of protest and free speech from your citizens isn't something undertaken on a whim. After all, we don't have rights because the government deigns to give them to us. The whole point of 'rights' is that they are ours to begin with; if an elected government wants to take them from us they'd better have clear, compelling arguments for doing so. Other governments of the world that have recently banned spontaneous protest include Zimbabwe, the Ivory Coast and the Sudan. You can't imagine the government would want to join a club with those three nations on a whim. So what possible reason could there have been to force them into such drastic action?

Section 132 was added to SOCPA in an attempt to evict one slightly deranged man, Brian Haw, after he'd spent over four years camped outside the House of Commons opposing the government, first on sanctions being imposed on Iraq and then on the Iraq war itself. It's hard to believe that a British government would amend a law in order to criminalize protest simply to put an end to one man's peaceful, non-violent demonstration outside the seat of our democracy, but that's exactly what they did.

On 25 March 2004 the Speaker in the House of Commons, Mr Michael Martin, told the front bench that he was losing patience with them for not dealing with Brian's protest. Apparently, Brian affected the running of the House whenever he expressed his views through a megaphone in the street outside. Some MPs said you could barely hear him, and even when you could it was impossible to understand what he was saying; others remarked that he wasn't as loud as Big Ben, which was far more annoying, chiming as it did every half hour. (Unlike Brian Haw, Big Ben wasn't spouting forth anti-government sentiments, so the great clock was allowed to stay.) Peter Hain MP replied to the Speaker that David Blunkett, the then Home Secretary, would bring before the House proposals to end the problem when they were ready, and attempted to allay the Speaker's fears that the issue would drag on. Mr Martin, who isn't the biggest fan of freedom of choice, having gone on the record to oppose abortion, replied, 'I want it dealt with as quickly as possible.'

On 3 November Peter Hain confirmed to the House that current legislation did not give the police the power they needed to control demonstrations and protests outside Parliament and promised new legislation that would, in the form of an addendum to the Serious and Organised Crime and Police Act. This Act was designed to give police increased powers to track down drug lords, human traffickers and gangsters; exactly why people protesting outside Parliament should be named alongside such criminals was far from clear to many MPs. Labour's John McDonnell commented, 'I accept the right of Brian Haw to make his statement out there. As soon as we start to undermine that process of free speech it becomes a slippery slope to intolerance.'[4] But not all MPs took the threat to freedom of speech so seriously, especially the architect of Section 132 himself, David Blunkett, who joked that introducing the thousand-metre exclusion zone just to get rid of Brian Haw was 'a sledgehammer to crack a nut'.[5]

Cross-party opinion began to unite against the government's attempts to force the amendment through. David Davis, the shadow Home Secretary, told the BBC, 'This is a contempt of democracy and a contempt of people's right to protest.'[6] Mark Oaten, the Liberal Democrat home affairs spokesman at the time, also saw it as a threat to democracy: 'This government has shown itself ready to play fast and loose with hard-won British freedoms.'[7]

Despite such objections the bill was passed into law on 1 August 2005, but not before Brian Haw's legal team had challenged it. They went to the High Court on 23 July. Outside the court, Brian told the press, 'For centuries, British citizens have had the right to protest outside the mother of parliaments. Now this is to be left to the diktat of the police.'[8] Three days later the High Court ruled that because Brian's protest pre-dated the Act – it had started in 2001 – he would not have to leave the designated area outside Parliament after all. So, the one man the law had been targeted to remove could now stay there indefinitely, while everyone else living in Britain would now have to seek permission from the police if they wanted to hold a demonstration within a thousand metres of their Parliament.

You would assume that the government would have been ashamed of the way they had tried to manipulate the parliamentary process simply to remove an irritating man with whose opinions they did not agree. You would imagine that once a High Court judge has told the government that their badly drafted law doesn't add up they would admit it was a terrible mistake and confirm to the public that those involved would resign. After all, you can't go around making up laws because you don't like the behaviour of one man when a High Court judge has ruled that he is simply exercising his right to free speech. Not in a democracy, at any rate. Think of the outcry! The public wouldn't stand for it. The government would be forced to back down.

The newspapers certainly got excited for a few days. Most people assumed the government would be forced to apologize – that's if they thought about it at all. Then we all got on with our lives and forgot about it. Socrates once said that people who work too hard don't have the time to fulfil their responsibilities as friends or citizens. Perhaps it was that. Perhaps it was a jaded sense of resignation drawing yet another veil between the people and their government. Whatever it was, the Cabinet didn't budge. They simply changed their reason for pushing through the amendment. From the moment Brian's eviction from Parliament Square was ruled out by the High Court the government stopped talking about Brian Haw when any-one asked them about the exclusion zone. It had nothing to do with Brian Haw, they said. Oh no. It was never about him, it was about something else entirely. It was all about security.

If you ask government spokespeople today about the protest exclusion zone they will lower their eyes, adopt grave expressions, utter their magic word 'terrorism' and expect you to walk away. If you press them for more information they will adopt even graver expressions, shake their heads and inform you that, tragically, the world has changed. If you continue to press them they will look around suspiciously before leaning in and whispering in your ear, 'You'll just have to trust us. We've seen classified information; we know what we're doing. The world has changed.'

It's changed all right. It's changed to the point that you can now get a criminal record for reading out the names of dead British soldiers by the Cenotaph.

Geoff Hoon, the Defence Secretary at the time, thought that anyone who found Maya Evans's arrest frightening was being 'hysterical'.[9] I find it frightening, but I don't consider myself to be 'morbidly or uncontrollably emotional' about it, which is how 'hysterical' is described in the dictionary. It's an interesting word to have chosen. Perhaps someone who advocates criminalizing an act of remembrance because of the threat of 'terrorism' is the one being morbidly or uncontrollably emotional.

No-one wants to trivialize the anguish and pain suffered by those who have been killed in, or who have lost loved ones to, an act of terrorism. Sudden inexplicable death and brutal murder must be an agonizing burden to bear. The media coverage of 7 July and accounts by bloodied and terrified commuters will be remembered by all who read, heard and witnessed them. And no-one would want to exploit the pain of the families concerned. Except, it seems, the government.

Terrorism is a frightening word. It's bandied around as the justification for ID cards, the increase in stop-and-search incidents, the illegal protest zone in the Serious Organised Crime and Police Act and many other laws that pop up later in this book, but how frightening is it in reality? The simple answer is that it's as frightening as you and the government allow it to be.

Lots of worrying stories about terrorism have appeared in the press since the attacks on the World Trade Center in New York on 11 September 2001. Old Trafford, the home of the richest, most widely known football club in the world, Manchester United, was recently at risk from an act of terrorism according to the frenzied coverage in the newspapers. That story turned out to be based on the fact that the police found posters of Old Trafford and a ticket to a United game in the bedroom of an asylum seeker who was arrested on suspicion of terrorism. The idea of the Theatre of Dreams being blown up was so horrifying that it became the headline story on that night's ITN news. The fact that the man in question was later released without facing a single charge received little publicity. The police and the government made no attempt to allay the public's fears when the story was blown out of proportion. They knew they had the wrong man but couldn't say anything because it would jeopardize their legal case.

Then there was the chemical weapons factory in London where terrorists were producing the deadly toxin ricin. Chemical weapons had arrived in Britain, or they had according to the *Daily Mirror*, whose front page featured a skull and crossbones over a map of the country under the headline THEY'RE HERE!, and the *Sun*, which led with the terrifying headline FACTORY OF DEATH. Tony Blair told reporters, 'As the arrests . . . show, this danger is present and real, and with us now, and its potential is huge.'[10] When the Prime Minister confirms the existence of terrorists making chemical weapons in London, we all get scared. You see, Tony has access to secret information, so we all slept a little less easily in our beds when he confirmed our worst fears. But there was no ricin. The police and the government knew there was no ricin within three days of the arrests (the mysterious substance turned out to be Brylcreem) but they didn't put the public's mind at ease for another two years because they didn't want to undermine their legal case in advance by revealing that they had no evidence. Needless to say, when the charges were dropped against four of the five defendants and it became clear that the ricin ring didn't exist after all, the *Sun* and the *Mirror* forgot to lead with the headline DON'T WORRY, THERE WAS NO RICIN HERE to make us feel safer.

No-one is suggesting that the government actively seeks out ways to terrify the public; newspaper editors are quite happy to do that by themselves. Anything goes if you're in the middle of a tabloid circulation war, but it all feeds into the greatest fear of all. The fear we all harbour. The fear that stops us shouting too loudly when the government suggests legislation that takes our freedom away. The fear that makes us all more and more dependent on our leaders, giving them ever greater power until they start to behave with impunity.

The unspoken fear we all share is a terrorist getting his hands on a nuclear or chemical bomb and choosing to use either of them in Britain. London vanishing underneath a mushroom cloud, or a chemical attack on the tube – that's what everyone is really afraid of. That's why so few of us grumble when the government start taking liberties. When Tony Blair stated 'The rules of the game have changed', we all knew that that was what he meant. But how serious is the risk of such a large-scale assault on London? After all, if Saddam Hussein couldn't get his hands on weapons of mass destruction what chance does a religiously challenged maniac from Dudley have? Or, for that matter, a millionaire on kidney dialysis who lives in a cave?

The only recent use of chemical weapons was on Tokyo's underground system by the Aum Shinrikyo sect in 1995. They spent billions of dollars building a massive chemical factory to produce nerve gas that killed a total of twenty-seven people, twelve of whom died on that one attack on the underground. Tragic though these cases were, they bore no relation in terms of scale to the scenarios the words 'chemical' and 'weapons' can conjure up if we let our imaginations run wild. Suddenly the thought of a group of men holed up in a small flat in Wood Green with a few bottles of Domestos and some hair wax doesn't seem so frightening. As for the nuclear threat, Dr Theodore Rockwell, a nuclear expert, stated in 2004, 'I don't think it [a dirty bomb] would kill anybody . . . You'll have trouble finding a serious report that would claim otherwise . . . The American Department of Energy has simulated a dirty bomb explosion and they calculated that the most exposed individual would get a fairly high dose [of radiation], not life-threatening.'[11] It should be noted that in order to arrive at that level of exposure the test results were based on the assumption that the individual remained at the site of the attack for an entire year.

And then there's Chernobyl. It's hard to imagine that a dirty bomb could kill more people than that reactor melt-down in 1986. Despite only two people being killed in the actual explosion, the world became convinced that those living in the region would die of horrible radiation cancers in the decades that followed. In fact, Chernobyl has been cited as the direct cause of only fifty-six deaths over the last twenty years, according to the UN agency the World Health Organization, despite press projections at the time running up to the 200,000 mark. And forty-seven of those were men from the clean-up crew who went to the site immediately after the explosion.[12] Nuclear weapons, of course, are a different matter entirely, but only renegade states determined to throw their weight around can afford those. Terrorists will find them much harder to get hold of – providing we don't sell them any, of course.

At the moment the most pressing risk to the public from terrorism has come from our government's response to it. We might not know much when it comes to terrorism, but we do know some things. We know that there is no way you can stop a terrorist detonating a nuclear or chemical bomb by searching anti-government activists outside the Labour Conference. Even advocates of ID cards – including Charles Clarke, the Home Secretary at the time –

admit they would not have stopped the London bombings of 7 July. Only a lobotomized man in a straitjacket would expect to find evidence of terrorism by searching the bicycle of a thirteen-year-old girl outside an American military base, but that didn't stop her being searched under the Terrorism Act. And people eating a picnic in Parliament Square every Sunday for months on end? They're pretty unlikely to be secretly planning to throw anthrax at Tony Blair's passing limousine, especially when you can watch every second of their protest live on CCTV. It's also a pretty safe guess that if someone really does want to detonate a conventional bomb badly enough, no legislation that takes away our freedom will prevent it from happening.

We certainly can't search every single cargo ship or flight that comes into this country to look for weapons of mass destruction. You can't stop and search everyone in the country every single day of the year in case they're carrying a bomb. On the other hand, you might be able to stop a terrorist getting his hands on a weapon like that in the first place through intelligence and diplomacy. You might be able to stop him wanting to do it in the first place by examining your nation's foreign policy, ending arms sales to some of the most hostile regions on earth, or putting money into the research of new energy resources so that we aren't reliant for fuel on an area of the world controlled by dictators. You might even be able to knock a dent in terrorism and lessen global instability by removing subsidies that protect a few thousand jobs at home but consign developing countries to the endless grip of biblical poverty. Terrorism is inevitable as long as we are dependent on cheap oil for energy and have to safeguard that oil supply through military action. But the power to solve these problems lies with our government. When it comes to the war on terror all we, as individuals and communities, can do is fight terrorism in our minds. How frightened we should actually be depends on evidence and statistics, and as enemies go, in terms of its body count, terrorism is actually pretty pathetic. In 2005 terrorism killed fifty-two people in Britain. Each one of those deaths was as violent and tragic as each of the nine deaths that occur every single day on Britain's roads. Fifty-seven times as many people died on the roads in 2005 as died as a result of terrorism. So even in the worst year we've known for terrorist-related fatalities since 1945, you should find the car in your garage fifty-seven times more frightening than the threat of a suicide bomber. Moreover, the fifty-two deaths caused by terrorism in 2005 represented a 5,200 per cent increase on the number of deaths in the UK from terrorism the year before, which was zero. Even if you took a figure of fifty-two deaths as the annual average it would still be dwarfed by the 132,000 killed every year by cancer, the 3,500 who commit suicide, the 1,300 killed by asthma, the 1,168 killed by MRSA and the 550 killed by flu.[13]

It's even outdone by the seventy people killed every year while at home doing DIY.[14] It's unlikely that the government would attempt to introduce measures to fight the evil menace that is B&Q but the facts prove that we should be more afraid of putting up shelves than of suicidal religious fanatics. Take ladders alone. Ladders kill one person every single week and another 100,000 people a year are so seriously injured as a result of using them that they require hospital treatment. Perhaps the government's next piece of legislation will force us all to live in bungalows. Ridiculous? Not when you consider the danger to public health posed by a flight of stairs.

You may well laugh, but stairs are a true modern foe, ten times as likely to kill you than terrorists were in the year Britain suffered its worst attack since the Second World War. So where, we must conclude, is the government's war on stairs? And if you really want to live in fear of something that is statistically terrifying, try being afraid of your job. According to the UN, work-related deaths kill over two million people a year around the world. That's two 9/11-scale disasters every single day, and far more than the 650,000 people killed globally every year by war.

Our reaction to terrorism is disproportionate in other ways too. After 9/11, I distinctly remember being asked to hold a three-minute silence for the victims of the Twin Towers disaster rather than the one-minute silence we have on 11 November for the millions massacred in both world wars. Is there now a pecking order for acts of remembrance? Victims of terrorism get three minutes and war casualties get one? Why the sliding scale? What are we so afraid of?

If the facts prove that we should be more afraid of Lawrence Llewellyn Bowen than Osama Bin Laden, what does terrorism really threaten? To steal a phrase, 'It's the economy, stupid.' On 20 September 2001, nine days after the attacks on the World Trade Center, George Bush addressed Congress and the American people. Towards the end of his speech, after outlining the new kind of war they were facing, he said, 'Americans are asking, "What is expected of us?"' Before urging them to pray, he pleaded for them to go out shopping. 'I ask your continued participation and confidence in the American economy. Terrorists attacked a symbol of American prosperity; they did not touch its source. America is successful because of the hard work and creativity and enterprise of our people. These were the true strengths of our economy before September 11, and they are our strengths today.' Shopping became an act of patriotism in the aftermath of the attacks on the World Trade Center. After the suicide bombings on the tube in London on 7 July 2005 there was a call for Londoners to show their defiance to the world by, er, going back to work. That's the way to show the handful of terrorists who are prepared to turn themselves into human bombs that we've got fire in our bellies. That will really show them we mean business. When we're under attack our leaders rally round and tell us to keep shopping and to go back to work. Those are the two foundations of our modern way of life to be safeguarded at all costs. That's what 'freedom' obviously means to our leaders – the freedom to work and shop. It's hardly 'we'll fight them on the beaches', is it?

Perhaps it's just a coincidence, but while the government is busy eroding our personal freedom in the name of 'terrorism' the rights of economic interests seem to be getting stronger and stronger by the day. It's almost as if the people of Britain are less important to the government than the people who want to make money here. Conspiracy theory nonsense, you may think. Well, don't take my word for it. Go and see the evidence for yourself. You could start by walking through your local town.

While I was compiling the book *Crap Towns*, two main themes emerged. One was that Hull really is the most turgid, desolate armpit of a town, and constantly smells of death. The other was that people felt councils and the government were more interested in the needs of those who wanted to make money in their town than the people who actually lived there. It was the same from Glasgow to Dover and Liverpool to Thorpeness. Britain used to be the land of Albion, but now it's Britain plc.

You've probably noticed a change in your own life. You should have, because the statistics about life in modern Britain make depressing reading. We spend more time propping up Britain's economy than we spend with our families. The surprising thing is that so few of us seem to have a problem with it. We now work an average of forty-three and a half hours a week, which is longer than any other country in Europe. Sixteen per cent of full-time workers put in more than sixty hours a week. This takes them into what's known in Japan as the *Karoshi* zone. *Karoshi* means death from overwork. According to the Department of Trade and Industry, twice as many UK workers would rather cut down their hours at work than win the National Lottery but the Confederation of British Industry say that the real problem is that we're not working hard enough. The CBI is always bleating on behalf of their members about the cost to the economy of people throwing sickies. They've worked out that the loss to the economy as a result of fake illnesses stands at around £1.75 billion a year. The Trades Union Congress, on the other hand, sees things a bit differently. They think unpaid overtime is a more pressing concern, and put its value at £23 billion a year. That's £5,586-worth of work everyone in Britain does for their boss every year for nothing.

Things are even more depressing when we're not working. Western society values busyness above all else, and they don't want any of us slacking off just because we don't happen to be at work. When we're not working we should be shopping. It's a patriotic duty, remember? And we've been taking our duty very seriously indeed. Now we're in so much debt we don't even understand what the numbers mean. As a nation, Britain is over £1 trillion in the red, and that figure is rising by 8 per cent a year. That's over £7,000 per household, and the figure excludes mortgages. I don't understand economics, but if we're supposed to be richer than ever before but we're in more debt than ever before, hasn't Gordon Brown, or anyone else for that matter, appreciated the fact that maybe we're not actually financially better off after all?

Remember the figure for suicides? It was 3,500 a year. That's nearly ten self-inflicted deaths every single day of the year. Derek Rawson, a forklift truck driver, owed £100,000 on sixteen credit cards and killed himself because he couldn't cope. Stephen Lewis owed £65,000 on nineteen credit cards before taking his own life. Ian Beech killed himself after the Halifax won a court order to evict him and his family from their home. He owed them £4,714.66. He was in the process of re-mortgaging to pay them what he owed but they wouldn't give him enough time. He killed himself because he thought his life insurance policy would leave his family better off financially, but of course the small print pointed out that an act of suicide rendered the policy worthless. Perhaps a war on suicide might be a good idea. It was sixty-seven times more likely to claim you in 2005 than an act of terror, according to the Office of National Statistics. Unless you're a pensioner, of course, then it's much more likely. According to the Prudential building society, 2 per cent of pensioners – among them the generation that was prepared to 'fight them on the beaches', no less – have contemplated suicide because they haven't got enough money to retire on. The government have lots of targets for economic growth, but what about the basic happiness of their citizens? Is that of any concern to them? Is that only achievable through an ever-expanding economy? You'd think so by the amount of time they spend talking about it.

Before we were knocked off our perch by China, Gordon Brown was very keen to point out that Britain had the fourth largest economy in the world. Now, as I said, I'm very naive when it comes to the economy. But if ten people are killing themselves every day, others are suffering neglect in nursing homes, the gap between rich and poor is wider than ever,[15] our pensioners are scraping by on £85 per week when their council tax and energy bills keep rising, people are dying because the NHS is more concerned with targets than its patients,[16] 1.6 million children are living in 'Bad Housing'[17] and we're all £1 trillion in debt, then perhaps being the fourth largest economy in the world isn't such a good thing. And while we're at it, where's all this money our economy is producing going if we are a trillion pounds in debt? I'm talking about the fruits of our economy. Where are they? They exist, we can be sure of that. We should have the fourth largest fruits in the world, for goodness' sake, but where have they gone? Where are they being hidden? I certainly can't find much evidence of them in Britain.

MPs seem to value the fruits of economic growth more than the happiness of the British people. It makes you want to question their priorities, and we all know where you have to go if you want to question an MP. The House of Commons. Parliament is where the power lies. If you want answers from your democratically elected government about the state of Britain, you have to go down there and ask the people in control. It's a great British tradition, after all. It's called freedom of speech and the right to protest.

Well, it used to be. Now, of course, unless you're prepared to fill out a form and wait six days to see if the police and the government's bureaucratic machinery will grant you the privilege of exercising the basic right of free speech, it's breaking the law.

# CHAPTER 2

People have always gone to Parliament Square to call the government to account. From demonstrations about slavery and women's suffrage to apartheid and the poll tax, protest has always been a crucial part of our democratic process. How often has something been denied the people of Britain by the government until the tide of popular opinion, through the act of protest, forced them to change their minds? Protest works. Demonstrations work. In a democracy, they are as important as the ballot box.

On the day the Serious Organised Crime and Police Act became law (1 August 2005), people with gags on their mouths assembled in Parliament Square holding banners bearing the words 'Freedom of Speech'. The police warned them that they were breaking the law. The protesters ignored the warnings and were promptly arrested, beneath the statue of Winston Churchill, who I'd wager would have found the sight of their being carted away for exercising free speech outside his beloved Parliament more disturbing than the time when he acquired a green Mohican. As soon as one group of protesters was arrested, another appeared to take its place. Then Mark Barrett and his friend Sian had an interesting idea. They thought the exclusion zone was sinister and ridiculous, so they decided to organize a weekly picnic in Parliament Square. They met there at noon with their fellow protesters, sat on the grass and ate sandwiches and cakes (with that illegal icing). At first the picnickers were arrested, then the arrests became sporadic. The law, it seemed, was being enforced on a whim.

Now I don't usually go around breaking laws. Although that's not to say I wasn't outgoing and interesting when I was younger. I drank alcohol before I was eighteen. I stole a rubber once when I was twelve. I've taken illegal drugs, broken the speed limit while driving, been drunk (although not while driving), ridden my bike on the pavement, and skateboarded where signs strictly prohibited me from doing so. But this law was different. This was one of those laws you could actually get a criminal record for breaking. Up to that point in my life I had also managed to exploit the middle-class force field that put the police off the scent if I was ever up to no good. My friend Greg took this idea one stage further. If the police ever paid him any attention while he was driving to a rave in possession of illegal powders he would simply turn on Radio 4 before they asked him to wind his window down, 'because it formed an impenetrable bourgeois sphere that the police simply couldn't penetrate'. But as it was, I didn't mind getting arrested. You see, it was all part of my plan.

Cecil Rhodes once wrote that being born an Englishman was like winning the lottery of life. Now, clearly, sentiments like that are rooted in the days of the British Empire which has become rather politically incorrect to admire today, but the exploitation and greed of the Victorian era aside, there is still an element of that quotation that has always made me feel a certain sense of pride. Whenever I heard it the Empire was certainly not what dominated my thoughts, just the simple idea that the things in life that mattered were still valued here. Looking around the nation in the twenty-first century, however, Rhodes's words seem increasingly hollow and out of date.

When my partner Rachel and I started a family the future into which our country was heading began to preoccupy our minds. It wasn't just the question of civil liberties being eroded, although that weighed heavily enough, it was the maternity ward with invisible midwives where our son was born; the grotty, leaking community centre down the road where the government's Surestart initiative was being implemented; our badly lit and nerve-racking local train station; the grimy local swimming pool threatened with closure; and the community police officers taking a breather in our local park instead of proper old-fashioned bobbies walking the streets.

Put simply, life in general has become based on its cost rather than its value. Every time you go out of your front door to go shopping you always get the feeling that you are about to buy what the shop can get away with selling you for the most money rather than something honestly priced that was made with pride. Hospitals are not valued by the services and the care they offer but by how much money they spend and the length of their waiting lists. (Pregnant women can't be put on waiting lists so midwifery is simply not a priority for spending in the NHS, such is the effect on the ground of the upside-down thinking of government policy.) Schools are not valued for nurturing new generations of children but for how well those new generations can be taught to jump through the same hoops, making it easier to compare, streamline and reduce schools even further from places of education into simple production lines for the job market or, increasingly, as cheap childcare for the millions of parents working longer and longer hours to help pay off those credit card bills.

If you have the good fortune to be alive, you'll certainly have spotted the huge disparity between the way we are told things are and the way your experience proves them to be, whether it's the difference between what the brochure said about your holiday and the holiday you experience when you get there; the pert, tight, seventeen-year-old bottom enclosed by that pair of size 6 jeans on the billboard by the bus stop as opposed to the way your thirty-year-old, size 12 bum looks in them when you get home; or the politician who tells you what you want to hear then mocks your naivety as soon as your back is turned. We live in a time when what our brains tell us has value is rarely reflected in the reality of the world being constructed around us, and I wanted to get to the heart of that basic question of truth. Why were the politicians and corporations that ordered our lives as workers and consumers striving to take away the faith we had in our own experience and ideas, and to make us reliant on the wisdom of their highly paid 'experts' instead? Rachel and

I were becoming terrified that our son would grow up in a country stripped of its values and sense of place. The government was certainly no longer fighting to protect it because they were the ones forcing the change. According to the newspapers, any meaningful political debate is now over anyway. 'All our political parties are fighting over the same ground' seems to be the conventional political wisdom. Worryingly, this new mainstream 'political consensus' appears to be that politicians no longer fight for the long-term interests of the people who elected them and the country of which they are the custodians but for the short-term interests of those who want to make money out of this country. I was determined to do what I could to preserve what I felt this country stood for so that my son could experience it and enjoy living in Britain too.

But what could someone like me do?

These days it's not enough to talk or write about something. People don't notice. They haven't got time. You've got to do something visual. You've got to make a statement by proving you can be stupid on a scale never seen before. We've seen many types of desperate behaviour to which people will lower themselves for celebrity status, but we've never seen anyone deliberately attempt to become a criminal to point out how far from real-life experience, how authoritarian, our 'democracy' has become. Well, not for a while anyway.

You may not think the idea of my deliberately becoming a criminal went down well at home, but Rachel was rather pleased by the change of direction my journey had taken. Breaking new laws rather than old ones meant that, among other things, I would no longer have to contract bubonic plague before attempting to hail a London cab, or try to take possession of a beached whale (all of which are owned by the Queen). In fact, the enthusiasm that seemed to fill her at the prospect of my being given a lengthy jail term made me think she was quite keen to get away from me for a while. Despite such misgivings, I took her enthusiasm as nothing more than simple, unconditional support.

And then my criminal life began. With a picnic.

Outside the YMCA a man with a feather in his hair was dragging on a cigarette. I was looking for a signal that I'd come to the right place, and a man with a feather in his hair was as good a sign as any. I snuck in through the door and sat next to a young man making notes in a Che Guevara notebook. So far all my prejudices were present and correct. The meeting was about to begin.

I surveyed the room with trepidation. These protester types were bound to be dangerous extremists. I remembered the riots in 1999 when a McDonald's and the futures exchange were ransacked during a rampage through the square mile. I remembered the 'guerrilla gardening' event of 2000 when another McDonald's was destroyed and Churchill acquired that green Mohican. I also remembered the seven-hour stand-off in Oxford Circus on 1 May a year later. These demonstrators were regularly portrayed as dogmatic, frightening radicals. Before the stand-off in 2001 Tony Blair set the tone for the approach the police would take by accusing the demonstrators of planning 'fear, terror and violence'. Most of the protesters were demonstrating against arms dealers and Third World debt, but Tony was unmoved, labelling them all as criminals with no genuine grievance. 'The limits are passed when protesters, in the name of some spurious cause, seek to inflict fear, terror, violence and criminal damage on our people and property,'[18] he was quoted as saying. Jack Straw, Home Secretary at the time, weighed in too, calling the guerrilla gardeners 'evil'.[19]

Being a good middle-class boy I was therefore a little nervous about the type of people I was sitting with in that room. I positioned myself by the door because it would allow a speedy exit if things became too radical. As I looked round, however, that idea began to seem rather unlikely. I had imagined lots of Doc Marten boots, slightly unsettling piercings, pointless anarchist drivel and that disquieting look of the pious anti-capitalist evangelicals you sometimes get stuck talking to at weddings, but the proceedings were remarkably polite and good-humoured, if a little earnest. But then they were discussing freedom of speech, which they clearly regarded as something of value. Having said that, there *was* an eighteen-year-old American anarchist who kept calling for us to storm Parliament and take over the state, bless him, but everyone else seemed surprisingly normal. In fact, it was a bit like being in a Benetton advert where diverse groups coexist happily. There were a few old rebels, a couple of legal experts, a few ladies who looked like schoolteachers and about fifteen young, angry men and women, all hoping that, after half an hour debating who would be the chair and the scribe, and what exactly the purpose of the meeting was, they'd start talking to one another.

It soon emerged that Matthew, the man I had sat next to by the door, the chap with a feather in his hair (Mark

Barrett, the original picnicker), and three others dotted around the room were the picnickers who'd been arrested. The rest were people like me, who had just turned up out of curiosity and a willingness to get involved.

After about forty minutes someone suggested that everyone in the room should explain why they had decided to come to the meeting. The same opinion came up time and again: the right to protest outside the Houses of Parliament was a democratic right that the government simply could not just decide to take away. It was clear to me by this point that these people were not dangerous radicals after all. Not unless by 'dangerous radicals' you mean people who are simply prepared to take responsibility for something larger than themselves. There was something else clearly apparent in that room too. They didn't just want to organize protests, they wanted to arrange them, wherever possible, in the pub, which was a price I was prepared to pay to further the cause of civil rights.

A brainstorm of ideas soon began. I put up my hand. 'What about having a teddy bears' picnic instead of a normal picnic? We could all dress up in teddy bear suits. Then the police would have to arrest teddy bears. It would be hilarious!' They wrote 'teddy bears' picnic' on the board of ideas to be discussed later. Then a man sitting in the corner suggested that protest itself should be celebrated as a vital function of human progress. By the end of the meeting it was agreed that for 6 November 2005 they would organize something on a larger scale than they'd attempted before. Email addresses were taken and jobs were dished out. Those of us on the periphery were told to keep an eye on the website for further updates.

\*

As a new father, I have to admit that the path down which I was about to travel felt slightly self-indulgent. I had no doubt about the importance of the political journey I was setting out on, but found it hard to balance that with my new responsibilities as a parent. I'd read Gandhi's auto-biography to get the inside track on this activism business and was surprised to discover that despite his amazing achievements he was, nevertheless, a totally shit dad. Going off to South Africa to save thousands of indentured Indians is all well and good, not to mention the enormous role he played in securing India's independence, but while he was off being a hero he left his wife to bring up his children single-handedly for years on end. Another of my heroes is Satish Kumar, who in the sixties embarked on a pilgrimage on foot from his village in India to meet the leaders of all the then nuclear powers to campaign for disarmament. In a village in Russia he came across a tea factory where a woman gave him four boxes of tea. She asked him to give one box each to the leaders of Russia, France, Britain and the USA and to plead with them to stop and make a brew if they ever found themselves contemplating pressing the nuclear button, hoping that this small act would remind them of all the ordinary people who would be massacred if they went ahead. After visiting Russia and France, in London Satish met Bertrand Russell, who wrote the original article that prompted his journey years before, then boarded a boat to New York to meet President Kennedy. But when he arrived Kennedy had just been assassinated and his long journey ended at JFK's grave. Satish then decided to carry on with his pilgrimage by walking to China.

It is a remarkable story, and his autobiography is a beautifully written account of a man with a vision of hope he wanted to share with the whole world. But, once again, despite being a remarkable man who inspired thousands of people, Satish turned out to be a crap dad to the child he'd had with his first wife who, like Mrs Gandhi, was left holding the baby at home while he went off on his grand adventure. From what I have heard about his current life in England, where he started a new family, this criticism may seem a little uncharitable, but the fact remains that it was clearly easier for these two men to contemplate and then set out on an epic adventure thousands of miles away than simply to stay at home and concentrate on being a good father. I decided I would not allow myself to lose sight of that fact whatever I came up against, and resolved to make sure that I was a family man first and political revolutionary second.

A few days later I headed for Parliament Square to attend my first illegal demonstration. The nerves started kicking in as I ambled along the pavement. I wasn't sure if I was ready. After all, making the transition from 'member of the public' to 'political activist' was something I wouldn't be able to reverse. At that moment I was completely unknown to the police. They didn't have my fingerprints, my DNA or even a photograph of me on file. I was just another faceless member of the public, someone who quietly got on with his life and who never stepped out of line.

I have to admit that I was utterly petrified of being hauled off and dumped in a cell. Now I know there have been lots of books about people spending time in real prison, criminal memoirs and that kind of thing, so my being scared of simply being arrested may sound a little pathetic. So instead of me contemplating a night in the cells, imagine if you were facing the prospect. I don't know you very well, but I'm guessing you're either an old hand at this protest stuff or an intrigued hand who has never done anything like this at all. If you're an old hand you're probably the kind of person who is so alternative you don't care about modern society and its values, but then you're also bound to be really paranoid about the power of the 'state' so you probably understand my wariness. If you're the intrigued hand, then you're the kind of person whose life would be completely turned upside down if you got a criminal record. Not entirely unlike me. I'm the kind of person who likes being regarded by authority as a decent, law-abiding citizen. My personality has been built on the foundations of the middle classes. I'm proud, not remotely ashamed, of where I come from. I'm not an outsider. After all, the police, the Establishment and the government are the middle classes too. It's probably uncool to admit that I admire the police. I don't, by and large, refer to them as 'pigs'. Even when I hear about them doing something awful my first thought is that when someone is out on the street waving a gun around and everyone is running away in panic the police show courage to walk towards the maniac holding the gun. That takes some doing. I know I couldn't do it, I respect them for it, and I didn't want to get arrested by one of those people. Of course that just made me even angrier with the government, because they had turned me into a criminal. I was being drawn away from my status as a law-abiding citizen because I dared to value freedom of speech.

My mind was running off in panic down Whitehall and losing itself in the streets of Covent Garden when I realized that if I stepped onto Parliament Square and joined the group of protesters it would be only a matter of time before the police had a file with my name on it. If I got arrested, which after all was supposed to be the whole point of the exercise, I would no longer be an ordinary member of the public; I would have become a 'trouble-maker' for the rest of my life. According to the Foreign Office, if I got arrested, regardless of whether or not I was actually found guilty of any crime, I could forget about ever visiting America because they routinely refuse visas to anyone who has had their collar felt.

It wasn't long before I'd managed to convince myself that if I so much as looked at the picnickers I would be dragged off kicking and screaming into the back of a police van. Back at the YMCA, Matthew had talked about people's fear of arrest. He pointed out that being with the protesters did not make you one. This was no comfort though, as my excessive flatulence began to prove. I literally trumped my way along Whitehall. Before long I turned the corner and saw the square. There were hundreds of tourists milling about, gazing up at Big Ben, but none on the square itself, which was surrounded by a moat of traffic. Parliament Square is an obvious place to come if you're a tourist visiting London. In fact Parliament Square itself is a World Heritage Site, which is one of the reasons why Brian Haw's protest was such a problem for MPs. On 19 May 2004, Sir George Young MP raised concerns in the House of Commons about the impact of Brian's presence: 'He [Brian] began by camping on the grass in Parliament Square, but was moved on by the Greater London Authority, which manages it. He has camped outside ever since, sleeping on the pavement under a plastic sheet, accompanied by an unsightly accumulation of placards, flags and hoardings, and assaulting the eardrums of anyone within range – audible graffiti on the walls of Parliament publicizing his mini-shantytown. This is not a conventional demonstration of the type that we know, accept and sometimes enjoy, but an unacceptable visual and audible intrusion that risks becoming permanent.'[20]

On 7 February 2005 Parliament debated suggested amendments to the Serious Organised Crime and Police Act which included one proposal to reduce the exclusion zone from 1,000 to 100 metres, an idea some felt was an entirely practical alternative. For five and a half hours MPs debated 'New Clause 18 – Demonstrating without authorization in the designated area', which later became Section 132 of the SOCPA when the bill became law. Sir Patrick Cormack MP commented in the House, 'I do not think that any individual has the right indefinitely to deface the centre of a great capital city, which is what we have seen over the past three years with Mr Haw.' Glenda Jackson MP was speaking as the debate drew to a close. 'I have heard people say that no such demonstrations as we have seen for the past three years should be allowed in Parliament Square because it is a World Heritage Site,' she said. 'It is a World Heritage Site not because of that rather scruffy square of grass or the statues at its corners, and it is certainly not surrounded by buildings of overwhelming architectural excellence, with the exception possibly of Westminster Abbey. It is a centre that the whole world comes to visit because of what has happened in this Parliament, and certainly what happened in Westminster Abbey. This building [the Houses of Parliament] is a symbol to the world of a democratic system whereby the rights of the individual were placed above those of, in the first instance, a sovereign, and, in the second instance, a state. Westminster Abbey is the great symbol of Christianity with its call to all of us to have compassion for those who are the lowest in our esteem. We should be—'[21] And at that point she was cut off and the debate was closed. The amendment to reduce the designated area to 100 metres was refused. It could only happen in Britain.

I wandered round the perimeter of the square looking for some way of getting across the road but I couldn't find a single pedestrian crossing. The only way to get over to it was to run across the road during a break in the traffic. I looked ahead for a smile and the waving hand of a fellow protester but there was no-one to be seen. It was 12.10 p.m. Surely the picnickers hadn't already been arrested and carted away? Brian was there, on the pavement, looking out towards Parliament and Big Ben. The wind got up, and I remembered Matthew saying how cold the protests had become. It was one thing having a picnic in August, but having one at the end of October was slightly less inviting. Perhaps they'd decided to call it off and save their ideas for the big event on 6 November.

I began to feel like a criminal staking out the joint as I

sat on a bench eating a sandwich I'd brought from home. After half an hour of introspection, gazing up at Big Ben and listening to the increasingly irate road rage of the passing motorists, I got bored and headed for home across Green Park. I crossed the road, walked round the corner and saw the entrance to the Cabinet War Rooms. I stopped and stared at it for a minute, feeling a strange urge to go in.

Now, comparing the threat of Hitler and Nazi Germany to not being able to have a picnic on Parliament Square seemed a little far-fetched, even for me. But World War Two *was* the last time the freedom of the people of Great Britain was truly threatened. It was also the last time the government brought in ID cards and a whole raft of other measures designed with security rather than freedom in mind. The difference then, of course, was that these measures were actually necessary. Britain was fighting for its life on foreign soil while back at home parts of London were being reduced to rubble by the Luftwaffe every night. It's hardly the same level of threat we have today when statistically you're more likely to be seriously injured putting on your socks[22] than by an act of terrorism. After the war most of these measures were phased out because in peacetime the price was no longer worth paying. But that makes it sound as though I was trying to justify going in when in fact I'm a great believer in wandering about aimlessly to see where coincidence and serendipity will lead you if you're prepared to spare them the time. The entrance fee, £10.50, seemed a little steep but I decided to go for it and joined a queue of American tourists.

I emerged an hour later feeling a little stunned and surprised. The War Rooms are slightly bewildering. In this day and age they seem rather quaint and sweet – the technology of elastic bands, paper cups and those old phone systems where a woman with conservative hair plugs and unplugs wires to patch you through to your caller. Apparently, during the war rats were a real problem, and they had no air-conditioning and pre-politically correct attitudes to smoking. It can't have been pleasant. According to one of the commentaries, Churchill was a bit of a cantankerous old sod when the War Cabinet met to discuss operations. He had a habit of feigning deafness when his ministers and advisers didn't agree with him, but to his credit, and unlike Hitler, he never went against the will of the collective even if he himself disagreed.

As I walked round those dark, cramped passages, it seemed absurd that the marauding Nazi empire had been held off for so long by this small band of people underground and those above ground in the country at large. There was a spirit in the land back then, a determination to stand up and fight for freedom. Of course, sixty years on, what they won the war with isn't in those passages any more, and you'll be hard pressed to find it out in the country either. After the war the rooms were sealed until 1970, and now they have been turned into a rather impressive, if slightly confusing, state-of-the-art museum. It's a shame we can't commandeer those rooms again today. Britain was conquered while they were closed, that's for sure. Conquered by an infantry pincer movement of overwork and over-consumption and the cavalry charge of consumer debt. We don't seem to have the stomach to stand up for ourselves any more. Either that or we're all just too busy. We never seem to have time to think. Which is a shame, because if people don't have time to think and hold their government to account you get to a stage where you can be arrested for holding up a banner that says 'Freedom of Speech'.

I got home earlier than I'd planned, relieved not to have been arrested. I visited the picnic website to see if there'd been any excitement I'd missed out on. There was no mention of any new arrests nor an explanation for the absence of protesters earlier in the day, but there was a message for everyone to come to a party in Parliament Square on 6 November.

They were having a teddy bears' picnic.

'It cost £94. Well, £104.92 including postage. It is a bona fide business expense though. I won't get taxed 20 per cent on the hundred pounds, so it's effectively only really £80.'

Rachel began to laugh. Wilf, our ten-month-old son, was sitting on the floor trying to reach my computer keyboard.

'You're actually going through with it then? You've bought a teddy bear suit to wear on Sunday in Parliament Square?'

I was feeling as though I might have overstretched myself and was looking for reassurance. I moved Wilf towards his large rocking snail.

'I suppose Wilfy will like having a daddy-sized teddy bear,' Rachel added. 'But I do think you're completely insane.'

I sat down and took a deep breath.

A notice had appeared earlier that evening on the picnic website:

*PRESS RELEASE 2/11/05*
*Federation of Teddy Protesters assert Freedom to Protest*
*The Federation of Teddy Protesters are becoming increasingly unhappy with the way their furless friends, the Parliament Square Picnickers, have been harassed by the police since the introduction of the Serious and Organised Crime and Police Act (2005) this year. This draconian law forbids demonstrations within 1km of Parliament without the prior 'authorization' of the police. To date they have made at least 19 arrests. Five of those arrested were our friends the Parliament Square Picnickers. Their crime? Simply daring to eat cakes with 'Freedom to Protest', 'Freedom of Speech' and 'Save our Speech' written on them in icing, for wearing T-shirts with slogans such as 'Make Trade Fair' and 'Peaceful protest is an essential part of democracy', for discussing the important issues of the day at their 'people's commons', for clapping in a provocative manner and generally drinking tea without prior 'authorization'. The T-shirts have been seized as evidence.*

*Being inanimate objects and therefore not subject to this outrageously undemocratic legislation, the Federation of Teddy Protesters (FTP) have decided to support their comrades by staging a 'Teddy Bears' Picnic' this Sunday at noon in Parliament Square. We call on all free-thinking Teddies who value free speech, and the right to drink any beverage without authorization, to join us in tea, cakes, party games and peaceful protest.*

I was on my third glass of wine, and the press release, coupled with the knowledge that the idea I had suggested back at the YMCA was actually going to happen, had made me bubble over with enthusiasm. Everybody would be wearing teddy bear suits! It would be hilarious! I *had* to get one. I couldn't be the only one without a teddy bear suit. Two minutes later I'd spent a hundred pounds. Teddies would take over Parliament Square. I could already see the newspaper front pages. It was genius!

There were, however, certain practicalities that I hadn't considered. Rachel pointed out one of them: 'How are you going to get it there? Are you going to get on the tube wearing it?' Wearing a teddy bear suit in public would certainly not be very dignified. And once I reached the square there would be no way of blending into the background as the police approached, that's for sure. Still, at least I wouldn't be the only one. That really would be humiliating. I rallied myself. If enough of us were prepared to look ridiculous we would definitely pull it off.

The next morning I bounded up the stairs with a large box containing my new teddy suit. Rachel, laughing again, demanded I try it on immediately. I cut open the box. A pair of paws and a pair of feet lay on top of the headpiece and finally the suit itself. It was enormous. I tried it all on and Wilf immediately began to cry. He crawled off down the corridor with tears streaming down his little face. Rachel looked horrified. 'You look really frightening,' she said. 'Since when do teddy bears have such scary teeth?' It was true. The headpiece did have a particularly nasty set of yellow gnashers. I'd managed to buy the only teddy bear suit known to man that actually looked intimidating. I took the headpiece off and sat down on the sofa feeling dejected. Rachel was right: it was complete madness.

Although, I began to realize as I stroked my fur, it was actually rather comfortable. I ran my hands over my furry arms and legs, scratched my furry tummy and reclined on the sofa. It would, I thought, be a brilliant lounging-around suit for wearing at home. Like the kind of thing you imagine everyone wears in the Playboy mansion. Well, *I* would wear one if I got into the Playboy mansion. It oozed a wonderful kind of class and sophistication born of reckless confidence. The tail was a little uncomfortable to sit on, there were no pockets and it wasn't the most flattering thing I'd ever worn (I suppose all teddies have pot bellies on account of all those picnics), but those things aside it was rather cool. Suddenly, normal clothes seemed absurd compared to this ultra-comfortable, warm and cuddly adult romper suit. I stroked my back and my shoulders and let out a little purr. Why had I never thought of getting one before? This was the comfiest thing I'd ever worn in my life! After twenty minutes the acrylic lining did begin to itch my legs, but I put on some track-suit trousers underneath, tucked them into a long pair of socks, and it was perfect. So perfect that I fell asleep on the sofa.

The day of the protest started rather badly. I had a terrible hangover following a firework party at a friend's. We'd got in at three, and I'd had to get up with Wilf at six to watch *Teletubbies*. Consequently, the early part of the day had a vaguely hallucinogenic tinge to it. Outside, inevitably, it was pouring with rain.

I was feeling rather nervous. Rachel's parents arrived to babysit Wilf so she could come with me and take some photographs. Her mum, Gail, asked me over breakfast if I thought Rachel would get arrested if she came with me. She was concerned what effect that might have on her career as a teacher and what the loss of her part-time salary would do to our small family. I assured her it would be fine, but it was a stark reminder that, however silly the whole business might have seemed as I tried on my teddy suit, we were about to go out to deliberately break the law and place ourselves at the mercy of the process of criminal law. We had decided that we should split up when we got to Charing Cross so that Rachel could arrive in Parliament Square on her own. That way no-one would suspect we were there together. Still, the paranoia that suddenly swept over us both at the breakfast table put SOCPA's exclusion zone into a context that I don't think either of us was remotely prepared for.

After a solid breakfast and countless mugs of tea I squeezed the teddy suit and a few tubs of chocolate muffins into my rucksack and we headed off for Parliament Square. By noon, only six other people had arrived. It was cold, wet and miserable. I felt like a complete idiot, and my teddy bear suit was still packed deep in my bag. I drank a cup of tea I'd bought nervously, wondering if I could sneak home and sleep off my hangover before anyone noticed, but then I saw Matthew walking over. It suddenly struck me that I'd bought my tea from Starbucks, the enormously profitable corporate chain, which was clearly not going to endear me to the protesting elite. Matthew didn't recognize me but asked if I'd come for the teddy bears' picnic. I asked if many people were going to turn up. 'Well, to be honest, I'm the only one who gets here on time,' he replied. 'They all seem to come at one thirty. We've got lots of people we can rely on, though.' He then added enthusiastically, 'We have got cold curry, and someone's bringing tea,' before marching off towards Brian Haw's stash of tarpaulin sheets.

Cold curry? Well, thank God for that.

Gradually, people I remembered seeing at the meeting began to emerge from across the road, but no-one seemed to recognize me. They converged on three pieces of tarpaulin that Matthew had laid out at the edge of the square. Still, I reasoned, once the other people in teddy bear suits arrived I'd put mine on and be hailed as a fellow protester. It was only a matter of time before I was welcomed into the fold.

It was at that point that I noticed everyone seemed to be unpacking small teddy-bear-sized teddy bears. I looked around, waiting for someone else to put on a full-size suit. There was a chap with long hair and glasses who looked like the type of guy who'd be prepared to throw himself into the spirit of things. But he took off his rucksack and began pulling flasks out of it until it was empty. I looked around desperately. Surely someone else had a teddy bear suit? Matthew certainly didn't, he was decked out in jeans and trainers. Then a few attractive young ladies emerged, but alas, none of them had brought teddy bear suits either. Tight jeans and trainers were the order of the day. Everyone huddled under umbrellas and talked in whispers. The light drizzle became dense and sharp. The sheets of tarpaulin were occasionally buffeted by exhaust fumes from the road. I spotted another person I remembered from the meeting. I looked at his feet, hoping to see fur poking out from under his tracksuit trousers, but he just smiled, sat down under an umbrella and started to read a newspaper.

I looked around for Rachel and saw her sniggering by the statue of Churchill. She began gesturing at the rucksack by my feet and raised her camera. She was laughing quite animatedly by now.

I opened my rucksack and looked at the furry humiliation I'd lovingly packed a few hours earlier. The tarpaulin in front of me now held about twenty slightly bedraggled small teddy bears in a heap. There were plates of sandwiches and cakes too. Someone began to assemble the teddy bears into a circle and gave them a tiny plate each. It *was* a teddy bears' picnic, but it was not quite what I'd had in mind. Doubt took me over completely. I looked around for support but was met only by strange blank faces. A few more people emerged and produced more small teddy bears, which they laid down with the others on the sodden plastic sheet. I'm not sure what I'd imagined. Perhaps a certain sense of camaraderie, smiling strangers unified in defiance of an unjust law. I'd always thought these protester types were full of kindness and good cheer. I put their unspoken hostility down to my Starbucks cup and the rain and began to unpack my suit. After all, what was the worst thing that could happen? I was hung over. I'd had three hours' sleep. I was standing in the rain with a load of people I didn't know and I was about to put on a teddy bear suit in an attempt to get myself arrested. What could possibly go wrong?

As I climbed into it I heard a few sniggers but still no-one spoke to me, no doubt suspicious of this unknown lunatic in their midst. Matthew appeared when I was fully dressed and began to laugh. I like to think that I brought some much-needed good cheer to the proceedings. At least I was up for it. Either that or they all thought I was some kind of desperate maniac and they were simply too terrified about what I might do if they didn't laugh supportively. At least my humiliation had broken the ice with Matthew. I started to quiz him about what had made him come to Parliament Square in the rain to eat a bowl of cold curry.

'Look who's talking,' he said with a smirk. 'I wrote to my MP about SOCPA and she told me I'd have to get arrested if I wanted to expose it. She said someone had to push it through the courts. I got done a few weeks ago for breaking Section 132 of the Serious Organised Crime and Police Act.'

At this point two policemen appeared on the other side of the road and began to walk around the perimeter of the square. Matthew pinned a sign on my back that said 'Serious Criminal?' There was no escape now. The sign had turned me from a random lunatic in a teddy bear suit into an illegal demonstrator.

'Those two policemen are going to come over and tell us to move,' Matthew said. 'They'll give us a warning.'

He looked completely unfazed. I felt my bowels twitch for the second time that day. I could see the headlines now: INCONTINENT TEDDY BEAR SECTIONED AFTER ARREST IN PARLIAMENT SQUARE.

I asked Matthew what had happened when he got arrested.

'When I first heard about the law I thought, "It's got to be a joke." But then I got arrested for having a picnic.

After they gave me a warning I made a decision not to do anything remotely protesty. So I just lay face down in the grass, literally doing nothing, and they still came back and arrested me – for not moving.' What would it mean for him to get arrested a second time? 'I think I'd be in a lot of trouble. I might get my bail conditions changed so I can't come anywhere near here. There is a small chance of being detained [he shakes his head] but to be honest I'm not going to get arrested again. It's not a good idea. I've got school.'

Matthew was sixteen. He was studying for his A Levels.

By this time the police had made their way over. Matthew leant over to me and whispered, 'That police-woman is particularly nasty. I know that from experience.'

This is an exact transcript of the exchange that followed:

**Policeman**: Hello, people, what are you having here? A teddy bears' picnic?

**Protester 1**: What do you think?

**Policeman**: That's what it looks like.

**Teddy Bear**: [to Scary Policewoman] Would you like a muffin?

**Scary Policewoman**: No. Thank you.

**Teddy Bear**: They're very nice.

**Scary Policewoman**: No, honestly. It's fine.

**Policeman**: Right. No protesting in this area at all. I will inform you of that. Right?

**Matthew**: Why not?

**Policeman**: You cannot protest within something like five hundred yards or something of Parliament without the permission of the CX [Charing Cross police]. If you do carry on protesting in this area you are liable to be arrested.

**Protester 1**: But are we protesting?

**Policeman**: Well, I don't know. You tell me. Are you protesting?

**Protester 2**: I'm not protesting.

**Protester 3**: I'm protesting!

**Policeman**: So this is a teddy bears' picnic, that's what you're telling me? If you're telling me that then I can tell my base that you're having a teddy bears' picnic on Parliament Square. You start shouting and screaming then those guys over there [pointing at the policemen on the gates of Parliament] are going to say, 'No, they're protesting. There's no teddy bears' picnic going on there.' Right? So I will tell them that you're having a teddy bears' picnic. Don't start charming me, right?

**Protester 2**: It's a stupid law. Why is it a law?

**Policeman**: Parliament brought it out. They brought it out to try to get rid of Brian but because Brian was here before it was brought in—

**Protester 4**: It's bollocks!

**Policeman**: Well, tell them that [he points towards Parliament]. They're the ones that brought it in!

The policeman and the scary policewoman walked off.

Now, I don't know about you, but these days, when I think of protesters being threatened with arrest, I think of large men wearing facemasks running at riot police or smashing up branches of McDonald's, not a group of bedraggled sixth formers, assorted adults and a man in a teddy bear suit sitting on sheets of tarpaulin in the rain. It was like some kind of school trip gone wrong. The policeman didn't seem to understand the exact terms of the new law but at least he knew why it had been brought in.

Then someone asked if they could take a picture of me in my suit. This turned out to be Prasanth Visweswaran, one of the people who'd been arrested a week after SOCPA became law. After spending over a decade running a taxi company in Madras, Prasanth was working in London as a 'provider of rare services' according to his business card. I assumed this was a euphemism for 'drug dealer' but when I pressed him about it he shook his head and laughed, 'Drugs aren't rare!' I then asked him why he had been prepared to flout the new law. 'Because this is Britain!' he replied. 'You expect these sorts of things to happen in other places in the world, but this is Britain! Britain is supposed to be the gold standard when it comes to democracy. The gold standard that everyone else aspires to. So it's more important to protest about it happening here than to protest about it happening anywhere else.'

Prasanth had gone on a protest about the police's shoot-to-kill policy after Jean Charles de Menezes was shot dead fifteen days after the 7 July bombings. Someone in the crowd during the demonstration told him that in the near future such a protest would be illegal. A week after SOCPA became law he went to Parliament Square with a banner. 'I found a quote from Noam Chomsky that said, "If you don't believe in freedom of expression for people you despise then you don't believe in it at all." I was just holding it in Parliament Square. I did get a warning. They were handing out leaflets saying, "You are breaking the law", then an officer came over and said, "Have you been given the leaflet?" I said, "Yes, I have." He asked, "Have you read it?" I said, "No." So he started reading it for me, and then he asked me if I understood. I didn't say anything, then he said, "The defendant has not made a statement," while another policeman made notes. Then they arrested me. And now I think I'm going to end up with a criminal record for holding up a banner made out of fridge packing.

'At the station they took my DNA, photographs and fingerprints. They bagged up my banner, wearing gloves, into an evidence bag. I spoke to the sergeant who was booking me and he said, "Well, you broke the law. Laws are not supposed to be broken." And he's right, there are laws, but there is also morality, and that's my main law. I don't have to follow a law just because it's a law. It's common sense. If I have a problem with the government there's no point arguing about it in Tesco or at home, or in my street. You have to go where the problem is. People should be able to say what they feel like saying. Anyone. Anti-war protester, pro-war protester, BNP supporter, whatever. That's what freedom is supposed to be about.'

The rain was falling steadily by this time. Rachel had disappeared for a coffee somewhere and just standing there now seemed pointless. A few of the protesters decided that the teddies should storm Parliament and rushed over the road to attach them to the railings. It was descending into a farce. It was time to leave before things became embarrassing. I removed my suit, falling over in the mud in the process, swore as the wind blew my paws off towards the road, chased after them, slipped over again because of a lack of grip on the underside of my teddy feet, finally gathered my soiled, furry suit into my bag and crept over towards Brian Haw with as much dignity as I could muster. I thought I should try to catch a few words with him, seeing as it was his plight that had, indirectly, brought me to Parliament Square in a teddy bear suit.

He looked as if he'd just woken up. When he saw me approach with a video camera he nodded, crouched down and lit a cigarette. I asked him how his cause was going and he literally exploded.

'Well, you're missing the point if you think like that. *Your* cause, you said. Whose cause is this? It's not my cause. It's *your* cause; it's everyone's cause. It's the cause of humanity! It's not right that only one person in Britain can be outside this Parliament protesting! They're not going to take away my right! I bloody fought for it. I've been to the Royal Courts of Justice twice now; I've had six court cases. It's six-nil now. Mr Ex-Barrister Blair doesn't have a very good track record. It's a good job he left the law, isn't it? They don't know law. They don't respect law. They have contempt for law. For them, law is about getting what they want and making you do what they say, and that's not law. It's what's right for me, what's right for you, what's right for all of us – that's law.'

I asked him whether he thought we should have a constitution to protect our rights and he shouted at me for interrupting him before letting me know his thoughts on whether or not we should have one.

'Yes, we should have a constitution. But unlike America we should actually practise it. "All are created equal."

[He rolls his eyes.] "What do you think of British civilization, Mr Gandhi?" You know what he said? "Yes, it's a good idea." It's still a good idea, isn't it? When are we going to bloody do it?'

I opened my mouth to say something but thought better of it. Brian looked up, smiled as if in recognition, and started talking again.

'Look at the Race Relations Act. It says we must treat people decently regarding their ethnic origin in this country. You must not abuse them verbally, physically. You must not do it, that's the law, it's on the statute book. But then we go and bomb the shit out of them everywhere else in the world. Isn't that nice? Doesn't that sound very British?'

Then, having said his piece, he gestured for me to go away, threw his cigarette into the gutter, and crawled back under his sheet of tarpaulin to shelter from the rain.

As I said, Brian Haw is slightly deranged. He seems to have paid a high psychological price for his staunchly held beliefs. But being deranged, or passionate if you're being charitable, shouldn't disqualify you from having the right of free speech. After all, a democracy has to have frayed edges if it is to be truly democratic. My few minutes with Brian reminded me of a quote I heard once, which at the time made me feel proud to be British. 'When I pass protesters every day at Downing Street – and believe me, you name it, they protest against it – I may not like what they call me, but I thank God they can. That's called freedom.'[23] (Tony Blair.)

## CHAPTER 3

If something so essential to our sense of common identity can be criminalized with barely a murmur from the British people, then do the people of Britain exist in any real sense any more? I found it hard to correlate this sense of despair with my own growing sense of excitement. Taking on the law, albeit dressed as a teddy bear, had awakened a certain spirit inside me. It wasn't a sense of power, or self-righteousness; it was more a sense of responsibility and exhilaration I'd never felt before. It was refreshing to be around people who were simply not prepared to accept the government's behaviour. I had stumbled on a group of people who were trying to reclaim what Britain is supposed to stand for, even though most of them would have baulked at the idea that they were patriots.

I was brought up on tales of King Arthur and the Knights of the Round Table and I had a vague sense that I had tapped into the spirit of something that was supposedly once found in every corner of this country – the spirit of Albion. I had no firm understanding of what Albion actually meant, but that hadn't stopped me being desperate to go there, wherever and whatever it was.

Albion has always conjured up an image in my mind of rolling hills, a free and tranquil England, punctuated by laughter and frothing pints of ale, but according to my friend John Moore that's probably what you'd come up with if you were trying to sell a beer called Albion. In reality, 'Albion' is just a feeling. A wonderful feeling of pride and hope in our nation and a nagging feeling that it is slipping through our fingers at the same time. It seemed to have become out of date. As though it belonged to a different age. A time of colour and happiness, perhaps, or the time of your life you could no longer expect to have.

As you may have seen at the beginning of this book, according to the *Concise Oxford English Dictionary* Albion means 'Britain or England, unrecorded'. I stumbled on it one night while looking up a word a politician had used on *Newsnight*. Taking that definition literally, it occurred to me that if I did record the ideas and values of people in Britain who felt they were not being listened to and had decided to demonstrate and protest – those few people who were taking seriously their responsibilities as citizens – I would be creating a map into 'Albion'. The thought made me as excited as a child waking to discover five inches of snow outside his bedroom window.

If you want to know more about Albion then you have to find a man with an enormous beard, a penchant for drinking frothing pints of ale and swearing like Father Jack. Luckily for me, I knew just the chap. John Nicholson is one of my more interesting friends. He has worked with Ant and Dec, has appeared in the Harry Potter films, *Gormenghast* and *Extras,* and was once photographed in the nude by David Bailey. John is also an amateur historian who specializes in dissent. And when I say 'amateur' I mean that he is not recognized as an academic, which isn't to say that he doesn't know more than anyone in Britain about riots, rebellions and revolts – a fact proved by his staggeringly impressive library that takes up an entire floor of his house.

Only talking to amateurs rather than professionals wherever possible was one of the signposts I'd decided to follow as I drafted my map into Albion. If the professional, recorded world was failing us then it made sense that some insight might be found in the unrecorded world of the amateur. I was hoping that the ideas of all the unrecorded people of Britain would reveal a different way of thinking that might improve the lives of all of us who live here. We all know the recorded world because it's the world we work in, the world where we stare at the clock willing the precious minutes of our lives away. Once we get home from the office and the mindset of work slips away – when we get to put our feet up, or enjoy a tipsy reunion with our closest friends – we become ourselves again. All of us are able to snatch a glimpse of Albion in the bits of time we haven't had to sell to an employer. This amateur world is where none of us really knows what we're doing but where most of our fun, love, joy and laughter lie. So I had decided to ask people who were not professional politicians questions about politics. Those who knew nothing about town planning would be the ones from whom I would seek advice about how to protect our towns and cities, and anyone not practising law would be my first choice for questions about justice. Because the amateurs of Britain are where you will find the soul and the conscience of the country. By embracing this amateur world, I hoped I would, at last, be able to turn Albion from myth into reality.

I got the train from London Bridge to Bedford, where John lives, with a clutch of newspapers under my arm. It was the day after Maya Evans became the first person to go to court under Section 132 of SOCPA, and the papers were filled with stories about her. The *Daily Mail* and the *Independent* were very unhappy about her conviction. Both had a picture of Maya on the front page. I had gone to Bow Street Magistrates Court for her hearing to offer moral support to Prasanth, who was understandably taking an interest in the proceedings. I'd also met Mark Barrett there, the chap with the feather in his hair at the first meeting, the original picnicker, who was also keen to see what would happen to Maya before his hearing in January 2006. In court, a surprisingly cool retro room with oak panelling (later in the year Bow Street was closed down and sold to a property developer to be turned into luxury flats), the magistrate found Maya guilty of breaching Section 132 of the Serious Organised Crime and Police Act of 2005. She was given a conditional discharge and ordered to pay £100 costs.

Maya Evans was not the first person to fall foul of Section 132, just the first of the cases to go to court. There were two other pictures beside Maya's on the *Independent*'s front page under the headline WAR CRIMINALS: one of

Douglas Barker, seventy-two, who had been threatened with prison for withholding ten per cent of his income tax bill in protest against the Iraq war, and another of Malcolm Kendall-Smith, a thirty-seven-year-old medical officer who was facing a court martial for refusing to go on active service in Iraq. This appetite for law breaking seemed to be getting sharper by the day.

As the train pulled away from London Bridge, half an hour late, my mobile phone rang. It was John. I answered with an immediate apology.

'I'm really sorry, John, I'm going to be late.'

'Oh fuck,' he replied.

'We'll have fun, though. I'll buy you some lunch.'

'Beer, Dan, beer. See you soon.'

I was hoping that John would be able to put the picnickers into some kind of historical context for me. Prasanth had told me that he thought demonstrators were true patriots despite always being portrayed as extremists in the newspapers. The dictionary defines a patriot as someone who is devoted to his country. Some may argue that devotion is following England's football or cricket teams across the world, or cheering wildly as the Queen rushes past in a bulletproof limousine, but for me, being prepared to get arrested to defend the principle of free speech is a bit closer to the mark. I had come to the con-clusion that far from being a bunch of idealistic radicals, these people were just fulfilling their roles as citizens. The seventy-two-year-old holding back part of his tax in protest against the war, the medical officer refusing to go on active service, they were just the tip of the iceberg. But why were people everywhere suddenly beginning to take a stand? It wasn't just the war in Iraq. Pensioners were refusing to pay council tax, demonstrations were being held against roads, airports, hospital closures and out-of-town supermarket developments. Was there something in the air? Where was this spirit coming from? Why were so many people beginning to feel they were under attack? Perhaps it was nothing new. Perhaps it has always been happening under the surface. Were these people just the latest examples of a pattern of behaviour going back centuries? John was just the person to give me some answers.

An hour later I spotted him in the waiting room at Bedford station. 'Ah, there you are.' He slapped me on the back. We walked into town for an all-you-can-eat Chinese and then made straight for a Wetherspoon pub called Pilgrim's Progress. John looked through the window at the beers they had on that day and didn't look impressed. 'There's another one up the road, let's see what they've got.' So off we went further into the town.

As we walked, people made no attempt to hide their surprise as John ambled along the pavement. Six foot five with long, wild, grey hair and an enormous beard, he's a hard man to ignore. It was John's physical presence that always got him his acting jobs, rather than any specific acting ability. 'I specialize in tramps, drunks and maniacs,' he told me once. Although it was just the beard that got him booked on *Ant and Dec's Saturday Night Takeaway*. One member of the studio audience had written in to *Jim'll Fix It* at the age of eight asking to throw a custard pie in someone's beard. John fulfilled the childhood dream live on TV thirty years later. He'd also been a vagrant for Graham

Norton. 'It's not very dignified,' he told me a few weeks afterwards, 'but you pay the bills any way you can.'

We found a quiet corner in a suitable pub and sat down with our frothing pints.

'What's all this bollocks about then, Dan?' he boomed, and drained his glass. I went back to the bar, got him another pint, sat back down and asked him what he made of the reputation British people had for having a stiff upper lip and being too timid to complain. He leant forward and raised his eyebrows, staring at me intently through his bushy grey face. 'A very quick glance at historical records will prove that that is total nonsense. That was actually the thinking behind the little pamphlet I produced called *The Primer of English Violence*,[24] which was just a simple chronological list of all disturbances from 1485 to 1974. The amount of material I assembled, which was by no means exhaustive, showed that there was rarely more than ten years without some kind of uprising, disturbance, riot or revolt of some kind. In fact, it's not been a tranquil five hundred-odd years at all. You see, it's in our blood to stand up against tyranny.'

I told him what Prasanth had said about British democracy being the gold standard and that I was beginning to think that the protesters I'd met, and the ones I kept reading about in the newspapers, were true patriots. He began to grin.

'Well, first you've got to understand what being British, or in reality what being English, means. The Scots and the Welsh would take issue with us all being lumped in together. Daniel Defoe wrote a wonderful poem about the True-Born Englishman where he says we're the mongrels of the world. You see, there's no such thing as the English. There's no true race of English. We're all a bit of this, a bit of that and a bit of the kitchen sink. You know, there's no *English*. It's wonderful, vitriolic stuff. If *English* means anything, it means everyone. This is why it's so absurd for all these nationalistic c**ts to bang on about racial purity all the time. Apart from their point of view being objectionable crap in the first place, it also proves that they haven't got the slightest clue about the nation they claim to be so passionate about.'

Being seen as a 'nationalistic c**t', as John so eloquently put it, always seemed to me to be the biggest stumbling block to anyone seeking to display any sense of national pride. The idea of reclaiming patriotism around a sense of liberty was an idea that had long appealed to me. Many people take a dim view of the British Empire and the numerous atrocities it has been associated with, but a national identity existed long before Britannia ruled the waves. The 'Empire' was the recorded empire of the ruling class: the aristocracy, the monarchy, the entre-preneurs of the Industrial Revolution. The selling of our labour by the hour in 'dark satanic mills' and factories, rather than the medieval practice of being more in control of your working life, was the beginning of our current way of doing things. In order to force people away from their lives as artisans, where many had incomes from different sorts of 'jobs' rather than the insecurity of one full-time occupation, the Church was brought in to preach hellfire and damnation from the pulpit to anyone who refused to enter the mills and factories of the new industrial age. In Britain today there are many campaigns each year to increase the number of bank holidays to bring us in line with the rest of Europe. In the days of 'Saint Monday' the idea that you couldn't just decide for yourself whether you went to work or not would have seemed absurd. In the early years of the Industrial Revolution people didn't need state-sanctioned public holidays because they only bothered going back to work on a Monday if their wage packet had run out. Work was seen then as a necessary evil that stopped you doing what you wanted to do rather than a 'virtue' in itself, as propagated by the Protestant work ethic that enslaved the vast majority of people in poorly paid, clock-watching jobs. As you can imagine, 'Saint Monday' didn't last long. The mill owners abhorred the notion that people should expect to be in control of their own lives. How ironic that the 'progress' of the industrial age has brought us to today where we have less control over our time than we had in 1760.[25]

When Gandhi told the people of India to burn Lancashire cloth and to weave their own cotton as a symbolic rejection of the Empire, the people in the slums of Britain supported him, appreciating only too well the reality of the Empire for those who were propping it up. When Gandhi came to England to discuss Indian independence it was no coincidence that he decided to lodge in the slums of the East End where he was welcomed with open arms. The unrecorded voice of Albion was as undocumented back in the days of Empire as it is today.

I returned from the bar swaying slightly, but with more frothing ale in my arms. As I sat down, John continued.

'The idea of English patriotism coalesced around the

figure of John Bull. Now he's a tricky one, because on the one hand he was the epitome of the brain-dead thug brandishing a cudgel to make his case. Nevertheless, he is still also the perfect image of English common sense – common sense being what the common people have. Forget democracy, it's a much more powerful sense, the common sense, shared by everybody in the country, everybody in society. It's embedded in the character. It's a very odd phrase when you think about it. One that we take for granted.'

Now I may be naive about the economy but I'm even more so when it comes to democracy. I know it's important, but I haven't seen much evidence of it in my lifetime. As we all know, in a democracy everyone not in prison who is over eighteen gets a vote. But under our current electoral system, unless you live in an area where the government's majority is under threat, no-one actually cares who you vote for. So living in a democracy, while it sounds wonderful, principled and ideal, doesn't always mean that your voice gets heard, unless, as I said, you live in one of the 'swing seats' Peter Snow's always talking about on TV. Labour held on to power in the 2005 elections by getting 22 per cent of the possible vote. It's hardly a ringing endorsement from the British people when 78 per cent of us either voted for someone else or couldn't be bothered to vote at all.

We don't actually live in a democracy anyway. The power of your vote depends on your constituency. For example, if you live in the less populous far reaches of Scotland your single vote is a greater proportion of the vote as a whole in your constituency than it would be in

Deptford, the constituency where I live. So one vote is not always of equal value to another, which surely is supposed to be one of the cornerstones of 'democracy'. Then, of course, we still have the House of Lords, which is not elected at all. All of this is so well known that I risk ridicule for writing it here, but these are the facts that so many of us seem happy to forget when we idealize our 'democracy'. To combat this, many people, including the Liberal Democrats, advocate the introduction of proportional representation – where one vote really is equal to another. But successive governments have thrown out the idea as unworkable, and it seems unlikely that the Liberal Democrats will come to power under the current rules and implement PR any time soon.

Common sense, on the other hand, is something we all share whether we vote or not. There is no official national forum to discuss what it is or what we all mean by it, but it is the one thing we rely on to protect our communities from the questionable actions of our democracy. At the moment common sense sits, fuming but impotent, in every house up and down the nation. It only seems to mobilize when a crisis occurs that forces people to take a stand in the small amount of time they have left when they get back from work – if a hospital is threatened with closure, for example, or a planned mobile phone mast threatens a local community. This is the closest our common sense ever gets to our political leaders, usually in the form of a defiant but unsuccessful attempt to halt a centralized government policy that has little or no consideration for local circumstances. When you think about it, these kinds of demonstrations are simply expressions of the public feeling the machinations of our democracy so efficiently manage to ignore. It seems a waste only to harness these thoughts, passions and ideas at a moment of crisis and not use that common sense opinion to give people more control of their lives at a local level. But as no practical legal means to protect your community actually exists (see chapters 4 and 6), when this collective common sense does mobilize for a local cause it nearly always ends in failure. It is hardly surprising, then, that people have less and less faith in the system, and interest in politics as a whole breaks down.

I returned, yet again, from the bar, flushed and grinning wildly, with more beer in my hands. John and I were working our way through our fifth (or was it sixth?) pint when he began to explain more about the True-Born Englishman.

'A good way to explain the idea of the True-Born Englishman is the famous Hogarth picture *Gin Lane*. It's not widely realized that it is part of a pair. Gin Lane is bad but the other one, Beer Street, is good. And *Beer Street* is an equally tremendous print. People think Hogarth was having a go at alcohol in general with *Gin Lane*, but gin was what was causing all the problems, not beer. Everything in Beer Street is paradise. The only one not having a good time in Beer Street is the pawnbroker, because beer is part of the true English birthright. They used to drink beer all the time! They had small beer, which was virtually non-alcoholic, but it was much safer to drink than water. Drinking water back then could kill you, but beer was safe. There was also the belief, which I learned from an academic a few years ago, that wine was seen by the English as being associated with Catholic Europe, whereas hops made beer, which was Protestant and English. So you also had this split between Beer–Good–Protestant and Wine–Bad–Catholic.

'This takes us to the other birthright of the True-Born Englishman – to defy tyranny, which was most clearly shown when England broke from Rome [in the sixteenth century]. England became the first world power to be non-Catholic. There had been non-Catholic outbreaks before, but England was the first sovereign state not to acknowledge the authority of Rome, which is why Rome tried to send Jesuits to undermine it, why the Armada was sent, why the Pope said he would bless anyone who assassinated Queen Elizabeth. So all this Protestant stuff, this isn't Ian Paisley speaking, this is our orthodox history that used to be taught in schools, which is now overlooked in the multi-faith era. There's nothing wrong with that, but this stuff used to be the proud boast of the orthodox view and it was taught up until the 1940s. It inspired the whole of the Churchillian period. It is an image we always cast ourselves in. We stand alone against tyranny. We stood alone against Napoleon, we stood alone against Hitler, and Thatcher tried to position herself standing alone against the communist menace until Reagan joined her.

'So the rights of the True-Born Englishman are to drink beer and defy authority. To defy tyranny whatever its guise. If tyranny raises its head it's our duty to challenge it and to fight it until it's overthrown. So your protesters are fulfilling their proper destiny. They are the ones carrying out England's role. They're the ones, wherever they might have been born, being true to

England's history, its character, its heritage and its culture.

'I'll give you one good example of what I mean. 1848 was a year of revolutions in Europe. We didn't have one in England; the best we had was the Chartists' petition, which failed. Now most of the revolutions in Europe were put down by the military, and in Hungary, Kossuth's independent uprising was suppressed by a real butcher general called Haynau. Haynau came over to England for an official tour of London and part of his tour was around the Barclay and Perkins Brewery in Southwark. Well, the draymen there heard who he was and they went mad. They got hold of him and beat the living shit out of him. As far as they were concerned he was a butcher so they beat the crap out of him and he had to be rescued. Palmerston [the Prime Minister at the time] sent a perfunctory apology to Haynau, but then extended a very warm welcome to Kossuth. This pissed the Queen off no end but made Palmerston very popular in the country at large. So as late as the mid-nineteenth century it was still there. It's still there to this day, but it was more noticeable then. Can you imagine the British Prime Minister welcoming the head of the democratic movement in China, if there is one, like that today? So your fellow with the gold standard, I love that. The idea that anybody who didn't behave decently who came to England would get the shit beaten out of them is something to be proud of. That's why we've got this reputation. Today, of course, those draymen would no doubt be labelled mindless thugs or terrorists.'

Being told that being English actually means being part of an inclusive mongrel race that has always thrived on diversity, and that your right and duty as a member of that race is to stand up against tyranny whatever its guise – government, corporations or anyone who tries to exploit you or take away your freedom – *and* drink large amounts of beer (rather than gin, or its modern equivalents, alcopops, flavoured vodka and those luminous shots you can buy in dodgy nightclubs), was all of great comfort to me. That was an idea of national identity I could get on board with.

The map into Albion was beginning to take shape. It was a place that felt like home. A tolerant country where people from all over the world are welcome, where you don't take any crap from people trying to exploit you, and where you have as much fun as possible, largely, though not exclusively, through drinking beer. That's my idea of Albion. Let's celebrate those principles next time it's 23 April.

Having discussed the overthrowing of tyranny, John and I decided to continue our exploration of the other part of our birthright and get thoroughly and defiantly pissed. I fell asleep on the train home, missed my stop and ended up in Brighton. I didn't stumble through my front door until two in the morning.

A few days later I was back in Parliament Square. Mark Barrett had phoned me to say that Cindy Sheehan was going to meet Brian Haw as part of her publicity trip to Britain. Cindy had become the most prominent anti-war campaigner in America after camping outside George Bush's compound in Texas, demanding an audience with the man she blamed for the loss of her son, a soldier who had died in Iraq. There was a great commotion in the square. A mob of people surrounded an inspector and ten police officers and there were press everywhere. People shouted at the police but they remained deliberate and calm. Most of the people were arguing that they were there to meet Cindy Sheehan and had no intention of protesting. One of them pointed out that there were no banners and no-one was chanting. The policeman told them calmly that in his view it *was* an unauthorized protest and that unless everyone left within half an hour they would all be arrested. Mark handed me a 'Protest Permit Holders Only' sign the picnickers had made and was immediately rounded on by a policeman who gave him one of the leaflets explaining that he had just broken the law. Mark took it from him and smiled.

Behind him, things were becoming increasingly fraught. People were trying to talk calmly but their frustration was clear. One of the women I'd seen at the first meeting who looked like a schoolteacher was doing her best not to lose her temper with a policeman: 'It's *not* a protest, we are allowed to stand here to wait for Cindy Sheehan. You have no right to threaten us with arrest! This is a public area! We are committing no crime!' The police backed off and stood away from the crowd, but they had made their intent clear. More officers appeared on the edges of the square. We all had half an hour to leave or the arrests would begin.

I told one of the officers standing a few feet away from the picnic blanket that I didn't envy his job enforcing laws as absurd as this one. He smiled. 'To be honest, it is a terrible law, but what can we do?' Another younger officer was less relaxed. He stood with his arms folded looking down his nose at the skirts and home-made cakes that swirled around him. I asked him what the definition of protest was so that I could make sure I wasn't doing anything that might make me liable for arrest. He looked at me in frustration. 'What do *you* think it means?' I said that it didn't matter what I thought it meant because I didn't have the power of arrest; it was what *he* understood it to mean that mattered to everyone there. I asked again. He stared at me, shook his head and walked away. This is the most absurd aspect of the legislation that created the protest exclusion zone. If you can't get a clear response from a policeman on what exactly it is you are doing that he is threatening to arrest you for, then what chance do you have of preventing yourself from breaking the law?

It was at that moment that Cindy arrived. The film crews and photographers outnumbered everyone else as Brian took her through his banners and posters. The photographs of dead children had her in tears. She held on to Brian as he guided her along the pavement between well-wishers and photographers. She said she thought he was a hero and hugged him time and time again. The police remained unmoved, staring quietly at Big Ben. They had told the crowd that they would start making arrests at half-past one. At 1.25 I walked over to the inspector who was going through the plan with one of his officers. 'At half past we'll ask them all to leave and if we're not satisfied that they are going to disperse I'll give the call and get the vans from around the corner and then we'll start making arrests,' he said.

One of the picnickers approached and asked for more

time to clear the food away. The inspector clearly didn't want to arrest anyone, but he would follow the letter of the law if he had to. 'Look,' he replied, 'if I can see that you're all making an effort to move on then I won't make any arrests when it gets to half past.' I went up to him and pointed out Peggy, a ninety-two-year-old peace campaigner, sitting in an armchair behind Brian's display of banners and posters. Brian had just introduced her to Cindy as 'their mother'. I asked the inspector, 'Do you think you could start by arresting her? It would do wonders for the publicity campaign.' He looked at me in horror. He seemed exhausted, shook his head and said desperately, 'But that wouldn't do me any good, though. Would it?'

Without getting too misty-eyed about it in retrospect, there wasn't an unreasonable person standing on Parliament Square that afternoon. Everyone sat or stood on that patch of grass acted courteously, even if their tempers were frayed. In the great history of Parliament Square, I can't imagine there has ever been anything quite like what happened that day. The police politely informing a group of twenty people that they were breaking the law; the same policemen agreeing with the people about the insanity of the law the people were breaking; police vans parked round the corner waiting to arrest people with smiling, laughing faces, having a picnic while a mother who'd lost her son in a war cried on the shoulder of a peace campaigner. Now that may seem like I'm laying it on a bit thick, but that was how it felt being there. I realized at that moment that I didn't want anyone to get arrested that day because I didn't want to do it to that police inspector. I could see that he simply didn't need the hassle of having to deal with Section 132 of the Serious Organised Crime and Police Act. He was being asked to treat teenagers, adults and grandmothers who believed in freedom of speech like criminals and load them up in riot wagons. Parliament hadn't just let down the people it was supposed to be representing by allowing such an undemocratic law, it had also severely let down the police who had more than enough to deal with as it was. After all, a good relationship between citizens and their police force is vital for any society. It was inexcusable for Parliament to make a law that contravened the principle of free speech, and it was just as inexcusable to drive a wedge between the people it served and the people entrusted with ensuring their safety.

I walked over to Mark and asked whether he was going to stay to be arrested. He shrugged. 'I'm not sure. I don't really want to spend eight hours in Charing Cross police station again. Do you fancy a drink instead? I'd love a pint.' I told him what I'd learned from John, that our birthright required us not only to stand up against tyranny but also to drink lots of beer. He smiled. 'Well, that's settled it. We can't deny ourselves our birthright.' And with that we all headed off to the pub.

# CHAPTER 4

Watford's is called the Harlequin Centre. Basingstoke opted for Festival Place. Reading decided on The Oracle (in classical antiquity, a place at which advice or prophecy was sought from the gods). Cumbernauld, meanwhile, kept it simple with Cumbernauld Shopping Centre, although residents, I hear, refer to it simply as 'Hell'. This disease has now spread to every town in Britain. The chainstore makeover was, seemingly, not enough. Now every town needs an absurdly expensive and pretentiously titled shopping mall to entice shoppers away from the identical shopping mall that's just been built in the town down the road. But Derby felt it was missing out, which is why its council opted for the Riverlights Centre, a 500,000-square-foot development which, according to the developer's website, would include '22 units of restaurants and bars, with premier operators, a Grand Casino, a 120-bed quality city hotel, and 150 high-quality city apartments'. The only thing in their way was a forty-two-year-old lady called Dorothy who was camping on the roof of the bus station the developers needed to bulldoze before they could start work. 'Of course you can come and interview me,' she said down the phone. 'And if you do come, could you bring me some cashew nuts? Oh, and white chocolate?'

I admire Dorothy for many reasons. Spending the night on the roof of a bus station in the depths of winter is not something you do unless you're desperate, but she'd already been there for eight weeks by the time I visited her, so she certainly had guts. But it was her bloody-minded defiance that really impressed me. The *Crap Towns* project had revealed a lot of things about the state of Britain's towns and villages. People cared very much about where they lived but seemed, in the main, resigned to the fact that their councils were more interested in companies that wanted to invest in their towns than in the people who actually lived in them. But Dorothy wasn't prepared to let her council's plans go unchallenged.

Before *Crap Towns* came out I went on a forty-day road trip to visit some of the places *Idler* readers had voted as the worst in the UK. It was a very interesting journey that took me all over Britain, from Dover in Kent to Thurso in the northern reaches of Scotland. I visited some truly surprising places: Blackbird Leys, the home of joyriding just outside Oxford; Winchester in Hampshire, the smuggest town on earth; the Bransholme Estate in Hull, John Prescott's back yard; Cumbernauld in Scotland, by far the most miserable and depressing hell hole in Britain, largely due to its poverty; and then, inevitably, there was Slough.

Good old 'butt of a thousand jokes' Slough. It means 'bog', by the way, but then if you've been there you've probably already guessed that. Slough was somewhere I had experience of because I used to work there as a weed sprayer. The job of a weed sprayer is to kill weeds. I had to wear a green boiler suit with yellow Marigolds and carry a twenty-five-litre tank of weedkiller on my back. I remember it well because working in Slough was actually a promotion from my previous job scaling motorway embankments spraying around the little trees that were being bullied by thick bramble and other violent plants. I learned a lot as a weed sprayer. Namely, that if you spend all day every day doing a job you loathe there are only two ways you spend the rest of your time – drunk or asleep. I also learned something about humiliation. It's the only time during my life I've been called a 'sad bastard' by both an incontinent bag lady and the driver of a souped-up Capri. Discovering that you are lower down in the social hierarchy than those two elements of society gives you a unique sense of perspective on life, I can assure you.

Economically, Slough is the perfect modern town, which should strike fear into the hearts of everyone living in Britain. It is near an airport, the local economy is thriving and provides plenty of jobs for local people, it is racially inclusive, it lies close to London and, at the same time, is also located near beautiful countryside. This is the British town that exemplifies the priorities of modern life. It's town-planning perfection. Slough is a microcosm that tells you everything you need to know about the things our country prioritizes, yet everyone in Britain who's ever been there thinks it's a shit hole. The BBC even did a series called *Making Slough Happy*, for goodness' sake. Slough is the kind of town Morrissey would have immortalized if The Smiths were around today. Slough makes you want to slit your wrists. Well, it made me feel like that when I worked there as a weed sprayer. As it happens, the guy I used to spray with did slit his wrists, but that's another story.

Returning to Slough on a book tour because it appeared in my book as one of the crappiest places to live in Britain was, therefore, quite a cathartic moment. At least it was until the end of the evening, when it also became rather enlightening. After the audience had laughed along politely to my slightly offensive judgment of their town, I asked them why they were all prepared to live in such a God-awful, depressing, ugly place. A woman immediately put her hand up and said, 'I've lived in seven countries all over the world and the reason I love Slough is because it's the most racially tolerant place I've ever been to. A friend of mine from Ghana came to visit us last year and he said when he walked down the high street he'd never felt so free of prejudice anywhere else in the world. He heard someone speaking his language, and saw people of all colours and styles of dress walking freely and without fear.' Everyone around her nodded sagely. Then someone else added, 'And no pretentious people would ever dream of living in Slough, unlike down the road in Windsor, which is full of c**ts.'

Now you can't really argue with that, can you?

But Slough aside, wherever I went on my journey the

complaints always seemed to be the same: too many super-markets, too many of the same shops, too many bars selling cheap booze, too much puke on the streets, too many councillors with their noses in the air and fingers in the till, too many planning applications approved for huge companies despite local protests, too few police on the streets, too much violence, too few schools, no voice and no sense of community. The other recurrent theme was the way our towns and cities are beginning to look. So many of them are irredeemably ugly. There is no in-spiration, no sense of being part of something. The places we live in have just become places to work and shop that masquerade as towns. A prime example is South Woodham Ferrers, just north-east of London. Go there and you'll get a surprise. It's Asda town, and all the streets are named after characters and places from *Lord of the Rings*. It would be funny if it weren't so tragic. I've always imagined the logic behind enormous supermarkets is that they are built to provide a service for people who live in the area. In South Woodham Ferrers you begin to realize that now it's the other way round: Asda isn't there for the people, the people have been brought in for Asda. On the day I was there the entire place was like a ghost town – until I went into the shopping centre and found hundreds of people milling about. There was nothing else to do in South Woodham Ferrers except spend money and get bored. The planners have learned from the success of Slough. South Woodham Ferrers is the town of the future.

When local worthies did rally round to defend their town's appearance in our book they always trotted out the same old arguments, blaming the building programmes of the fifties and sixties. My friend Fin concurred in the case of Hull, claiming, 'Its best town planner was Hitler.' But you can't blame everything on the architects of yesteryear and the Luftwaffe. It's hard to imagine that no-one working in town planning over the last fifty years saw the generic, every-high-street-is-indistinguishable land we now live in looming on the horizon.

I called a friend of my mum's, Honor Gibbs, a retired architect and landscape architect, to ask how we had got ourselves into such a mess. Honor pointed me in the direction of a book published in 1955 by an architect called Ian Nairn, aptly titled *Outrage*, which I tracked down on the fantastic website abebooks.co.uk. *Outrage* is a combination of a prediction, a call to arms and a plea for planners, designers and ordinary people to appreciate the enormous impact our environment has on our lives. It is a savage premonition of a country that is almost identical to the one we find ourselves in today, the country of crap towns, or as Nairn described it, 'Subtopia'. Right from the start, Nairn is clear about who is to blame for things going wrong:

Public Authorities are responsible for nearly all of the faults exposed in this [book]; they have most power and often least awareness of the visual responsibility that should go with it, but they are only a corporate reflection of what goes on in the mind of each one of us . . . this is a prophecy of doom – the doom of an England reduced to universal Subtopia, a mean and middle state, neither town nor country, an even spread of abandoned aerodromes and fake rusticity, wire fences, traffic roundabouts, gratuitous notice-boards, car-parks and Things in Fields. It is a morbid condition which spreads both ways from suburbia, out into the country, and back into the devitalised hearts of towns.

What interested me most about *Outrage* was that Nairn saw a direct cause and effect between our sense of unhappiness and the places we call home. In essence, the crap towns we live in are a physical reflection of our mental state. The more unhappy and unfulfilled we are as people, the worse our towns and villages will inevitably become.

For Nairn, the world was split between what he called the self-conscious world of man and the unselfconscious world of nature. It was possible, he wrote, for these worlds to co-exist providing each was treated with care and attention. Instead, the reality was that man had levelled off these two worlds, morphing them into one indistinguishable and unpleasant 'mean which is a threat not simply to our felicity but to our continued development as more than an order of termites. The environment is an extension of the ego, and twentieth-century man is likewise busy metamorphosing himself into a mean – a meany – neither human or divine. And the thing he is doing to himself and to his background is the measure of his own mediocrity. Insensible to the meaning of civilization on the one side and, on the other, ignorant of the well-spring of his own being, he is removing the sharp edge from his own life, exchanging individual feeling for mass experience in a voluntary enslavement far more restrictive and permanent than the feudal system ... it is man enslaved dragging down his environment to his own level.'

We have certainly done that to the way we think, confusing the ideas and principles of driving the economy and our overwork ethic with our sense of safety, happiness and contentment. As Nairn predicted, the result of this way of life has manifested itself physically in every identical town in Britain. All the complaints people have today about the way their communities are decaying is simply a reflection of the way our values and sense of happiness have been eaten away by our slavish acceptance of an ever-expanding economy with its work, debt and consumption.

But even if we don't care that we're becoming an order of overworking and over-consuming 'termites', chasing mass experience, *Crap Towns* at least proved that people really do care about the places they call home. Civic pride is alive and well in Britain, but small local groups don't get to fight the corporate world on a level playing field. Planning law exists to ensure equal treatment, but if it was ever intended to protect our communities or the people that live in these areas then it has catastrophically failed. We may be growing blind to the damage the corporate vision has done to the way we live on a day-to-day basis, but we are not blind to the way this corporate vision has redesigned our country. Our environment, the unrecorded world of Albion, has been pushed, bulldozed and ransacked, and the only chance we have to reclaim and protect it is to start listening to, and recording, the common-sense opinions of local people.

For Nairn, the origin of our downward spiral, when our misery directly began to destroy the world around us, was clear. 'Any hope of intelligent interpretation was lost when planning was tied down step by step with local government, and made into another unrewarding office job,' he wrote. 'This chained it to the very points where democracy is most likely to give the lowest common denominator, not the highest common multiple: corporate Subtopia with all the planning rules as its armoury, perverted to make every square mile indistinguishable.'

A friend of mine, an architect called Jason, confirmed this was still the case today when I spoke to him about the problems he faced with local planners in South London. 'You can't find people to do the job who have any stake in the local area, that's the problem,' he said. 'I'm always coming up against planners who are twenty-somethings from Australia or New Zealand. They're nice people, but in six months they'll be back at home.' What should have been a sacred, valued job became the domain of pompous local dignitaries and local planners who often had no long-term interest in the area they were responsible for. The design and appearance of our nation was surely something we all had a stake in. How had it become so devalued in our minds?

Nairn was an architect so he couldn't be accused of being anti-development, far from it. He was just desperate for people to realize that an area of life that required enormous care was receiving very little attention indeed. The crimes were there for all of us to see, in the housing estates, the high streets, the failed urban regeneration plans and the decimation of the countryside, but for some reason, then as now, we just shrugged our shoulders, went back to work and assumed an 'expert' somewhere was taking responsibility for these things on our behalf.

I read further into the book and came across a

phenomenon that thousands of people had written about in the nominations we received for *Crap Towns*. Nairn showed nine pictures of suburban streets, listed the names of nine towns and asked the reader to decide which was which. The point was that this was impossible. From Carlisle to Southampton, everywhere looked the same. This has developed one stage further today with our uniform high streets and out-of-town shopping malls. Every town in Britain has become a sinister replication of the same place, and it's getting worse.

At the end of his book Nairn made his call to arms, and it's worth reprinting here because little has changed: 'The action is needed NOW. So the attack must come from outside. That is a job for all of us, and the only qualification we need is to have eyes to see . . . if you think they represent a universal letting down and greying out; if you think that they should be fought and not accepted . . . Use your double birthright – as a free-thinking human being and as a Briton lucky enough to be born into a country where the individual voice can still get a hearing.' Don't expect the answers to come from the 'experts' – they've had their way, and look what they've done. The answers will come from the opinions and thoughts of ordinary local people. The systems are actually in place to protect and preserve our communities, but we'll never be able to use them until we start to reclaim our time from the world of work. After all, who can attend a public inquiry for months on end to try to save their local community if they have a full-time job? The way we live – the reason for the mess in our minds that's reflected in our environment – will need a radical rethink if we are to stop things from getting worse.

Thankfully, some people are fighting against Nairn's Subtopia. People like Dorothy in Derby, for example, who decided to camp on the roof of the bus station because she didn't want luxury apartments and a casino complex built on top of a flood plain. She was a sign of hope, and I was desperate to meet her. I asked Mark Barrett to come with me so that I could find out why he'd been moved to protest, and because I knew he'd find Dorothy's story inspiring.

Spontaneity is one of those wonderful things that has all but died in the professional world. A fellow Idler, Daniel Pemberton, bemoaned the lack of it in his life in *Idler 36*: 'it has been extremely depressing to discover more and more of my friends unable to do anything without a three-week warning, preferably backed up by some typed confirmation.' Thankfully for me, Mark was someone capable of being spontaneous. He may not have had much cash but, because time is so much more valuable than money could ever dream of being, he was able to decide on a whim to come with me on a little adventure.

I met him at St Pancras station. He was wearing a pink hat with tassels that hung down below his ears. I bought a cup of tea for myself and an espresso for him, and we headed off to platform 13 to get our train.

As it pulled away I asked him to tell me about his life and why he had decided to start the picnic protest. He was certainly driven, and unlike me, he wasn't scared of getting arrested. For a revolutionary intent on re-establishing a 'people's commons', his background turned out to be quite a surprise. Mark graduated with a first from law school and took up a work placement to secure the final part of his qualification. This involved working in Dubai for an enormous law firm he'd prefer I didn't name. That's the same Dubai that is now desperately marketing itself as the place professional footballers go on holiday. 'It was so depressing, seeing all these brilliant minds spending every single day trying to find new ways of helping various billion-dollar oil and media corporations worm out of paying tax,' he told me. 'And the contrast in the way you were treated if you were white rather than local was hideous. It was the undiluted, untamed corporate world. I couldn't bear it. I had to leave.'

He travelled extensively, lived in Mexico, where he fell in love (he got married in Vegas), then moved to Canada for a while and took part in the famous 1999 protest in Seattle, which gave him faith that a different future was possible. A period on a commune in Devon followed, he got divorced, stayed in monasteries for a while, then went to India and had an affair with a Bollywood film star and ex-Miss India who told him he was about to discover the 'main course' of his life. 'I decided then that I wanted to stand for community. Human rights are always about individual rights, but why don't we have the right to live in a community? The market doesn't provide communities, it breaks them down, so when the market doesn't provide something that humans really need, that's when the government needs to step in and facilitate it.'

When he returned to England he began to take an interest in Brian Haw's vigil in Parliament Square and felt compelled to get involved. 'I began watching the situation because I knew that if they banned protest in Parliament Square I would have to fight it. I knew that. The law came into force on 1 August. There was a Stop the War event on that day which I didn't go to because I don't really trust the Stop the War/Respect organization, it's hierarchical and undemocratic, but on 7 August there was a mass act of defiance planned. There was no ideology, it was just "this law is wrong whoever you are", and that was more my cup of tea. It was like the anti-war march in February 2002. There was a spirit then that I recognized from back in North America, dealing with a serious issue like the war but with fun rather than aggression.

'So on 7 August I turned up in Parliament Square in bare feet giving out flowers to people, and I persuaded a load of strangers to throw teabags into the Thames with me, like the Boston tea party. It was a demonstration of support for the Tobin Tax, which is this idea that if you impose a 0.01 per cent annual tax on the trade of buying or selling currency, just in Britain it would create three billion pounds a year that you could ring-fence for international development, famine and so on. Forget Geldof's "Give us your fucking money" nonsense. All these millionaires telling us to make poverty history by offering to cancel Third World debt, but only for countries prepared to sell the family silver by privatizing their infrastructure and the basis of any future economic power to western corporations – forget that. Three billion just from the money exchange! Imagine what you could do with it! That was where the tea party idea came from, which became the picnic for protest itself, rather than just being my protest that the government won't implement the Tobin Tax. The *Independent* ran a big feature about the picnic a month or so later, and you know what the quote in the paper said about where the idea came from? "It started as a joke for Mark Barrett." The media is so frustrating. Anyway, my friend Sian, who was also there that day, suggested we hold a picnic every week to protest against SOCPA's exclusion zone, but for me it's also about re-establishing the people's commons. Because our commons is just not there any more. It's gone.'

Mark now had a part-time job as a guide for American tourists visiting Europe. He worked during the summer and spent the winter doing his own projects. He was planning to train as a citizenship teacher the following September.

The train picked up speed.

'I'm convinced that everything will work out in the end though,' Mark concluded. 'I've got this theory that the road to heaven is paved with bad intentions.'

Mark was 'for real', as Manic Street Preacher Richey Edwards would carve in his arm. I think a legal expert who wears feathers in his hair is just the kind of person the world needs more of.

We arrived in Derby and walked down towards the town. It could have been any town in Britain. It was full of elements of Nairn's Subtopia – uninspired, grey and functioning only as a place to work and shop. The footpath signs leading from the station constantly contradicted themselves so we spent the first half-hour wandering around in circles. Then we came to a roundabout and the pitifully ugly Eagle Shopping Centre. It contained an empty covered market with huge ceilings and odd Christmas decorations. No doubt at one time it too was heralded as the answer to modernizing Derby's shopping experience. We then walked down a claustrophobic passage that led us out towards the high street. The usual suspects were there. Again, it looked like any other high street in Britain. If you looked up you could see beautiful buildings above the shop fronts, but lurid branding obscured anything worthwhile.

I rang Dorothy to find out where exactly the bus station was. She gave us directions to the Court House, which had a huge Make Poverty History banner hanging from the entrance. The bus station itself was surrounded by fences and signs explaining its imminent closure. The road adjacent to it was full of temporary bus stops and miserable people waiting for buses that never seemed to arrive. We had planned to get up on the roof with her, but she explained that it was far too windy for the ladders so we'd have to do the interview from the ground up through the skylight. We walked round the side of the station until we spotted a gap in the fence. We clambered through and saw Dorothy's tent on the roof above.

The bus station had fallen on hard times but the building itself was solid with faultless brickwork. Art deco architecture is beautiful. If it was in a town that had vision, or any appreciation of our architectural heritage, it would be preserved and celebrated, but it had been neglected for so long that it looked run down and out of date. Allowing a building like that to rot for a few years is a good way of avoiding complaints from the public when the council finally suggests pulling it down so they can sell the site for millions to a developer. People get so sick and tired of perfectly good buildings falling into ruin that a nice illustration of glass and steel seems far more appealing than preserving something that's been left to die. It also makes a developer far more money than they would get for simply repairing the existing building.

Dorothy peered down through the skylight and handed down a bit of rope she used for hauling up provisions. I sent up the bag of cashew nuts and white chocolate buttons. 'Oh, thank you,' she said. 'I've lost so much weight up here because it's so cold.' Then she paused. 'Oh, you naughty boy, these are Nestlé.' But she was too hungry and cold to throw them back.

In Derby's local press, opinion was divided between whether Dorothy was a local hero or an insane eco warrior, but Dorothy's objections to the development stemmed from the lack of local consultation and the fact that the proposal was simply unsustainable. 'For a start there was no public inquiry,' she told me. 'Outline permission for this was given ten years ago and we've been fighting it ever since. There was no public consultation about this development. There were models in the town and in the market telling us how it was going to look, but that was it. The planning application was made, which went through with a nod, and then we were told what was going to happen and that was that. It got to the point where the bulldozers were moving in and the only way we could make our view heard was by taking non-violent, direct action. I've now been up here for eight weeks.'

The Riverlights website talks about 'city-living style on the waterfront', a 'relaxing atmosphere' and 'more choices'. Presumably that's more choices in how to spend your money. But because of Dorothy's protest the developers were having problems making these claims a reality. 'The developer has to build a new bus station first, which will be on the bit of road you've just come past,' Dorothy explained. 'The development is supposed to be made of steel and glass, and as you know the price of oil is soaring and the price of steel is soaring as well. So the developer isn't too keen to start building the new bus station if he's got no takers for the rest of the site. They can't open bars now because there are no liquor licences. There were twelve that were originally granted, which had to be renewed every year, but we appealed against them and won. So now the whole project is becoming a white elephant. Now no-one will be able to open a bar.'

Dorothy's protest wasn't about halting Derby council's plans to enhance its citizens' shopping and leisure experience; she was more concerned with the practical implications of what they were trying to build. 'I'm not just up here because I love the bus station,' she said. 'It's about sustainable development. Where we are now is an air quality management area. Thirty-four thousand cars a day use this area here and it's also a flood plain. The River Derwent is right at the back of us. It's flooded three times in the last thirty years. In 2000 it almost broke again, and in 1965 it flooded most of the city. They want to have a casino, nightclub, bars, apartments for about eight hundred people, and underground car parking as well. They haven't told the potential investors that when the river floods all their nice cars are going to get a bit wet.'

I asked her why the council was so keen on pushing the development through. 'A lot of the time I think the councillors are just told by the planners that something will be good for the economy of the city, and good for jobs, and therefore that makes it the right thing to do,' she replied. 'The economy is what they serve, not the community, and it's not the same thing. In a lot of other cases they are simply ignorant and don't know what they're talking about. I mean, there are still officers and councillors here who don't believe in climate change.

'We did lots of demonstrations, we went through all the "proper" channels before we got to this point, but why should they care what we think when we don't have any actual power? I've written to most of the big brewery chains that were thinking of moving in to show them a copy of a letter from the Environment Agency, which recommends emergency evacuation procedures for all the establishments on the development in the event of a flood, which would have made something of an impact on their decision to invest, I'm sure. But the hypocrisy of the council is astounding. The block of apartments is supposed to be built on an area our own Environmental Health Department has said is not suitable for residential use. It's dead noisy at night – I can confirm that one – and you've got the weir, the cars, the lorries at night and the guildhall clock, which chimes every quarter of an hour. I have to wear earplugs and ear protectors at night to get any sleep.

'Of course, this could all have come out if the people had been consulted. There is a new planning thing the council have to apply in cases like this called the "statement of community involvement" but it's not worth the paper it's written on. We had to nag the council to put the word "participation" in it, and even then it's like Kryten trying to lie in *Red Dwarf*. They just can't say the word. "Par . . . parti . . . partici . . ." Yet the new strategic environmental assessment directives say that they have to allow the community to participate well before they get in touch with the developer.'

Participation is one of those words politicians don't like to use because everyone is absolutely clear about what it means. If you have to promise someone participation then they will assume they'll get the chance to participate. If they subsequently don't get a say, faith in the system understandably begins to break down. 'A lot of the time you discover the council have been discussing something with the developer months and months before even the councillors get to hear about it, let alone the actual community,' Dorothy added. 'That happened with the incinerator we are also campaigning against. The developer was being consulted eighteen months before the local people were told anything about it! The future doesn't get a voice, that's the problem, which is why things *have* to be sustainable. The government pays lip service to the idea of sustainability but their actions prove they don't know what sustainability means. Why was the Sustainability Commission set up? Why did they define sustainability? What is the point of all these commissions, all this legislation, if all they do on the ground is act against it? We have a City of Derby local plan, for goodness' sake, which states that buildings like this bus station will be reused! Recycled! Refurbished! As if! It also says that wildlife corridors, like the one at the back here that's going to be ripped up to make way for a casino, should be protected! At the moment the council is consulting on its natural history strategy! They wouldn't know their natural history if a branch whacked them in the face!'

Despite the odds stacked against her, and the fact that people regularly referred to her in the local news as a lunatic, Dorothy was confident that her protest would work. 'Eventually I think the developer will drop out, make a new agreement with the council to modernize and refurbish this bus station and hopefully turn this into a social enterprise and give it back to local people. The people who care about it are the people that use buses. No-one on the council uses buses, none of the planning officers use buses. They don't care about public transport.'

I told Dorothy that I thought she was a true patriot, and she looked at me in a strange but thoughtful way. 'That's a funny thing to say. I've never really considered whether or not I'm a patriot. I'm actually of Polish extraction. I love living here. I don't want to do what I'm doing but it's got to be done. Someone's got to stand up and fight these things. This development takes no heed of what will happen in the future. The Deputy Prime Minister's Planning Office's statement says that every new development like this has to calculate its carbon dioxide-producing potential. This development is huge. This area, the bus station and the coach park, is enormous. But the new bus station will only fit into a third of the area that it takes up at the moment. The rest of it's going to be under-ground car parks, flats. It's town cramming not town planning, reverting back to the dubious designs of the seventies.'

Before we left, I asked Dorothy if there was anything

else she wanted to tell me, if there was anything specific she wanted me to record in my search for Albion.

'There is one thing.' She paused, and seemed unsure whether to continue. 'I don't want to sound melodramatic, but during the last twenty years of campaigning over various things, I can see . . . I was going to say a creeping totalitarianism, but it's not creeping. It's here, and it scares me. We had a protest here in Derby when the G8 met up in Scotland [in July 2005]. The police spent millions on getting extra police for the protest and in the end the scale of the effort prevented lots of people coming because they were simply too afraid. That's not good for a democracy if people are afraid to come out and express their opinion. We got two hundred in the end, which wasn't bad. But there was a cycle ride from the station that day and the police thought some of the cyclists were cycling too slowly so they started dragging them off their bikes and throwing them in the back of police vans. In the paper the next day there was a picture of a policeman and a woman, a protester, standing apart. The angle of the photograph made it look as though they were closer than they were, but you could see from the perspective they were about eight feet away from each other. The headline was PROTESTER SQUARES UP TO POLICEMAN. The only violence that day was when the police dragged people off their bikes. Before the protest the papers were full of stories predicting lots of violence. All the shopkeepers boarded up their shops in anticipation, the little statue in the memorial garden got put in a little box. It was weird, because protesters are always portrayed as being violent now, but it's not violent extremists who want to protest.

I'm sick of being portrayed like that. We just care about our communities.

'I've been involved with Friends of the Earth for twenty years, and in the campaign we're running now we've got an engineer, a train driver, a gardener, a nurse, a teacher, and I wouldn't have seen that twenty years ago. I've even got a lawyer advising me with the liquor appeals for this development. I think it's becoming normal to protest and be "radical", which is probably why the government deal with protest in such a heavy-handed way, to scare away normal people from demonstrating their point of view. It's becoming mainstream to demonstrate and the government don't like that. But people have had enough, and that's one of the best feelings I have noticed since being up here. I've had enough too, but now I'm actually fighting and doing something about it. I'm going to carry on fighting. I will not roll over. I'm not going to give up and let this develop-ment happen. I just hope lots and lots of other people will start to think, "I'm not going to take it any more" where they live too.'

The media do often portray protesters as lunatics who are violent and dangerous, and we've already seen that the government shares that view. Being arrested for eating cakes in Parliament Square may strike you as absurd, but it's surely also frightening. But is it frightening on a George Orwell scale? From Dorothy's point of view it seems to be heading that way. Protesters are not weird extremists who don't fit into our society. My experience with the ones I'd met so far proved that. They were not violent. Angry, yes, but not mindless thugs or, in Jack Straw's words, 'evil'. What they were doing was more often than not incredibly sensible and well thought out, if you stopped, listened and actually recorded what they had to say. It's not that these people are out of place in normal society, it's that the priorities of society are becoming out of place for the few of its people who are actually behaving like responsible citizens. It is genuinely alarming that things around us have changed to the point where someone demonstrating against a council's plans to build a huge development on a flood plain can be dismissed as insane. What Dorothy said just sounded like simple common sense to me.

We left Dorothy and headed into Derby's town centre. Mark had pointed out that now we'd met someone who was standing up against tyranny, it was time to enjoy our other birthright – by drinking beer in the pub.

After a bit of searching, Mark and I found a pub adorned with St George's flags that looked more conventionally patriotic. We were looking for a pub that seemed in spirit the opposite of Dorothy, in the hope (and in my case presumption) that we would hear a few opposing local points of view about her protest. It looked like the kind of place where fights are seen as just another way to socialize. When we walked in everyone stared at us. They seemed a little anxious about Mark's pink hat. There were pictures on the walls commemorating England's 5–1 defeat of Germany in Munich in 2001, and gruff old men propping up the bar smoking impossibly thin cigarettes. I bought a pint of bitter for me and a pint of Guinness for Mark.

We sat down at a small table by the door. The barman asked whether we'd be more comfortable over there, and pointed to another room on our right full of empty tables. We moved, somewhat nervously, next to a man with a shaved head whose arms were covered with England tattoos, and began chatting about Dorothy. I was convinced everyone in the bar thought we were gay, and on the basis of the decoration I'd made another presumption that that wouldn't be seen as a good thing. After a while a chap standing at the bar came over and asked if he could join us. He was wiry, with black hair and a black eye. I felt even more nervous. Mark seemed delighted. He moved his coat from one of the seats and took off his hat.

The man was called Adam and he worked at the pub. He was waiting to start his shift but had an hour to kill. It turned out that he'd been listening to our conversation about politics and Albion, and it soon emerged that he wanted to be a writer but had given up on doing anything about it beyond deciding it was something he'd like to do. 'I can't write. I'm crap,' he said of himself, dismissively. I asked him what he wanted to write about and he began to tell us about his life. 'I'd like to write a book about working here, in the pub. I've got loads of stories. I don't know if you can see this' – he pointed at the enormous bruise around his eye – 'but my missus did this. She came in with three blokes and they dragged me outside so she could beat me up. She's eighteen stone! She can punch!' He started laughing. 'Then I had to go to court for my lad and I got everything I asked for. She asked the judge for me to have a drug test and I said, "Oh yeah, fine, as long as she has one too." And then I passed it but she failed! Now I get to see him whenever I like. I always take my lad down the river to feed the ducks and swans, down by that old bus station.' Adam hadn't heard about Dorothy's protest, but he was worried about a development stopping him from taking his son to feed the ducks along the river. I told him to buy a notebook and write down his ideas but he had no faith in himself and just shook his head. 'No, I wouldn't do that. It'd just be a load of rubbish.'

I doubt whether Adam is alone in thinking that his thoughts have little value. Being allowed to have ideas is another thing that's been professionalized now. Tom Hodgkinson, the *Idler*'s editor, wrote a fantastic piece in the magazine about the joy of notebooks: 'You may feel a trifle self-conscious when you first get the notebook out. You may worry that people will think you have ideas above your station. You may think that the very act of jotting down thoughts in a book implies a sort of arrogance – that you consider your thoughts to be worth jotting down in the first place. Ignore these negative emotions, which have been produced in your mind by years of conditioning by the industrial society, conditioning that says only the experts have got anything to say . . .'[26]

Before long Adam had to start his shift. I told him I'd send him a copy of *Crap Towns* to read, but I didn't. I sent him a notebook instead.

By this time Mark and I were half sozzled – only because we hadn't eaten, I hasten to add – and he was busy waxing lyrical about how real democracy would save the world. He soon caught the eye of another man sitting at the next table who looked over at us shiftily. 'Are you two politicians or something?' Mark told him we were not. 'Good. I'd have beaten the shit out of you if you had been. I was listening to some of the stuff you said, about politics.' Then he looked slightly embarrassed.

Mark tried to draw him into the conversation. 'What do you think of politics, then?'

'It's a load of shit,' the man replied, 'but nobody's interested in what I think, anyway. I been in prison. I fuckin' hate politicians.' Mick (as we soon found out) came over to sit at our table and carried on talking. 'My sister, right, she's twenty-one, she's got two kids and she needs a house, but she was told she can't have one because they've got quotas. They have to house forty immigrants a month and they're ahead of her in the queue. Now, I grew up in Normanton all me life, and so did she. I'm proud of where I come from. I'm a mongrel, me: my gran was Polish and my granddad was German. Imagine that! But there's all sorts in Normanton. Of my best mates only three are white. I got black friends, Pakistani friends, Indian friends, friends from all over Europe, and every-one's always got on fine. I'm proud of Normanton, because it's where I'm from, but I wouldn't live there now. It's been ruined by these Albanians and their fucking prostitutes. I got nothing against anyone coming here if they're in danger, but they're fucking taking the piss. There's no space for 'em. They can fuck off. People born and bred in Derby should get priority over immigrants. But no-one gives a fuck what I think.'

The rage was now literally bursting out of him. 'I'm no racist, right? How many friends you got who aren't white?' I admitted that apart from Prasanth, who I'd only just met, I had none. 'I'm a mongrel myself,' Mick continued, 'but we haven't got enough down here to start sharing it with immigrants. Now, no-one gives a shit what I think,

I've been a cracker and I've been in prison, and if I thought you two were politicians I'd tell you to fuck off and job on, but if people read what I think in your book then they might listen. So write about that.'

I'm the kind of person who thinks immigration is good for Britain, but at the same time I have to admit that immigrants don't actually get placed in houses near to where I have always lived. I'm also the kind of person who assumes that people who vote for the BNP because of immigration issues are racist idiots, but if the BNP are the only party prepared to defend these communities from the problems Mick talked about then it's hardly surprising they achieve electoral success. The poorest places in Britain don't have enough for themselves, let alone anyone else. Again, it's common sense.

I bought another round, and Mick told us more about his German grandfather who had suffered terrible racism during the war and for the rest of his life. Mick said that today people would be able to tell he had depression, but he felt such an overpowering sense of obligation to his family that he kept on struggling despite everything he had gone through, first his escape from Germany and then becoming a target of persecution here. His daughter got engaged on her twenty-first birthday; the next day, Mick's grandfather hanged himself because she was no longer dependent on him for her survival (his wife had died a few years earlier). Mick wanted to know more about where his family came from so I suggested he go to the Public Record Office in London. He seemed intrigued, but soon started shaking his head. 'Sounds great, but that stuff's just not for people like me,' he said.

Mick had a copy of that day's *Derby Telegraph* so I began leafing through it to see if it mentioned Dorothy's protest. It didn't. The front page was full of praise for Derby's council instead. That very day it had been awarded four stars by the Audit Commission which made it one of the best-performing councils in the country. The council leader, John Williams, said 'We've put a lot of effort into making sure we do things as efficiently and effectively as possible and this shows we deliver high-quality services when and where they are needed.' The council was clearly very successful in acting according to the government's remit. It was the remit itself that left a lot to be desired if Dorothy's struggle was anything to go by.

After a few hours of drinking and chatting with a couple of facially tattooed lesbian DJs Mark got us talking to, we left and made a dash for the train. By the station we grabbed some fish and chips from a girl behind the counter who, memorably, 'fuckin' hated havin' to touch fish' and climbed on the 8.02 train back to St Pancras.

# CHAPTER 5

In 1797, John Hetherington walked out of the shop he ran on the Strand in London wearing his latest invention. As he walked down the road he created quite a stir. Ladies fainted, men booed and a young boy accidentally had his arm broken as a crowd surged forward to see what was going on. Before long, Hetherington was arrested and hauled before the Mayor of London, who found him guilty of breaching the King's peace and fined him £50 (more than a skilled textile worker or a policeman earned in a year). As he passed judgment, the Lord Mayor condemned Hetherington for 'wearing upon his head a tall structure having a shining lustre and calculated to frighten timid people'. He was warned that a repeat offence would see him sent to prison.

His invention was a top hat.

In 2005, a sixteen-year-old boy in Portsmouth was given an anti-social behaviour order by a local judge which prevented him from wearing a hood or a baseball cap on his head. After the case, PC Andy Montague said, 'Some people see baseball caps and hoodies as intimidating.' Earlier in the year another sixteen-year-old boy from Manchester had also been banned, again using an ASBO, from wearing a hoodie. He was told that if he wore one again within a five-year period he would be sent to prison.

There's over two hundred years of legal progress for you.

In a speech about anti-social behaviour in 2003, Tony Blair outlined the argument for introducing ASBOs as part of the government's 'Give Respect, Get Respect' initiative. 'First, anti-social behaviour is for many the number one item of concern right on their doorstep – the graffiti, vandalism, dumped cars, drug dealers in the street, abuse from truanting school-age children,' he said. 'Secondly, though many of these things are in law a criminal offence, it is next to impossible for the police to prosecute without protracted court process, bureaucracy and hassle, when conviction will only result in a minor sentence.'[27]

But not all ASBOs have been given to people committing acts like those outlined above. In November 2005, police threatened Vic Moszcyznski with an ASBO because of the Christmas lights he had put up on his home. Apparently his display was attracting too many visitors seeking the spirit of Christmas. David Gaylor, who had been banned from entering any branch of Asda, was found guilty of breaching his ASBO and fined £50 for sitting at a bus stop he didn't realize was on land Asda owned. Christine Boswell, a sixty-year-old woman who is partially sighted, was sent to prison after she breached her ASBO by swearing. Eileen Davies was threatened with an ASBO for feeding the birds in her garden. Eileen is seventy-two. Mark Devlin was jailed for breaching the conditions of his ASBO, which outlawed him from riding his bike. Stefan Noremberg was given an ASBO that forbids him from moving furniture in his house if anyone can hear him doing it from outside. Mitch Hawkin was threatened with an ASBO for posting a joke about the Pope's death on his website. Caroline Shepherd was given an ASBO for walking around her own house in her underwear. Eight months later she was found guilty of breaking the conditions of this ASBO and was evicted from her council home. Roger Trotman found his neighbour's penchant for parking on a blind corner on his road irritating and dangerous, so he went round to complain and was given an ASBO for his trouble. The five-year restraining order forbade him to go near his neighbour, and he was also ordered to pay £1,200 in compensation and court costs. The council subsequently earmarked the blind corner in question for double yellow lines because it was unsafe to park there. David Boag, a fan of *An American Werewolf in London*, likes to go into his garden and howl like a wolf. He got an ASBO for that and was given a four-month jail term over Christmas for breaching its conditions. Janice Lee, thirty-seven, was given an ASBO for singing in her own home. Paul Henney was given an ASBO for slamming doors too loudly. Alexander Muat, eighty-two, is not allowed to be sarcastic to his neighbours. So far he has breached his order three times. Teresa Webb, thirty, was given an ASBO for playing Peter Kay's version of 'Amarillo' too often. In Aberystwyth, a woman was given an ASBO for trying to kill herself thirty-six times by jumping off the town's pier. If she attempts to go anywhere near the beach or the sea she'll breach her ASBO and be sent to prison.

It's a long and ludicrous list, and ASBOs have certainly made headlines, though probably not the ones the government intended. Especially in the case of Paul and Gary Doyle, whose ASBO conditions memorably included banning either of them from saying the word 'grass' anywhere in England and Wales.[28] Thank goodness these 'criminals' are no longer able to evade justice.

Fear of crime is a very powerful thing. Personally, I've got to the stage where if I'm ever walking home late at night and I see more than two young people hanging around I immediately become convinced that I'm about to be stabbed. I work on the assumption that all young people carry knives and anyone wearing a hoodie is potentially a drug-addled maniac. One evening in February 2006 I was walking home in the dark pushing Wilf in his pram when I came to a railway footbridge that leads to the road we live on. The bridge is caged in, presumably to stop people throwing things down onto the line. Standing on the other side were a group of six teenage boys wearing hoodies, all of whom were mooching around shivering, smoking and swearing. I felt very intimidated, which according to Hazel Blears, the government minister who defined anti-social behaviour as 'whatever the victim thinks it means', meant that these boys were being anti-social. I walked towards them with trepidation. When I got within a few feet of them I slowed down, hoping they would move out of my way, and to my surprise they did. One of them leant over the pram and said 'boo' to Wilf, making him giggle, and then drew back his head to blow out smoke over his shoulder. I thanked them all profusely for letting me through unscathed and the one blowing smoke said with a shrug, 'We're not monsters, you know.' After that experience I started to look at what the actual risk of violent crime is today. Statistically, our fear of crime is almost as absurd as our fear of terrorism. According to the British Crime Survey, 73 per cent of people believe crime rates are rising when in fact they have dropped by 17 per cent since 1999. A third of elderly women feel 'very unsafe', but only 0.00025 per cent of them will actually be assaulted, according to *The Times*.[29] And it's always young people wearing hoodies that they, and we, seem to be most afraid of.

ASBOs have been sold to us by the government as a way of controlling the feral children running amok in our communities. Statistically, these are the very people at the highest risk of being the victims of violent crime – of each other's violent behaviour. According to the Youth and Crime Unit, which was set up in 2001 to reduce youth crime across London, 'young people are over-represented as both perpetrators and victims of street crime in the capital . . . The peak offending time is between 3 p.m. and 5 p.m. weekdays when children and young people are leaving school for home.' The British Crime Survey found that 20 per cent of men aged between sixteen and twenty-four will be victims of violent crime every year. This is double the risk for women of the same age group.

As we have seen, your best chance of avoiding violent

crime is to be a woman over sixty-five. Being well off is another way of protecting yourself from it. One in thirty owner-occupiers as opposed to one in ten people living in rental properties will suffer from violent crime. Here's the British Crime Survey again: 'The group most likely to be subjected to violent crime was single adult and child households – 11 per cent of this group were subject to some form of violence. Around three-quarters of the assaults committed against single adult and children households were of a domestic nature. The type of area in which people live can affect their likelihood of being a victim of violent crime. In general, those households located in council estates and low-income areas were the most likely to have been victims of violent crimes.' So poverty and the level of violence present in your upbringing seem to be the deciding factors where violent crime and anti-social behaviour are concerned. It's a shame, then, that under this government the gap between rich and poor in Britain is now wider than it was under Margaret Thatcher.

Are ASBOs actually improving the quality of life in these poorer communities? Are they reducing crime and cleaning up the streets? To find that out I met a youth worker who works with children in one of Britain's problem estates. She wanted to retain anonymity in case speaking to me affected her job. I started by asking whether ASBOs had reduced crime in her area. 'No,' she replied. 'Instead of hanging out on a bench on one side of an imaginary line, the kids hang out on one on the other. All ASBOs have basic elements – you're not allowed to verbally abuse another person, you're not allowed to make threats against any other person, you're not allowed to assault any other person, and every one I have ever seen has always had an exclusion zone, although they don't have to by law. The exclusion zone has to be relevant to where they're making a nuisance, so it's usually town centres. If anyone hears a young person who has an ASBO swearing in the street they can be arrested and will immediately be taken to court for breaching their ASBO. The magistrate can't order a one-month prison term in a youth court like they can in an adult court. The minimum sentence for young offenders is four months, so they are punished far more severely than adults. We just had three lads who breached their ASBOs by swearing and they all got given six months in prison.'

Do these kids understand the parameters they are dealing with? 'We go through it with them and they do understand, but they just think, "Great, I'm not allowed to do anything for the rest of my life", which gives them a "what's the point?" attitude. The minimum ASBO they can get is two years and the maximum is five years. What tends to happen is that a child will be given an ASBO that takes them up to their eighteenth birthday. This means they're being told that they can't go into their local town, or wherever their exclusion zone is, for three or four years. Under any circumstances. They gave a lad I work with an ASBO and he wasn't allowed to go into the town centre. So he had to go miles out of his way, walking around the perimeter of the town, to go to school on the other side. A report by the Youth Offending Team pointed out that going to school was his best chance of avoiding trouble, but because he wasn't allowed to walk through the town to get there he didn't bother going to school. I suggested taking him through the town in my car, but they said, "No, he's not even allowed to travel in a car through that area." He wasn't allowed in a school bus either – it runs to the workshop where the kids fix cars – and he wasn't even allowed in a council van with teachers present. So he just stopped going. I also had a lad on an ASBO who has Tourette's syndrome. He wasn't allowed to verbally abuse anybody but found that quite difficult to stick to. He got done for breaking the swearing conditions and was given community punishment orders. If that was any other disability . . . imagine telling someone in a wheelchair that they have to stand up or else you'll give them community punishment orders. You'd have people screaming about discrimination. It's utter madness.

'The police can also apply for temporary exclusion zones anywhere they like. If any young people hang out in an area the police can come in and move them on. But that's what young people do. They hang out with each other. They say things to me like, "Where are we supposed to go? What are we supposed to do?" It's going back to that idea of "whatever the victim feels is intimidating behaviour". They don't mean to be intimidating, but the fact that there are a lot of them in one place is intimidating to some people. But they can't help that. It's not their fault that they wear clothes other people find frightening. They wear them because it's fashion.'

The Rowntree Foundation researched the lives and experiences of families living in the outskirts of Glasgow, one of the most deprived areas of Britain. Their study found that young people hang around in groups to protect themselves from being victims of violent crime. Having seen the statistics, you can see why they are so afraid. 'Young people took responsibility for keeping themselves and their friends safe by sharing knowledge, looking out for each other and moving around together,' the report concluded. 'They used their detailed local knowledge to avoid or minimize hazardous situations. Some were aware that certain adults saw such self-protective groups as threatening.'[30]

The youth worker I spoke to said that the minority of children causing most of the problems in her area behaved in an anti-social way simply because they were living anti-social lives. 'The majority of the kids' anti-social behaviour is directly linked to drugs and alcohol use, and their drug and alcohol use happens because there is nothing else to do. There's no great mystery about why people take drugs. They have a laugh when they're drunk and on drugs. A lot of them have parents who don't really give a shit about where they are late at night and that's why they're out late at night drinking, or they have parents who are drug and alcohol users as well. Most of them live in terrible poverty. A child that lives that lifestyle can't change overnight. You can't just say to someone like that, "You can't swear any more in a public place or we'll put you in prison" because their language *is* swearing. It's not meant to cause harassment or to be intimidating, it's just the way they speak with each other. Being in a group swearing at each other has now been made a public order offence which they can get locked up for. So the government has effectively criminalized youth. I can understand that something serious has to be done if people are making someone's life a misery, but I don't think ASBOs are the answer. They deal with the consequences of a situation but make absolutely no attempt to prevent the situation developing in the first place. You can't expect kids who've been up all night because their parents don't care or their parents are arguing or their parents aren't there to concentrate on schoolwork the next day when the most important thing in their immediate life is, "What's going to happen to my mum when I'm at school?"'

I also wanted to know what she thought the children she worked with would make of the government's 'Respect' agenda. She smiled uneasily. 'The trouble is that these kids just don't live in the same world as you and me. That is the problem that no-one is prepared to address. I'll give you an example. An old friend of mine used to teach in a primary school in the area I work in now, and one day he told me about this sweet little three-year-old boy he remembered who used to cycle up to the school, which was half a mile from the little boy's house, looking for his older brother to play with. Their parents were alcoholics and just spent all day at home drinking on the sofa doing God knows what. They didn't have a clue where he was half the time so he was fending for himself from the age of three. Well, that boy is now one of our clients. He's fourteen and he's in a young offenders institution because he breached his ASBO conditions by swearing. He didn't stand a chance. People are fed up of hearing what they think are excuses but they simply don't understand what life is like for these kids. It's not always an excuse. For them it's reality.

'A lot of them have suffered abuse. That's a big, big part of it. It's just horrible. Chucking them in prison is absolutely pointless. The cost of keeping a young person in prison is phenomenal. We've got a secure unit that costs £5,000 a week per young person. If they got a six-month sentence they'd do three months inside. Spending £60,000 on kids who don't recognize our society, kids who never had a chance to begin with, when it's guaranteed they'll re-offend, because they always do, is complete madness. For that you could set them up in a halfway house, a safe place to live, and give them a role model who does care where they are, who can teach them to look after themselves and give them just a fraction of a chance that people who don't like swearing got when they were children, and then they might start understanding what the government mean when they talk about respect.'

I put it to her that some of these kids must just be little monsters who don't care about anything other than causing mayhem, but she shook her head. 'I know how this sounds, but they have *all* got something going for them. On a one-to-one basis they are brilliant, but it's a pack mentality when they are all together that causes the problems. They have no self-esteem and are desperate to be accepted by each other so they just go along with what everyone else is doing. They become each other's role models in the absence of any others, and that means they try and impress each other all the time. It's about them feeling part of something, part of a group. If you combine that with drug and alcohol use then, unsurprisingly, you're going to get anti-social behaviour.'

Finally, as part of my continuing search for Albion, I asked her if there was anything she felt was going unrecorded.

'It's people's perception of young people that really bothers me,' she replied. 'There is a level of fear that is just totally unwarranted. The government and media have criminalized young people just for the way they look. It's totally demonized them. A hoodie is not meant to intimidate people. They are just kids.'

Recent research by Bath University's Dr Phoenix, who spent two years looking at youth justice in Britain, backs up the youth worker's views:

The 1998 legislation which gave birth to ASBOs and Youth Offending Teams was supposed to create a youth justice system in which those in need of punishment were punished but which would also help those with welfare issues to escape a life of criminality.

What we have today is a youth justice system that metes out increasingly stringent punishments on young offenders and fast-tracks them through harsher and harsher punishments.

Information on the desperate welfare needs of young offenders is available to all those who make decisions about young offenders – police, Youth Offending Teams and magistrates – but in practice they have only punitive measures at their disposal.

The fact that young offenders are first and foremost young seems to be of little consequence in our youth justice system . . .

The overwhelming common denominator amongst the majority of young offenders is poverty; poverty which has introduced them to homelessness, alcohol abuse, drug abuse and crime from a very early age.

Once they become involved in the youth justice system, state interventions are inevitably focused on some of their emotional difficulties rather than their practical needs. Anger management classes are no substitution for attempting to do something about their home situation.'[31]

So how *do* you improve things in the most impoverished parts of Britain, the communities that are cursed with the majority of the country's anti-social behaviour? Well, you could do worse than ask the people who actually live in these communities what they think rather than adopt well-meaning ideas handed down from central government that generate headlines but don't address the root causes of these problems.

I went to visit Blackbird Leys, often credited as the birthplace of joyriding, to meet a local councillor for the Independent Working Class Association who lived there. The IWCA sounded a bit *Socialist Worker* to me, but Stuart Craft is unashamedly only interested in helping the working classes who live on estates like his. His view is that the political party they used to vote for, Labour, has deserted them, so they have to start looking after themselves.

It was a boiling hot day when I got on a bus in the centre of Oxford and arrived, twenty minutes later, on the edge of Blackbird Leys. It felt like being dropped off by the helicopter in *Platoon*. I was absolutely petrified. I'd heard lots of horror stories of crack houses and syringe-scattered streets; I imagined I'd be gunned down within moments of arriving. The first thing I noticed was a group of youths using the Perspex windows in a bus shelter as a punch-bag; the second thing I noticed were dried-out bunches of flowers attached to various lamp-posts and railings. I gulped and wandered around looking for Stuart's house. Before long I came across a new cul-de-sac of orange-brick houses, and I soon spotted the one I was looking for. Stuart opened the door with a suspicious smile and welcomed me inside.

It took Stuart only five minutes to dismantle my middle-class prejudices. He reacted with disdain to my description of how awful life must be in his community. It had its problems and the residents needed help, he conceded, but the idea that it was beyond saving was insulting and absurd. Talking to Stuart, I began to realize how places like Blackbird Leys have become de-humanized. We think of them as hopeless worlds. Most of us don't understand them, which is probably why we do so little to help them. Stuart told me about his attempts to shut down the crack and heroin dealers on the estate who openly sold drugs outside the 20p-a-ticket cinema he helped to organize for local children. As a result, the heroin dealers were evicted. In a survey carried out before the local elections in 2002, Class A drugs were the residents' main concern, so Craft also organized a picketing campaign outside the houses of known drug dealers to scare them off. His critics talk about human rights violations – the people being targeted haven't been found guilty of any crime – but Stuart is unmoved, pointing out that you can tell if someone's using a house to deal heroin without proving it in court. A local gang of teenagers was terrorizing local residents, so the entire community – men, children, mothers with prams, everyone who was sick of the gang's behaviour – held a demonstration against them on the park in the middle of the estate. They held banners asking for 'Freedom for our kids to walk in safety', and the gang hasn't been seen since.

The IWCA took three seats off Labour in the last local elections so the community has obviously seen an improvement in their daily lives. The local Labour Party, however, are less happy. So unhappy, in fact, that in 2005 they resorted to dirty tricks to try to derail the IWCA's progress. In the run-up to local elections, Bill Baker, Oxford City Council's deputy leader, sent out leaflets about the IWCA with the headline WATCH OUT FOR EXTREMIST GROUP. He also accused the IWCA of being linked to Irish Republican nationalists. The allegations were groundless and Baker was forced to pay £15,000 to the IWCA in damages and to make a grovelling apology.

Stuart is also unpopular with the local council for fiercely opposing Oxford's European Capital of Culture bid, accusing them of being more interested in tourists than the people of Oxford. 'The last thing Oxford needs is more tourists,' he insisted. 'We don't have anything against tourists, but tourism is an area which is generally self-funding. Regeneration, however, would be more than welcome . . . yet the working-class estates of East Oxford stood to gain nothing from the Capital of Culture bid.'[32] People like Stuart believe the answer lies in helping local people to improve the quality of their own lives rather than boosting the attractiveness of a town for its tourists. There is a long way to go, but things are changing in Blackbird Leys.

I went to two other notorious problem estates on my

journey around Britain, Cumbernauld outside Glasgow in Scotland and the Bransholme Estate on the outskirts of Hull.

As I've already indicated, it's hard to see much evidence of Britain's thriving economy if you spend any time walking around Cumbernauld. Except, of course, the identical brand names and shop fronts you'll find everywhere else in Britain. In *Crap Towns*, Cumbernauld was described as an 'unrelenting collection of dismal, crumbling, concrete housing schemes populated by shellsuit-clad maniacs and terrified pensioners'. The first-hand accounts of living there give an insight into the experience of the locals and the priorities of the local council. 'My mum and I were walking back from my older sister's house, at midnight, after babysitting my newborn niece, only to be confronted with a guy with a chainsaw cutting down his neighbour's front door,' one resident told me. 'When he spotted us he charged at us with this saw. If it hadn't been for the fact that the saw cut out so he had to try to start it again and then fell on his arse in the process, I wouldn't have lived to tell this story. Needless to say the armed police swarmed the area and the guy was apprehended, but only after he had been cutting up his neighbour's house for forty-five minutes without anyone doing anything.'

Things didn't improve after Cumbernauld came second to Hull in *Crap Towns*. 'It seems the council of Cumbernauld have since woken up after coming second in the first *Crap Towns* book. Yep, the big shake-up has happened, and boy, what a shake-up! Instead of building a cinema, a decent shopping centre or anything else of worth for the residents, they decided to build "Fat Street".

On this street, beside the ever-present Beefeater pub, we now have a new Pizza Hut, a new KFC, a new Burger King, a new tanning salon, a new Global Video and a new Domino's Pizza. I thought today's kids in Cumbernauld had no future with the lack of opportunity and soul in the place – how wrong I was! They can now stop off at Pizza Hut for a stuffed-crust pizza, then KFC for a quick snack, flash the fake ID for a sneaky few bottles of Hooch in the Beefeater, pop into Burger King for a whopper and fries, then into Global Video, hire out *Gregory's Girl* [filmed in Cumbernauld], order a pizza from Domino's to eat while watching it, nip in for a tan while they wait for the pizza to be cooked, and head home only to have to stop at the roundabout with severe chest pains followed by a cardiac arrest and a large dose of death. All at the ripe old age of fourteen.'

Then I went down to Hull, which didn't have a very good reputation long before it was featured in our book. I found the Bransholme Estate on the outskirts of the city a far more frightening and desolate place than Blackbird Leys or Cumbernauld, largely because of its terrifying size. Locals complained of reduced bus services into Hull's city centre, but because Bransholme has its own shopping mall its residents don't actually need to go into the town itself, making the estate a modern-day ghetto of poverty on the edge of the city. Hull's local council had been failing the people of Hull for many years, and most memorably spent hundreds of thousands of pounds installing central heating systems in homes on the estate that had already been earmarked for demolition. When I visited, great swathes of homes had already been flattened.

It wasn't a pretty sight. The ubiquitous grilled crack-houses were everywhere, but so were well-tended gardens, brightly coloured flowerbeds and a few lonely garden gnomes.

A few years ago Hull was one of the richest councils in Britain after it sold a large part of its stake in Kingston Communications, the only privately owned telephone exchange in the country. The council then embarked on a £263 million spending frenzy; £40 million was spent on the local football club (just a year later the receivers were called in) and £32 million was spent filling a 'funding gap' in the council's day-to-day spending. Within three years the council had managed to blow a grand total of £650 million and council tax bills were rising again.

I did an interview with Hull's local TV news when it emerged in our book as the crappiest place to live in Britain. I asked a councillor on air about what was being done for the people living on the Bransholme Estate. She replied by pointing out how nice Hull's brand-new aquarium, The Deep, was and how many tourists it was attracting to the city. But spending millions on an aquarium in a place like Hull is rather like installing a swimming pool with a gymnasium complex in a house without a roof. Later, at a bookshop event in the town, I met a youth worker from the estate. He'd seen the local news and pointed out that that was the first time anyone had ever asked such a question in the local media. He felt Bransholme had been dehumanized to the point that it had become an embarrassing and unmentionable part of Hull's community.

After a damning report from the National Audit Office,

Hull's council got rid of many of its worst councillors and now things are beginning to improve. Let's hope they've learned some lessons. At the time of writing, the council has decided to sell its remaining shares in Kingston Communications, giving them another £200 million windfall. The people of Hull will be watching what it gets spent on closely this time.

It's common sense that places like Cumbernauld and Bransholme shouldn't exist in modern Britain. If being one of the five most powerful economic nations in the world can't eradicate such levels of poverty and deprivation then perhaps a constantly expanding economy isn't the holy grail of human development. The fact that places like Cumbernauld and Bransholme still exist proves that we live in a country where we have very little respect for one another. And a national sense of community doesn't stand a chance if things are allowed to break down at a local level. Local and national communities then become fragmented. People hide at home in front of the television, scared out of their wits by hysterical news coverage that makes them fear for their lives if they walk out their front door, whether the reason for the fear is violent crime, terrorism or bird flu.

But it's not all bad news. High levels of public fear are actually rather good for the ever-expanding economy, as Brian Dean, editor of the excellent anxietyculture.com, pointed out in *Idler 25*: 'There are strong vested interests in keeping public anxiety at a high level,' he wrote. 'Anxious people make good consumers. They tend to eat and drink compulsively, need more distractions – newspapers, TV, etc. – and more external buttressing of their fragile self-image through lifestyle products and status symbols. Insurance companies and the whole financial services industry make billions from our insecurities. The unsubtle targeting of our fears is evident in adverts for vehicle recovery services, cars, alarms, security systems, mobile phones, private healthcare, chewing gum, deodorant and so on. Employers benefit if the workers fear losing their jobs as fearful people are less likely to complain or rebel. Studies show that people are more suggestible and compliant when anxious. Politicians quote "public fears" as justification for more freedom-eroding legislation. Insecure populations also show a tendency to elect authoritarian governments.'[33]

We're certainly working harder than any other country in Europe to pay off the highest amount of personal debt owed by any country in the EU. That trillion pounds of unsecured debt we racked up through over-consumption will now have to be dealt with through more and more work, which gives us less and less time for our communities.

Every day, those of us in employment make a transaction to sell seven hours of our lives for a specific amount of money. For most of us time is only ever measured in money, and as we all know, you don't get money for nothing so our communities, because they can't pay us, can no longer expect any of our time.

This is something Sergeant Gary Brown, who has come up with a novel way of helping his community, noticed in the small town of Spilsby in Lincolnshire where he lives. 'The demands placed upon you by people who don't actually want to do anything for themselves are quite intense,' he told me. 'I had a lady who came to the police station the other day and said, "What are you doing about a school crossing patrol? Because it's dangerous for the children." And I said, "Well, we're struggling to find anyone who'll do it." And she said, "Well, I think it's disgusting," and turned to leave. I said to her, "Do you work?" She said, "No." So I said, "Why don't you do it, then?" She looked horrified and left in a hurry.'

That's the way you behave if you're a consumer, because the customer, we are told, is always right. But we are not customers of our communities. We can't allow our daily lives to be reduced to the working mindset of one transaction of consumption after another. Communities are not about economics. The break-up of our 'way of life', the lack of respect shown by the 'youth of today' and the 'throw-away culture' all came from somewhere, and in my view they came from the moment when every decision we made stopped coming from us as citizens of this nation and came from us as consumers of this nation instead. If you apply the logic of 'the customer is always right' to a nation, you'll find yourself living in a country where everyone deals in their own self-interest rather than the interest of the places they call home. And if your community begins to collapse then everyone living in it loses out, regardless of their income, the status symbols they've acquired or the height of the fence they have built around themselves for protection. A community where everyone is interested only in themselves will inevitably break down and people will begin to feel sidelined, frustrated, left out and angry. Those left adrift may even start feeling a little anti-social. Well, I would. Wouldn't you?

The more our government embraces the corporate vision of Britain, the more we become customers of our country rather than its citizens. As consumers we are always looking for a bargain, but getting a bargain from your country is not the same as getting a bargain from a large corporation. When you get a bargain from your country your community will always bear the brunt of the cost. When you get a bargain from a large corporation someone else's community, increasingly one in the developing world, bears the cost instead.

The government can't have it both ways. They can't sit back and allow the economic circumstances for anti-social behaviour to flourish and then hammer their fists on the table and talk about 'respect' when our communities inevitably break down. I believe that by allowing a market philosophy to invade every facet of our lives our government is directly responsible for the fragmentation of our communities. People are uninterested in politics for a reason. If voting turnouts are anything to go by we have given up looking for a leader to guide us out of this mess because we know deep down that the answers lie locally, in doing things for ourselves. The struggle all of us face is regaining control of our time so that we can actually fulfil our roles, rights and responsibilities as citizens and members of communities.

It may sound absurd, but the medieval way of life was, in some respects, far more civilized than the way we live today. Sergeant Gary Brown is the man behind the 'Knight School' project designed to prevent anti-social behaviour by teaching children about the codes of medieval chivalry and their role in a community. When you first hear about it, it sounds a ludicrous approach, but in the two years since his project began crime rates in the area have halved. 'Everything we do has been based around the whole idea of returning to the concept of a medieval society, one in which people rely less on their local authorities and more on themselves and their neighbours to turn around their town.'

Gary holds Knight School sessions for local children aged between six and eight and teaches them about courtesy, manliness, nutrition, health, behaviour, respect and their place in a community. 'The parents are actually the most important part,' he told me when I visited him to find out how Knight School had begun to reshape his home town. 'I tell them that they must engage in what their children are doing. That I'm going to teach their children not to swear and if they are planning on swearing at home then I don't want their child coming to Knight School. The problem for the parents is that the five- or six-year-olds see their friends walking away from Knight School with swords, badges, shields, tabards and medals and they all want to come. We've had a few situations where children couldn't come because their parents weren't up to standard, and then suddenly the child has a lever on their parents and can say to them, "I want you to behave, so I can go to Knight School." Our experience from the last two years is that the parents actually change their behaviour far more than the child because the parents' level of understanding is higher. We tell the parents that if they smoke, drink and gamble then their child is more likely to as well. And all parents love their children, so they are prepared to change to make their children happy. So we're engaging with parents, which is very important.'

Session one is an introduction. Gary's approach is that as the children are entering a new world they should be given new identities. The theory behind that is that because he's a policeman he will inevitably recognize some criminal family names and if a five-year-old appeared with a name he knew then psychologically it might change the way he treated the child. So he never allows himself to find out their real identities. As soon as they arrive they are given names like Galahad, Lancelot and Guinevere, and that's all he ever knows them as. 'They're not allowed to use their real names at any time and that gives them a whole new start. Anything that was in the past is in the past, and they're looking into a bright new future. Then they get given their Knight School toothbrush, and that's because it's the first thing they do in the morning and the last thing they do at night. It means they go to bed dreaming of it and wake up living it. It's quite interesting as toothbrushes go, because it's got the logo of Knight School on it and the bristles are in the shape of a shield. They're not allowed to choose the colour because humility is part of the training, and they can't choose their name either. They get it and they have to live with it. Some of them don't like their names because they're just plain horrible, but they can't complain because they're not allowed to.

'In the seven other sessions we go through their nutrition – we were teaching nutrition to them and their parents long before Jamie Oliver – their health, what pride, courtesy and respect are, and what constitutes good behaviour and bad behaviour. We go through all those things in a very structured way. Then at the end of the course they are all given a script to learn, and at the closing ceremony in a local castle they stand up on a podium and recite their own personal part of the course. At the very end, the children are knighted.

'The schools are always amazed by the transformation in the children, especially the ones who are difficult to control. But they're dealing with thirty children at any one time in school; I'm dealing with twelve. I am able to give them all, pretty much, my full attention. That makes them feel important as human beings, and if they feel like that they will do anything for you.'

Sergeant Brown's ideas don't stop when the children have 'passed out' from Knight School either. 'Some of the first kids to go to Knight School are now about eleven, so we devised this thing called the Green Knight for them to move on to. The Green Knight is a method to help them engage in community life. They pick a project and get a Green Knight workbook that includes the "magic formula". The magic formula is that they must be motivated, they must analyse what the problem is, they must set themselves a goal, they must innovate – to make sure the problem doesn't happen again – and then they must communicate what it is that they've done. We produced a lovely workbook – well, I would say that because I made it, but everyone who reads it says what a fabulous thing it is. Anyway, these children get this and they send it off to the Green Knight, this mythical character, who then sends them their certificate. Now I'm the Green Knight, so I see what these children will do to get a certificate.

They start picking up litter and doing all sorts of things to improve where they live. It's been wonderful. What I've noticed, though, is that "officials" will start throwing things like health and safety at me, risk assessments, that sort of thing. One councillor even raised the issue that the more we pick up our own litter the less the district council will do it for us. The problem is that people will actually listen to him and say, "He's got a good point there." So then people see no point in picking up litter if they know someone else is going to do it for them. That's the kind of mentality we're up against.

'I also wrote a book called *The Road to Camelot* which outlines a lot of this stuff. The aim is to get that book to every single child in Britain, but I thought I'd better start by getting one to every child in Spilsby. What I found was that if an official authority gives these books away, like a school or the police, there's less likelihood that the children and their parents will actually read and digest them. So now these books are given out by the British Legion and various other local clubs and societies instead. They're 50p each. As soon as they were coming from their own community rather than being imposed by an official authority, everyone started snapping them up.

'When the children started doing the Green Knight workbook I found that a lot of their literary skills were really poor, so we introduced the Dragon – the Pen-Dragon. He's a dragon and he's got a pen. After Uther Pendragon, of course, King Arthur's father. The Pen-Dragon is a writing competition we hold here for children to win the Pen-Dragon award. And there are more badges they can earn. We do presentations for them in school and that has driven up the way they write because they want to earn a badge.'

I asked Gary about the results he'd seen so far. 'My experience here suggests that it has a major impact on crime figures,' he replied, 'but we don't really understand why that is, other than that for every single child you meet you also meet their mum, dad – if they've got a dad at home – grandparents, aunts and uncles, who all engage with you as a policeman who is helping their child. So that's been a very positive effect. The sense of community has really changed and I'm sure that has to be a part of it. It used to take me ten minutes to walk from one side of Spilsby to the other, now it takes me about an hour and a half. You've got to bear in mind that this is just one of about thirty measures we've put in place. The Knight School images are in pre-school and they are outside every pub here. It's all part of a twenty-year strategy to improve behaviour so the kids will grow up with these images and these ideas around them. Everything about it is focused on citizenship.'

I'd read a few articles in the newspapers about Knight School but none them had got much beyond the image of children walking around with swords. Gary's excellent work was regularly being portrayed as something of an eccentric joke. I wondered if he found the media's coverage of his project frustrating. 'God, yes. It doesn't matter which newspaper or TV programme you're talking about, every one I've spoken to professes to be the voice of the people and to give out real news. Then they get down here and without fail they *all* just want to see a child dressed up in a knight's outfit. That's all they're interested in. They don't really want to report on what's behind it all, they just want that image. But I've found that the public actually want the opposite. The public want an answer to their problems. They want a real-time solution to what's happening in their communities. They understand the concepts behind what I'm trying to do and they can see beyond the glitz of a child in a knight's outfit. The media just don't understand that the public are actually interested in the ethos behind what it is we're trying to do.'

Towards the end of our time together I asked Gary what he thought of ASBOs. He went quiet for a moment. It was a question he was being asked a great deal, and as a policeman it was a difficult one for him to answer. 'Someone said to me recently that when it comes to modern behaviour we're travelling in a ship full of holes,' he said. 'ASBOs may well fill a few holes temporarily, but what we're doing here in Spilsby is building a brand-new ship.'

Finally, I asked him whether Albion meant anything to him. 'Absolutely nothing, to be totally honest with you,' he replied. 'Although . . . hang on a minute . . . there is a pub round here. Now, what's its name? It's called The Ship Albion. How about that then, eh?'

## CHAPTER 6

You can't embark on a quest for Albion and not have Glastonbury in the back of your mind, but John Nicholson had warned me about 'the mystical shit' that seems to surface whenever that town is mentioned. The theory goes that Jesus's uncle, Joseph of Arimathea, visited Glastonbury with the young Jesus in tow and that there the two of them built the first true Christian church. This is what William Blake writes about in his stirring anthem 'Jerusalem'.

As delightful, or not, as it may seem for the English to be the chosen people of God, it wasn't something I wanted to get too mixed up in. I was desperate to keep Druids, crystals and middle-aged men in flowing robes at arm's length. I couldn't escape the feeling that, as interesting as the myths and legends of ancient Britain are, if I went down that road it would be a long time before I came back to the surface or found anything that would be relevant to today. But speaking to Sergeant Gary Brown had put the idea of King Arthur back in my head. Perhaps there was a role for our ancient history, traditions and values in modern life.

It was Easter, and Rachel, Wilf and I spent a few days in a hotel near Glastonbury with my mum and some of her friends. They were going to walk and cycle, and we were looking forward to eating, drinking and catching up on some sleep. John had described Glastonbury as a 'theme park'. We were too close to avoid it completely, but we limited ourselves to a cheap lunch and a half-hearted amble through the vast array of mystical bookshops. I bought a few books about England from Oxfam for a fiver, we went back to the hotel, and that was the end of that.

But when we got back home a few days later I began to dream about King Arthur. I seemed to see his shadow lurking in my mind in the tortuously early morning light while Wilf watched *Muffin the Mule*. I became convinced that there had to be some way of fitting Arthur in without turning this book into some kind of mish-mash of visionary weirdness. Which was when coincidence decided to lend me another guiding hand.

Rachel and I both work part-time so we get to spend lots of time with Wilf. We don't have much money as a result, but we do have plenty of time. The week after we got back from Glastonbury, Rachel was supply teaching in New Cross Gate. For some reason, because I had never even thought about doing it before, I decided to push Wilf down to meet her at the end of the day at half-past three. The school was little under a mile away, so I looked at the *A to Z*, worked out the route in my mind and left home giving myself half an hour to complete the journey. It really wasn't very far, but I still managed to get myself lost and I started to drift aimlessly through the beautiful but battered streets of Brockley and New Cross Gate. I began to wonder what Arthur would make of the row upon row of terraced houses, some done up like those in Notting Hill while others, often next door, had been left to rot. No doubt he would be pretty unimpressed with the land of Albion today, the land of the Britons he supposedly rescued from the Anglo-Saxons back in the Dark Ages. But then I chastised myself for being overly romantic. Arthur was from a different world, if he was ever of this world at all. The problems we face are the problems of today; hiding in some lost mythology of fifteen hundred years ago would surely not make any difference to Britain now. I put my recent obsession with him down to reading *The Sword in the Stone* once too often and resolved to dismiss the whole nonsensical idea from my head once and for all.

But at that exact moment he appeared on the pavement in front of me. Or rather, I saw the word 'Arthur' in bright red lettering on the cover of a book in a cardboard box at the end of someone's drive with a note attached that said 'Please take me!'

As I say, coincidence can be a daunting thing if you have enough time to pay attention to it. I had never walked down that road before. I didn't even really know where I was. I picked up the book, read the cover – *The Trials of Arthur - The Life and Times of a Modern-Day King* – and felt the backs of my legs tingle. I looked around for some explanation and began to shake slightly. It's not often that you find a box containing a book at the end of someone's drive that potentially offers an answer to a question exercising your mind at that precise moment, but there you are. Maybe it was a sign of something. As I said, if you have the time to let serendipity and coincidence guide you they can lead you to some interesting places.

I read the book's blurb. Its subject wasn't King Arthur of Round Table fame, it was about a modern-day hairy tattooed biker and Mensa member called John. He'd had an interesting life, having served in the army before getting into all sorts of trouble with the police, and after years of adventure he became convinced he was the reincarnation of King Arthur. After all, according to legend our great king never actually died: he is sleeping in a cave somewhere until his country needs him again. Finding the book had freaked me out slightly, and it's very easy to dismiss a man who thinks he's the reincarnated spirit of King Arthur, but the way I'd come across his story made me give him the benefit of the doubt. I put the book in the pram. Later, when I got home, I started to read it. It was a staggering tale of one man's battle to save our heritage and old traditions. Once John had decided to let his 'old' self emerge, he changed his name to Arthur Pendragon through deed poll and, to cut a long and un-believably funny and surprising story short, went round the country looking for his sword, Excalibur.

One afternoon Arthur was with his girlfriend driving through Farnborough and Aldershot with the sword on his mind. After all, he could hardly claim to be King Arthur if he didn't have Excalibur. He knew the roads like the back of his hand, having spent so much time riding around there on a motorbike in his youth. All the same, he managed to take a wrong turning and was about to correct himself when the lights went red and he brought his van to a shuddering halt. At that point his girlfriend, Angela, spotted a shop down a side road called the Casque and Gauntlet and suggested they stop and go in. Arthur was unmoved, assuming it to be a stupid medieval re-enactment shop, but she insisted they park and have a look. When they got to the shop a few minutes later, as chance would have it, there was Excalibur sitting proudly in the window. And when I say Excalibur, I mean the sword that was used in the 1981 film. Arthur became rather agitated and went inside to speak to the owner. He pointed at the sword and said, 'I want to buy it.' The owner flatly refused. It turned out that he'd made lots of lightweight copies for the actors to use in the film, and he let Arthur hold one of those instead. The one in the window weighed a ton and no-one had been able to handle it. (Sound familiar?)

'No, I don't want that one, I want the real thing,' said Arthur.

The man looked at him. 'Why do you want that?' he asked. 'Anyway,' he added, 'I promised I'd only sell it to the real King Arthur, if he ever returned.'

Arthur threw his passport down on the counter. 'I'm the real King Arthur,' he said, 'and I've got to have that sword.'

The man opened up the passport and looked at it. Then he looked up at Arthur. You could see the gears shifting in his brain, the cogs whirring. He looked back at the passport and let out a little soft laugh of resignation.

'I can't argue with that. How much have you got?'

'I've got a hundred quid.'

Even Arthur knew this was silly. The man had charged the film company £5,000 for it. He'd already told him that. It had gold on the pommel and the hilt, and gold inlay on the tang. It was sprung steel, a real fighting blade. Aside from that, it was a film artefact, and worth even more because of that. The man looked at him again and laughed bitterly. You can't refuse fate.

'Go on then. A hundred quid and it's yours.'[34]

So from then on Arthur carried Excalibur in a scabbard attached to his belt as he travelled around Britain.

I read the rest of the book over the next few days and by the end of it I'd discovered a man who welcomed anyone who wanted to join his 'Warband' as long as they came across it through some kind of strange coincidence and were interested in protecting Britain. He also didn't take himself too seriously, was into drinking in a big way, and was prepared to stand up against the tyranny of the government's attempts to remove our civil liberties. This stance had led to his being imprisoned many times over the previous fifteen years while fighting for our right to use Stonehenge and then against various road developments that threatened the British countryside. On the occasions when he did find himself threatened with prison his lawyers successfully argued that Arthur Pendragon and his followers should swear an oath on Excalibur rather than the Bible when giving evidence in court. You can imagine him in the dock, wearing full ceremonial robes and a crown on his head, swearing on Excalibur in a court of law in the twenty-first century.

It makes you wonder, idly perhaps, what King Arthur would do if he actually reawakened in modern Britain. It's hard to imagine that he'd spend his time in Parliament or Buckingham Palace. Somehow the idea of him tied halfway up a tree thrashing at the police to protest against a road development, or riding from one pub to the next on a Harley Davidson, or managing to persuade the legal establishment in court that his sword is Excalibur and that as King Arthur his oath sworn on it is as valid as anyone else using the Bible, seems a little more likely.

I told Rachel the whole story and I could see a look of horror begin to spread across her face. 'It is a very odd coincidence,' she agreed, then trailed off. When she spoke again there was an air of determination in her voice. 'You're not about to tell me you want to go off to join King Arthur though, are you, Dan? I mean, I think I've been pretty supportive with all this criminal behaviour since you started this book but I'm going to lose patience if you suddenly start claiming to be one of the Knights of the Round Table.' I have to admit that the thought had occurred to me, but in the end it wasn't to be. I tried to track down King Arthur through my new radical contacts but he eluded me. Either that or he had done his job as a signpost on my journey already. It was certainly reassuring to know he was out there somewhere fighting for Albion. I like to think I will meet him one day.

As chance would have it, King Arthur's first anti-road protest turned out to be my first one too, the M3 extension at Twyford Down outside Winchester. His experiences there as the fight drew to a close prepared him for a much greater role in the protest at Newbury, where he settled his travelling 'Camelot' on part of the proposed route of the bypass. My first brush with protest began back in 1993, at the age of eighteen, when the Twyford Down demonstration became a regular item on the national news. It was a protest that redefined environmental activism and radically altered the then Major government's road-building programme. It was also a defining moment in my life because it all took place seven miles from the town where I grew up.

Despite deriding Winchester as the fifth crappest town in Britain a few years ago (for its violence, growing heroin problem and insufferable smugness), it was, back in the early nineties, one of the most beautiful cities in England. According to Sir Thomas Malory, who collected the Arthurian legends into one volume in 1470 and whose work was condensed into a single book by William Caxton's new printing press in 1485, Winchester was actually the site of Camelot. As with lots of the Arthurian legends there is no actual proof, but the view of the city from Twyford Down was certainly something to behold. Professor Martin Biddle, president of the Twyford Down Association, described it before the road-building began: 'the proximity of downland, water meadow and city produced an intimate and rare backyard, perhaps unique in providing a thriving modern city with a visual perspective reaching deep into its remote past. Here, perhaps alone in modern urban England, it was possible in the course of an hour or so to walk from the twentieth century to the prehistoric past, or even to glance from one to the other in the course of a moment at work or in school.'

I remember flying kites on the hill as a child and listening in wonder when I heard it was considered by some to be the final resting place of King Arthur. Now, cynicism aside – there have to be at least five 'resting places of King Arthur' up and down the country – if you'd sat on that hill and looked down on medieval Winchester, once the capital of this country, on a summer's evening you'd have agreed it wasn't so far-fetched. There was something in the air of that place, which is probably where the delightful guff about King Arthur came from. Whatever it was, it was something the local residents were damned they were going to lose without a fight.

Barbara Bryant, one of the key campaigners, wrote a book, *Twyford Down: Roads, Campaigning and Environmental Law*, about the experience she and her fellow protesters went through while fighting the development through the proper legal channels. She wrote it to give an insight into the process to anyone considering taking a similar stand elsewhere. Bryant was an unlikely campaigner who didn't dispute that the road needed to be built, or even, in the end, where it should be built. She and the huge team of dedicated campaigners that swelled around her simply wanted a tunnel so that the road could pass under Twyford Down rather than the brutal white scar that now cuts right through it. After all, the proposed cutting meant obliterating an area of outstanding natural beauty which contained a site of serious scientific interest and two scheduled ancient monuments, including an Iron Age settlement. Miriam Rothschild, a valued supporter of the campaign, wrote at the time, 'It is extraordinary that if a famous picture comes on the market and is about to be sold, a large sum of money is immediately made available to retain it in this country. Yet, a picture merely changes walls, and other people, say in America, can enjoy it. Yet at Twyford Down the same authority [the government] destroys forever thousands of years of irreplaceable beauty and the enjoyment of countless generations.'[35]

The project to extend the M3 from Basingstoke to Southampton was first considered in 1970. A route was proposed that passed to the west of Winchester, through arable land, and joined the north-west outskirts of the city of Southampton. It made perfect sense to everyone in and around Winchester with the exception of the wealthy landowners on that side of the city. Quite without explanation, that route was suddenly dropped. In 1971, a new route was proposed west of the old bypass and straying into the water meadows between St Catherine's Hill and Winchester. A public inquiry was held in 1976 to look at the compulsory purchase of the land involved, much of which was owned by Winchester College. The college, along with other residents, formed the Winchester M3 Joint Action Group, which successfully lobbied for other routes to be considered. In 1981, Kenneth Clarke MP announced that the engineering company Mott, Hay and Anderson were doing a 'fresh study'. They came to the conclusion that the only viable route left was a cutting through Twyford Down. Of course by this stage the government was getting sick of dragging its heels and decided to push it through despite local opposition. More public inquiries followed, but according to Barbara Bryant 'the problem with road-building inquiries is that for it to get to that stage ministers will have been advised that the best solution is the one on the table to be discussed. They will have given it their support; the public inquiry is just rubber-stamping or giving lip service to the idea of public consultation. So any new ideas or protests have a formidable opponent. If you successfully make your case a lot of powerful people will be left with egg on their faces, and powerful people don't like that.'

An example of the hopeless task facing you if you wish to engage in the public inquiry system was the tunnel Bryant and her team proposed. They submitted a drawing of what the tunnel could look like but had no idea how anally retentive the system would turn out to be. Any alternative plans submitted by the public had to be costed by the inquiry to see if they did offer a practical alternative. So the tunnel Bryant and her team submitted was costed, exactly according to the submitted drawing. Now the drawing was supposed to give an indication of how much better a tunnel would look rather than being an actual architectural plan, so the idea was thrown out because in the drawing the tunnel was set too high up on the hill and tons of earth would have to be moved to raise the path of the road up enough to pass through it. It never occurred to the inquiry to get an expert in building tunnels of this kind to look into the proposal seriously and set a tunnel at the correct level. They just looked at the submitted drawing, worked out that the cost would be prohibitive because it wasn't a perfectly workable plan designed by an architect, then threw out the idea completely.

If playing by the rules and involving yourself in the

public inquiry system is unlikely to alter the government's decision, you can forgive people for using more immediate and physical methods to get their views across. But the then Conservative government had something up their sleeve to combat that tactic too.

I wasn't actively involved in the protests that took place at Twyford Down, but I do remember the influx of people with strange coloured hair and eccentric clothes in Winchester's town centre. I can also remember political graffiti appearing, and that was not the kind of thing you usually saw in Winchester. All of it said just one thing: 'Down with the Criminal Justice Act'. I remember at the time thinking that these oddballs must all be criminals if they didn't agree with a bill designed to clamp down on criminal behaviour in the name of justice, which, in the light of its name, was what I took the contents of the bill to be. But as the protests continued and the debate about the road intensified, the scales began to fall from my eyes.

The environmental campaigner George Monbiot wrote in the *Times Literary Supplement*:

At the 1993 Conservative Party Conference, Michael Howard announced a Criminal Justice Bill which would create a series of new offences criminalising both peaceful protest and certain forms of homelessness. Crude, ill-drafted and repressive, it succeeded in uniting all the disparate factions whose interests or activities it threatened. Hunt saboteurs, peace protesters, football supporters, squatters, radical lawyers, gypsies, pensioners, ravers, disabled rights activists, even an assistant chief constable and a Tory ex-minister, joined the broadest, and oddest, counter-cultural coalition Britain has ever known.

Twyford Down, protesters pointed out, was destroyed because there were no legitimate means of defending it. Public inquiries for trunk-road schemes take place after the decision to build the road has been made; all the inquiry can discuss is where the road should go. Both the Department of Transport's objectives and the potential alternatives to road-building, such as public transport or traffic management, are ruled outside the inquiry's terms of reference, and the Department is both the promoter of the scheme and the final decision-maker. Prompted by the Criminal Justice Act, campaigners began to see similar glaring democratic and constitutional deficits underlying our environmental crisis.'[36]

The Criminal Justice Act was the SOCPA of its day, and after its success various governments have become even more confident in the policy of using the police not just for public safety but social control. The CJA criminalized dissent in a way that even the presence of middle-class demonstrators couldn't overturn. It created a whole new raft of offences and gave the police unprecedented powers to deal with anyone actively voicing dissent. Suggesting legislation that erodes civil liberties to 'solve' some kind of moral panic only for the police to then use these new powers to stifle protest and dissent is now a powerful policy. (This approach has reached its zenith today, as you will see definitively in chapter 8.)

Ironically, the bill that would help quash the protest over the M3 extension at Twyford Down was something for which the middle classes had clamoured to bring an end to the free parties of the 1990s rave culture. These free parties were simply not acceptable to the public at large, mainly due to misrepresentation by the media of what went on at them. The moral panic that ensued gave the then Conservative government the support they needed to add a clause to the Criminal Justice and Public Order Act of 1994 banning groups of more than a hundred people from congregating where music 'wholly or predominantly characterized by a succession of repetitive beats' was played, and another that would later prove problematic to road protesters called 'aggravated trespass'. Section 68 of the CJA explains that anyone trespassing on land in the open air who intends to intimidate or prevent people going about 'lawful activity' (i.e. road-building contractors and their workmen) will be liable for three months in prison and a fine of £2,500. This section of the Act, when coupled with the public inquiry system, effectively gives the government the power to do whatever they like when it comes to large-scale developments, whether they're for roads, airports or shopping centres. It is now impossible for local people to fight such schemes with any realistic chance of success, and certainly virtually impossible to oppose them effectively without breaking the law.

Of course, the CJA brought an end to the free outdoor parties where people took drugs that made everyone smile and where no-one (except the dealers) made any money. Something that had evolved through youth culture in an unofficial way, from the ground up, to which people could go for free and which was clearly an offshoot of drug culture but built around loving each other and having fun, unlike the official violent drug culture taking place in city centres every night through the use of alcohol, was over. If you look at the consequences of that legislation, you begin to see its purpose. It was not the drug culture the government wanted to bring to an end, despite the moral panic about the use of Ecstasy and acid in the media, because that continues to this day; it was the unofficial actions of people looking for ways to bring fun into their lives that could not be sanctioned. To anyone who attended one of these parties, Britain's rave culture was one of the most empowering and positive youth movements of the twentieth century. Sadly I didn't go to any raves myself because I had developed an interest in heavy metal and was spending my afternoons dressed in black while singing along to songs about Satan.

The cutting through Twyford Down is a monument to ugliness and stupidity. A better physical manifestation of the effects government policy has had on Britain you will never see. The fact that Twyford Down had such historical value, and was loved and treasured by the people who lived there and in the surrounding area, counted for nothing because the road had to be built for the sake of the ever-expanding economy. The new motorway link from London to Southampton simply could not be kept waiting any longer. Even though it had been fought against so bitterly and so bravely.

After the huge public outcry at Twyford Down the government lost confidence in its road-building programme and the view that our environment has a value that can't just be assessed in financial terms began to grow. Although battles still rage today against airport and road extensions a victory had been won, at least in the minds of the public. Legally, however, things are far worse today, and the threat we now face is more frightening than ever.

As George Monbiot pointed out, the battle for Twyford Down exposed a much wider disease running through our political system, not just something limited to environmental policy. It highlighted the new logic the state would apply to any kind of dissent: the police and the law should not only be used for public safety but also for public control. The government has now effectively turned any member of the public who doesn't agree with its policies and is prepared to protest against them into criminals. It is not doing it in an explicit way, because if they announced 'protest is illegal' everyone would complain, but that is increasingly what the police are using their new terrorist powers for. How else can you explain eighty-two-year-old Labour Party member Walter Wolfgang being manhandled out of the 2005 Labour Conference for shouting 'Rubbish!' at Jack Straw and then being detained under the Terrorist Act when he tried to re-enter the building? Or the child whose bike was searched by the police under the Terrorist Act, and all the other terrifying examples you will read about in chapter 8? The Serious and Organised Crime and Police Act and associated anti-terrorist legislation show how much faith the government has acquired in making use of all shades of moral panic to stifle any kind of political dissent. It's ironic that while embracing this tactic so wholeheartedly with one arm they're busy holding the other one up in disbelief, lamenting the fact that so few people in Britain are engaging with the electoral process.

Back at Twyford Down, twelve years after the road was

completed, the sides of the cutting are still enormous cliffs of off-white chalk, despite assurances from the government at the time that they would soon 'green over'. You would imagine that some kind of lesson must have been learned from the whole miserable episode, but recently there was a horrible twist in the tale. As part of the government's initial proposal the old road that became obsolete after the M3 was finished was given to the people of Winchester in perpetuity. Permission was granted for it to be turned into a meadow, to become a haven for butterflies and other insects and wildlife. It wasn't much but it was something, and in the decade after the cutting was finished it thrived. A few years ago, however, the local council decided that this piece of land should be covered in concrete and tarmac so that Winchester's park-and-ride car park could be extended. Apparently, Winchester's council and businesses wanted more shoppers to have access to the high street. Again there was a demonstration, and again people complained. After all that had gone on at Twyford Down, how could they have the nerve even to think of doing such a thing? Once again the protesters couldn't stop it and now the council have their new car park. I bet the local business leaders and councillors are pleased. And they wonder why so many of its own residents nominated Winchester as a crap place to live.

I have another friend who played a role at Twyford Down, Chris Yates, the famous fisherman, writer and Master of Idleness. He lives a fairly frugal existence taking photographs, writing books and making radio and TV programmes, but he's by far the most content person I have ever met. Chris was something of a protester in his youth, particularly when the building of new roads threatened to obliterate important parts of the country-side. He was also the one person I knew who had some conception of what it was like to live in Albion. His house is like something from a fairy tale, with woodland behind it and a well in the front garden, and his four children are as delightful, fearless and creative as he is. I went to see him to find out about the tactics he had used to fight road developments.

I boarded the train at Waterloo one bright spring morning and felt my shoulders relax as I passed out of suburbia and into the lush countryside of southern Wiltshire. Chris lives a few miles away from a small village called Tollard Royal. It gained the 'Royal' in its name from King John of Magna Carta fame, who spent a great deal of time there from 1200 to 1213 and often hunted in nearby Cranbourne Chase. I took this news as another signpost that my journey was following the right track. An hour and a half later I spotted Chris dozing in his battered car at the train station. He beamed from ear to ear and greeted me. 'I put some rods in the car, shall we go and see what the fish are doing? We won't be long.'

I don't fish myself, but I've spent many hours standing behind Chris in long grass listening to him say 'One more cast' again and again for several hours at his preferred lake. Sometimes he brings an interesting book from his dusty study for me to peruse in the reeds while he stalks carp. (One of these contained a short story by Edgar Allan Poe that actually referred to the lake itself, something of which, at the time he gave me the book, Chris had no knowledge.)

His preferred fishing spot does happen to be near a rather splendid pub too, so he never gets any complaints from me. After standing behind him again for a few hours at his favourite lake we drove up to the pub, ordered a few sandwiches and tucked into a few pints of local ale. Chris mined his memory for me, and soon stories of past protests were flowing out of his mouth between heartfelt guffaws.

'My favourite one has to be the stink bombs. We were fighting the M25 extension years ago and we'd got hold of this eminent scientist who was prepared to fly in from America and testify about the dangers of lead in petrol and what effect this would have on the environment if the road went ahead. Anyway, the public inquiry was scheduled to close on the Friday but our man couldn't get there until the Monday, so we had to find a way of making the inquiry overrun.

'The night before, all the various campaigners came together for a meeting to work out how we could do it, and I had this great idea to let off stink bombs in the hall. It would take ages to fumigate the building, the inquiry would be forced to shut early for the day and then it would run over to the following week and we'd be able to get our scientist to give his evidence. Everyone agreed it was a brilliant and hilarious plan, but the problem was you were always searched when you went into the room and there was no way we'd be able to smuggle in stink bombs without Security noticing. We thought about trying to break in overnight to stash them somewhere but we didn't want to get done for breaking and entering. Then, at the back of the room, this little old lady who was sitting with three others stood up and pointed out that none of their hand-bags had ever been searched by security when they visited the public inquiry. She sat down again and started whispering to the other three, then she stood up and said, "We'll take them in and set them off. No problem." Everyone collapsed laughing. I mean, can you imagine it! These sweet old ladies stuffing their handbags with stink bombs! But of course it was the perfect plan.

'The next day we all went into the inquiry as normal and all these butch anti-road protester types were being searched by the doormen – it took them ages to search us all – and meanwhile these four old ladies were ushered through and took their seats down the front. A few minutes later we were all in and they started letting the stink bombs off. There was a terrible commotion and people began running out of the room as fast as they could. The fug was unbelievable. Well, of course they had no choice but to suspend the inquiry and extend it. Our man flew in, gave his evidence, and it was the final piece of evidence we needed. The extension was refused and we won! It didn't stop there, though. His evidence about lead in petrol was so compelling that it got everything rolling to ban lead in petrol altogether. So everyone in Britain owes a lot to those brave and reckless grannies with their stink bombs.'

When I first met Chris and discovered the staggeringly relaxed pattern of his life (despite being a single father of four) I told him he was a Master of Idleness and he looked at me in surprise. 'But I've never even had a job.' 'Exactly,' I replied. I asked him how he'd managed to do it and he gave me a typically Yates-like response. 'Well, you see, in my experience you have two choices in life. You can have money or you can have time but you can never have both. I've always been happy because I've always chosen time.'

I pressed him for more stories but he had other ideas. He told me the first thing I needed to do was to forget all about work, and he threw my dictaphone into the general detritus collecting in the back of his car. Then he showed me a brand-new, enormous wind-up aeroplane he'd just bought. He was desperate to try flying it on the hill behind his house so we went off and did that instead. Later that night, after spending the afternoon playing with his new plane and re-enacting Southampton's recent defeat of Portsmouth with a small pink football, we stalked badgers and drank red wine while three of his children, Ellen, Alex and William, stared up into the sky looking for shooting stars. The badgers had got used to Chris on his moonlit walks and came out in a little line late that night, dipping their noses into the scraps of our dinner which Chris had put out for them.

It really struck me, sitting there that evening, how few of us ever actually have the time to work out how to live. I had read a little book on the train by the Roman philosopher Seneca called *On the Shortness of Life* which argues that people are always fretting about extending their lives when in reality we are given plenty of time to savour being alive, we just waste most of it. 'Men do not let anyone seize their estates,' he wrote, 'and if there is the slightest dispute about their boundaries they rush to stones and arms; but they allow others to encroach on their lives – why, they themselves even invite in those who will take over their lives. You will find no-one willing to share out his money; but to how many does each of us divide up his life! People are frugal in guarding their personal property; but as soon as it comes to squandering time they are most wasteful of the one thing in which it is right to be stingy.' He then went on to say, 'learning how to live takes a whole life, and, which may surprise you more, it takes a whole life to learn how to die.' Sitting there on a log chatting with Chris, I began to understand exactly what it was that Seneca meant. For a brief moment I got a glimpse of a life completely emptied of fear.

Chris was an example of someone who had found his own way to escape the clutches of corporate Britain. The lesson from him seemed to be that our own time, inspiration, sense of creativity and desire to have plain old-fashioned fun are what you should rely on if you are looking for a different kind of life. Artists and creative types seem to be the only kinds of people who ever get to live in such a relaxed and free way. I'm becoming convinced that our obsession with celebrities simply reflects this desire to be in control of our own time. When you look at the gossip magazines that sell hundreds of thousands of copies every week they are always filled with pictures of famous people doing surprisingly tedious and mundane things: going shopping in Sainsbury's on a Monday morning perhaps, having their hair done on a Thursday afternoon, or just going clothes shopping whenever they like. It's almost as though it's not them we lust after but the fact that they can pretty much do what they want whenever they like. All the while the rest of us rot in offices, tied to desks and commuter trains by an umbilical cord of debt, fear and anxiety.

The only other person I know who seems to have found his own kind of creative Albion is the artist/musician/poet Billy Childish. Not that he found it without a struggle, though. I once heard a story about Billy, which I found particularly shocking and inspiring. When he was sixteen he started working at a dockyard in Chatham. He had no qualifications, had suffered a hellish and sexually abused childhood, was an alcoholic and couldn't read or write. One afternoon he was chatting to an old man next to him in the yard. He told the man that he would only be working there for a few months because he wanted to go to art school. The story goes that the old man started laughing, so Billy asked him why. The man replied, 'Everyone says they're going to quit. I said that when I started here at fourteen, now look at me. You'll never quit. You'll get used to the security.' Billy apparently then walked over to a block of granite, picked up a three-pound club hammer and pounded his left hand with it four times, mangling it into a bloody pulp. A year later he was in art school.

He is now a successful artist and writer, but his music is what made Kurt Cobain one of his biggest fans. Beck and the White Stripes tried to get him to support them on tour, but he refused. He and his band won't use modern equipment because it alters the authenticity of their sound. Terrifyingly, the only reason most people have heard of him is the least interesting thing about him: he once went out with the artist Tracey Emin.

I went to see Billy in his home town of Chatham, to the east of London along the Thames. He greeted me with a smile perfectly framed by a wide Victorian moustache, led me into his kitchen and made a pot of green tea. We began by talking about how, rather than inspiring people to do things themselves, official culture actively seems to prevent normal people from bringing creativity into their own lives. 'You see, culture is meant to be about communication and not about elitist groups,' Billy said. 'The whole idea that anybody can be anything is a limitlessness, which means that no-one can find where they are because there are no boundaries and nothing really to aspire to. You should actually enforce limitations on yourself as rigorously as you can so that you don't end up with despotism. We've got a vaguely despotic, throwaway commercial society which sort of imposes in a very subliminal way lots of rules on people's behaviour. What you should do, what's cool and what isn't. The important thing in contemporary culture is to show that you're a bit wise, you don't really care, you're not really bothered. You don't show any vulnerability. That's the most important thing in contemporary culture, and that is its great weakness, its adolescent attempts at nonchalance. It doesn't matter that these things exist, of course, what is important is what you choose to align yourself with. A lot of artists have been interested in taking sponsorship from alcohol companies and that shows their desperation and lack of integrity. People don't like moving towards integrity because they are afraid of failure, but failure is what they should be trying to embrace because that shows you your humanity and weakness.

'People find it very, very difficult because we have no proper spiritual grounding. In school they don't teach or instruct the value of truth, how we really are and what the purpose of being alive is, which is to grow and be better people and not be obsessed with materialism – which is another myth, by the way. Materialism isn't even materialism now because quality doesn't matter. At least the Victorians were into proper materialism. Quality has never mattered less. I mean, I make books and you can't get decent paper now because decent paper costs two or three pence more per page. Decent paper doesn't exist any more because no-one gives a flying shit if a book's got that paper in it or not because they're chucking it away anyway, or no-one's going to buy it. I just did a three-book collection of poetry and I tried to do it on slightly more expensive paper – although it's hard to find good stitched paper – but it means that you have to spend more to begin with and you're not going to get as much money back as quickly. So it means you actually have to be interested in what you're doing to be bothered doing it. And most people are very, very cynical about that sort of stuff and they won't make something that they want out in the world. If you go into a restaurant or buy some clothes somewhere you get the feeling that what you get is what the people think they can get away with selling you. They won't say, "Well, how would I want this sort of thing to be?" It's always, "Well, this'll do. They won't notice." What you have to do is do things differently yourself. That's why it's important. It's all very well seeing things, but once you've seen them, don't do it, or endeavour not to, because then you don't become part of it.'

I pointed out that even when people have dreams they get hijacked into thinking that they must make a million pounds out of them. We all seem to equate winning the lottery with happiness. 'Well,' said Billy, 'I always say, "If they've got what you want, then they've got you." People working like that are unfortunate in the sense that they don't have the time or the inclination to work out what they really want in their heart, or what they need. And I'm not some kind of puritan. I'm as greedy and have as many problems as everybody else, and I've been an alcoholic, but I'm just very fortunate in life in that I lack ambition. I don't mind if I'm successful or not because I know what I'm doing is right. I look for myself in what I do and I try to be truthful to that. I've always been protected by not having any breaks, but I've never tried to change what I do or what I think. I've never tried to outwit or pre-guess anything. I never try to scheme.'

One of the reasons I find Billy so fascinating is because he occupies a strange position in our culture: he's almost the ultimate in cool because he has no interest in 'cool' whatsoever. I asked him if he found it odd that so many famous musicians kept name-checking him. 'Not really, I'm used to it. It doesn't make any difference to me. Look at the group I'm in. We cannot become what other groups become because we refuse to do the things that other groups do. We cannot be a stadium group because we refuse to use that equipment. I'm available to talk so people cannot make me into something that I'm not. The fifteen feet most groups want between them and the audience we're always dismantling. You can see the holes in everything we do because we don't hide behind PA systems and volume. In the same sense, I'll talk to you because if I talk to people they can see for themselves that I'm not anything like they expect. I'm totally ordinary, and I'm just doing something I enjoy.

'Someone said to me recently that I'm a minor celebrity. I refuse to be a celebrity. Celebrity is completely idiotic. I don't think artists are special, I don't think writers are special, I don't think people who work on magazines are special, I don't think there's any specialness about it. If people think they're special because they are artists then they are liars. They are egotistical and they are losing themselves. If a few people realize that and see that it's about our right as human beings, our nature to be creative – that's all it's about, and everyone is equal in that – then we wouldn't have this obsession with celebrity. It's about people doing things for themselves. Look at The Milkshakes [one of Billy's bands]. We gauged our success on the number of people who came up to us and said, "We liked your group so much that we decided to form a group." Things are meant to be inspirational. If they're not then they're not of any use.

'What you're talking about, if people think I'm cool they're getting the wrong end of it. All I try to do is be authentic and not be original. Originality is completely overrated and a complete waste of time. All that matters is authenticity. And I'm not authentic all the time. I fall down sometimes and make mistakes, but my intention is authenticity and that means looking at yourself and trying to do what is right for you. Having a community and integrity of communication is paramount. It should be about moving towards inclusion. I don't do exclusion when it comes to music. The writing is not about excluding people. People ask me about writing and I say you get a Xerox machine, you write your stuff and you do it. And you make a book and I'll show you how to do it if you want, but you've got to do it, I'm not doing it for you. Look for authenticity that speaks to you. Keep low to the ground. If you're looking for inspiration then everything's already inside you, it just needs to be unearthed and looked at. The problem is this false notion of originality, which is used to hamstring everybody. Originality is the least important thing there is. Authenticity and integrity are what matters.'

Before I left Billy in his attic, where he was hand-painting the boxes for his latest collection of poetry, and ambled off down the road to the station, I asked him what he thought about the state of Britain and how things could be improved. 'Well, I'd go for reduction in everything. I'd go for community policing and community shopping. You want decentralization in everything. Britain almost doesn't exist any more. Sometimes I can't believe I'm not in America.'

On the train home my phone rang. It was Mark Barrett.

'Dan? Where are you? Charlie Chaplin has just been arrested outside Downing Street. The police even took his "You have the right to remain silent" sign off him, so I guess you don't have that right any more either.' I was used to odd things coming out of Mark's mouth, but this was strange even for him. 'He's coming on the march tomorrow. Are you around? I've told him all about you. Come to the London Eye at four o'clock.'

The exclusion zone around Parliament Square was beginning to attract more and more people who had come up with ever more creative ways to make a stand. Chaplin was an interesting icon to choose, a man of the people who was always keen to kick officialdom up its backside whenever he had the chance – which was very often, if you're familiar with his films.

The next day Rachel, Wilf and I got to the London Eye on time but couldn't see Charlie. Mark, dressed as a clown in military apparel, was having some kind of altercation with a few gruff-looking security men while other clowns bounced and wheeled around him. A few minutes later more people began to emerge, and then I spotted the tramp, limping along with his walking stick, wearing a suit and bowler hat. I went over and introduced myself. He put his fingers to his lips and said, 'I'm not supposed to speak but I've got something for you.' He pulled out a thought bubble on a stick from the back of his jacket; it had 'Free Speech' written inside it. If I carried it within the exclusion zone I would no doubt be guilty of Britain's first thought crime.

We hobbled together over Westminster Bridge behind the mayhem Mark had organized, communicating only with nods and supportive smiles. By the time we got to Parliament Square Neil Goodwin's lips had loosened up a little, although he still only spoke in a whisper. 'My girl-friend says she'll leave me if I get arrested many more times, but do you fancy going up to Downing Street?' Mark and his assortment of beautifully dressed clowns were dancing and singing in Parliament Square but were attracting little attention from the police. I wondered what they would make of Charlie Chaplin outside Downing Street so soon after his arrest the day before. Neil still was-n't speaking much but he smiled broadly as he shuffled his way up Whitehall with me and my family in tow. We had no idea what would happen next.

Crowds of tourists seemed to think that he was some kind of official attraction and began to ask for photos. Neil duly obliged. A few tried to give him money afterwards but he ushered them away with that little hobbling walk I recognized from *City Lights*. As we got nearer Downing Street he leant over to me and said, 'Chaplin was the man, you know.' A few minutes later I began to understand exactly what he meant.

The tramp is not one of the most widely loved icons of cinema for nothing. Despite many of Chaplin's films being over seventy years old and having had no major cinema release in generations, everyone still knows and loves his characters. The tourists by the entrance to Downing Street laughed and clapped as Neil took up his spot outside the gates. They queued to have their photograph taken with him, but the police were not amused because he was holding a sign that said 'Not Aloud', which, because of the ludicrous nature of SOCPA's exclusion zone, meant he was breaking the law.

Within minutes an armed officer called over to him. 'You can't stand there, mate. It's illegal.' Neil shrugged as though he didn't understand. The policeman tried again. 'You can't demonstrate. Move along or you'll get arrested.' The crowd of people began to boo at the policeman. 'Doesn't he have the right to remain silent?' I offered. The crowd laughed. The officer angrily looked at me. 'Are you trying to be funny, mate? Who are you? Are you with him?' I shook my head and he turned back to Neil, who was doing his best to look scared, which was drawing sympathetic noises from the crowd. One of them called out, 'Leave him alone, he's only standing there!' Someone else put in, 'It's a free country, isn't it?' Neil shook his head with a rueful smile and the crowd began to applaud and cheer.

The policeman spoke into his radio. I decided to explain to everyone that because he hadn't got permission from the police 'Charlie' was actually breaking the law for holding an illegal demonstration. A man behind me laughed. 'You're joking, aren't you, mate?' Others seemed astounded. One woman looked at me as though I was deranged. 'You can't be serious?' she said. 'Protest can't just be made illegal!' The policeman rounded on me, 'Look, who are you? Can you just move along?' I refused and pointed out that I wasn't breaking the law. He became contrite and lowered his voice. 'No, you're not breaking the law, I'm just asking you out of courtesy if you'd move along because you're adding to this disturbance.' I refused again and he said into his radio, 'There are two of them holding an illegal demonstration. Can I have back-up?'

At this point, again to a vast array of boos from the crowd, another armed policeman emerged and asked Charlie his name and if he had any ID. A group of lads who looked like builders began to laugh, and one of them called out, 'What's his name? His name's Charlie, you muppet!' Again the swelling audience fell about. The policeman pleaded with Neil to move a few yards away to stop the crowd blocking the entrance to Number Ten. Charlie shuffled along, only for another two officers to approach him and ask again if he had any ID. Neil let go of his sign, revealing that it was chained to his wrist (so it wouldn't get confiscated like the last one) – cue more laugher from the crowd – and began theatrically to look through his pockets. Eventually he found a scrap of paper which he unfolded as if he had all the time in the world and turned its contents towards the crowd. 'No Comment' was written on it in large black letters. There must have been fifty people at this point and they all began to cheer. Even the armed policeman laughed. 'Well, he is funny, I'll give him that.' Two officers then ushered him a few yards further down the street. Neil was given a piece of paper that outlined the exclusion zone and explained about Section 132 of the Serious and Organised Crime and Police Act, which solicited a huge guffaw from sections of the crowd. The policemen told Neil that if he was still there in half an hour they would arrest him. Neil shrugged his shoulders.

Part of the crowd began to disperse. More tourists emerged and had their pictures taken, but none of them could believe that he was about to get arrested. One of them came over and chatted to me to learn what was going on. I explained that in a few minutes' time Charlie was going to get taken to Charing Cross police station for hold-ing his sign. The man was incredulous. 'They can't arrest you for just standing there, can they? What about our rights?' He was about to see exactly what had happened to our rights. A police van pulled up, the two uniformed officers emerged, and Charlie Chaplin was read his rights and manhandled into the back of the van. The passer-by turned to me with a look of shock on his face. 'That's fucking terrifying! They can't do that, can they?' I shrugged my shoulders and looked at Rachel in disbelief.

It was the first time I'd actually seen anyone get arrested and it was an unpleasant and alarming experience. One of the picnickers, Elizabeth, had told me that everyone should know what being arrested feels like to get some idea of what protesting in today's Britain actually means. The notion that Neil was a criminal left me baffled. As he got carted off in a police wagon the funny side of Section 132 of SOCPA seemed to go with him. The crowds seemed unsettled too. Their laughter gave way to bewilderment and shock. If only the architects of SOCPA and all the MPs who voted for it in Parliament had been on hand to explain to us all why there was nothing sinister about a man dressed as Charlie Chaplin being arrested outside Downing Street for carrying a sign that said 'Not Aloud'.

I'd had enough. It was time to get off the fence and put something on the line myself.

# THE 'ASHES' OF THE MAGNA CARTA

## CHAPTER 7

In terms of journalistic integrity and expertise you have to be careful not to overstep the mark when it comes to your story. Happily I'm an amateur, so that rule doesn't apply to me. Besides, I was more taken with an approach I'd heard from the artist Damien Hirst: 'Sometimes you have to cross the line if you want to find out where it is.'

From my journey so far and the people I'd met I had come to the conclusion that the problems we face in Britain exist only because so few people have the time or inclination to do anything about them. So, having done nothing since getting dressed up as a teddy bear, I decided it was time to get my hands dirty again.

But what do you do if you just want to do *something*? Conventional wisdom states that you need the press to poke people into action, and these days it has to be a grand and clever gesture to persuade the media to get involved. After watching others from the sidelines, I had begun to develop a few ideas about what might make a successful protest. I was convinced that the first step to getting your message across was not to give anyone an excuse to ignore you, whether that's through having too many piercings, wearing tie-dye trousers, or looking and sounding like a politician. If you want anyone to listen you have to be wary of the pigeonhole you will put yourself in before you utter a word. Of course I was already in the most powerful pigeonhole I could be in, the one for white middle-class men, but I decided to make patriotism the other feature of my plan.

Patriotism seemed a good idea because everyone is patriotic to some extent, whether it's to do with sport, hating the French, the Americans, or anyone else for that matter (in a humorous rather than racist way, you understand), or because of Thomas Paine, the Diggers, Guy Fawkes, Stephenson's *Rocket*, Brunel's bridges, Jeremy Clarkson, Princess Diana or Margaret Thatcher. We all love our country, even if we do reserve the right to think it's a bit crap some of the time. People care about Britain because there is something in the air or the light of this land that you can't quite put your finger on. George Orwell wrote in an essay entitled *Why I Write*, 'One day Patriotism and Intelligence will come together', and I wanted to do something to try to bring about that change. Overt displays of national pride seem to single you out as some kind of moronic bigot, but I'm proud of my country, I'm not a moronic bigot, and I'm sick of being told I should be ashamed of our flag. So that became my plan, to bring the fight for freedom of speech and liberty within the realm of patriotism.

I also recalled, after the success of his school dinners campaign, Jamie Oliver saying he suddenly realized one day that anyone who didn't agree with him that children deserved good food from their schools was a 'wanker', and from that moment on he knew he couldn't lose. That's an ideal cause, something that reduces your opponent to the status of 'wanker'. For me, the right to free speech and the right to protest outside Parliament is the political equivalent of Jamie's gastronomic campaign. Of course free speech can incite hatred if it's used out of context. You could hardly complain if you went to a wedding and started shouting 'This is absolute cock!' at the top of your voice and found everyone slightly nonplussed when you explained that you were simply exercising your right to free speech. But if anyone living in a democracy, especially a member of its Parliament, tries to argue against the right to protest and free speech outside its seat of power then they are simply 'wankers' too. So the campaign was perfect. All I had to do was not ruin it.

However, Jamie Oliver is a celebrity so he had that other vital thing on his side, a media profile. That was something I didn't have, but I did have a few tricks up my sleeve. Nationalism in this country today means you're a racist or you're talking about cheering on England in a sporting event. When SOCPA became law on 1 August 2005 England was on the verge of winning the Ashes on home soil for the first time since 1985. Everyone in the country went cricket crazy because of the typically English way we went about winning it. The iconic moment when Freddie leant down to console a distraught Brett Lee after we'd won the Edgbaston Test was as

English as you could get. Our team was strong and creative and it fought till the bitter end, despite having to carry a few plucky, but ineffective, team members. Now I don't usually go in for tacky sporting metaphors, but in this case I thought it appropriate, so in an attempt to harness some of that feeling I decided to organize a protest cricket match in Parliament Square.

A cricket match on its own might tempt the tabloids but I doubted it would work for the broadsheets, so I had to come up with something clever to interest that audience as well. Which is when I hit on another idea: why not organize a protest cricket match in Parliament Square for the 'Ashes' of the Magna Carta, seeing as the government had binned its last few remaining clauses in the name of protecting us from someone statistically less dangerous than Linda Barker? That made the whole thing highbrow, funny and mainstream. For a bit of added zest I wondered whether we could do it on St George's Day. Then we really could bring patriotism into the mix. On paper I was convinced it was genius. A celebration of nationalism based on our status as the mongrels of the world, where we have always thrived precisely because of a diverse ethnic mix, mongrels who fight tyranny wherever it dares show its face and who drink too much ale when it doesn't. That was what I wanted to celebrate on St George's Day.

There was only one problem. Being charged with organizing, rather than just participating in, an illegal demonstration carried the risk of a possible fifty-one-week prison sentence. Now I was prepared to do just about anything to get people to read this book, and that included being arrested, but being jailed for a year was pushing it. If only I knew someone prepared to go to prison.

'Hey, Mark, where are you? I've had an idea . . .'

Mark Barrett was very keen on the plan. He had already been thinking of organizing an alternative to the right-wing flag-waving spectacle our national day has become. His plan was suitably unconventional. 'I was going to call it St George in Drag. Getting drag queens to hold aloft the cross of St George in Parliament Square would be truly subversive and would highlight the problem of the exclusion zone at the same time.'

We met in a pub a few days later, and as we became lubricated the plan trickled off into strange places. I wanted to go on a pilgrimage before the match, because I was drunk and I thought it was the sort of thing Gandhi would do, and Magna Carta Island was only thirty or so miles from Parliament Square along the Thames. Mark was very excited. 'We could bring a replica of the Magna Carta to Parliament Square before burning it and playing for its ashes!' Admittedly, this meant the plan was beginning to get a bit Spinal Tap in its complexity, especially as St George's Day 2006 happened to be the day of the London Marathon. The runners would arrive inside SOCPA's exclusion zone after their professional marathon with the legal corporate sponsorship message 'Flora' on their shirts; we would arrive after our amateur marathon for liberty and end up inside the exclusion zone with the illegal political message 'Terrorism: It's Just Not Cricket' written on ours. We hoped that by the time we got to the square (teatime, naturally) the press would be bored of photographing exhausted runners and would cover our protest cricket match instead.

Everything seemed to be falling into place until I dropped a plate on my toe while cleaning Wilf's sick off my T-shirt at two o'clock one morning. It wasn't actually broken but it hurt like hell and I couldn't walk very well. So that was the end of the pilgrimage. Mark was philosophical. 'Don't worry, we can do the pilgrimage in June instead, which is when the anniversary of the original signing of the Magna Carta is, anyway. I've got in touch with some cyclists and they want to cycle the route, so they can bring the Magna Carta with them instead.' So the event became a cycle/march to Parliament Square from outside the exclusion zone, a patriotic tea party, and then an illegal cricket match before a night in the cells. If Neil got arrested for standing on his own with a placard, surely we'd get banged up for organizing such a blockbuster event. And if we got arrested for playing cricket on St George's Day then surely even the *Sun* would be moved to make some kind of response.

So we were all set. I got some T-shirts printed with that Tony Blair quote, a cricket bat, stumps and a ball. I even got hold of some proper cricket clothes and a flag with the cross of St George to carry on the march. Mark had planned for us to meet in the Peace Gardens by the Imperial War Museum, which was outside the exclusion zone, at one p.m. Then we would have some food before marching to Parliament Square for the tea party and the cricket match once the marathon was over.

I drank a cold beer the night before and prepared myself for the day ahead, but then the apologetic phone calls and emails began. By ten p.m. a large chunk of my cricket team had cancelled. A few blamed family commitments, one had the cheek to cite the weather forecast, others had got cold feet at the prospect of being arrested, but afterwards they all admitted the reason was work. They were all terrified of being sacked if they ended up spending a night in the cells. One of them told me, 'It's all right for you, you'll never have a regular job, but I just can't have a criminal record. I've got a family.'

In the weeks and months leading up to the event people had been very keen to be involved. All the people I spoke to about the exclusion zone thought it was a disgrace, but as the day loomed the threat of arrest began to change their minds. SOCPA's exclusion zone was working. When it came to the crunch, people were now simply too afraid to voice their opinion outside Parliament. They felt they had too much to risk. Only a handful – Jamie, John Mark, Katie, Alan, Edward and some of his mates – were still prepared to come. 'Well, someone's got to keep an eye on you, dude,' Jamie wrote in an email.

I found this change of heart fascinating. I love my friends dearly and don't blame a single one of them for not coming, but their reluctance to participate made me realize that I had already crossed a line. One of them even said 'I really admire you for doing this, it's really impressive' after apologizing for not being able to make it himself. I rang Mark and told him about the second thoughts I'd encountered, which were beginning to affect me too. 'Oh, for God's sake,' he said, 'we won't get arrested for playing cricket!' But Mark had stepped over the line a long time ago and didn't understand the reticence of people who had mortgages, credit cards and children to feed.

As I hung up the phone I felt proud that I had changed slightly in the eyes of my friends. The local elections were just around the corner and the polling card, printed on bright orange paper to try to make it stand out from the junk mail when it came through my front door, seemed rather pointless in comparison with what I'd discovered on my journey around Britain so far. I would vote – the Greens had a chance of getting in down in South London so my opinion could actually have an impact, and I wanted to play whatever part I could in giving New Labour a bloody nose – but the reason I felt politically awake was the cricket bat and rucksack full of T-shirts in my front room, rather than that piece of orange paper pleading for my attention in the hallway. I didn't care how silly it might seem to other people. For once I was actually going to do something I cared about. I was putting something on the line for what I believed in, and I had never, ever done that before.

It was then that I realized why we, as a nation, have such little interest in politics. We simply don't know what it means any more. Politics has got nothing to do with voting once every four years. It isn't about red, yellow, green or blue. It's about how you spend every single day of your life. That's your political allegiance – what you actually do with the short time you get to spend on this planet, not just what you like to think you believe in. You don't vote by placing a cross by someone's name on a ballot paper, you vote by having the courage to be who you are, to live the life you want to live and to stand up and say 'No!' to people who want to control and exploit you, whether it's the government, your boss, credit card companies, the people offering to consolidate your debt, careers advisers, newspaper editors or the purveyors of satellite TV. Politics isn't about Parliament, the House of Lords or MPs. The Palace of Westminster is just a big place full of jobsworth bureaucrats desperately trying to tick all the boxes their bosses have asked them to tick so that one day they can become bosses themselves. Rather like Ian Nairn's problem with the planners of yesteryear, politics has also been reduced to the lowest common denominator, the mindset of a tedious office job instead of the amateurism and hope of life.

Politicians have managed to make us believe that they have the answers to our problems and that paying a subscription to a political party, being a member of one, or even just voting for them once every four years means that you have an interest and a voice in our political system. The truth is, they don't have the answers. You do. When you act on something yourself rather than allow yourself to be paralysed by fear – of terrorism, poverty in old age, bird flu, Lawrence Llewellyn Bowen or Osama Bin Laden – you suddenly become a citizen of this country rather than a consumer of it. Then you have a stake in something larger than yourself and you begin to forge your place within your community. That's the moment when your life will begin to change beyond measure.

The morning of the protest arrived, and the day started well. Henry Porter, the *Vanity Fair* and *Observer* writer who had been fighting passionately to defend our civil liberties in a newspaper column, had been having a frank exchange of emails on the subject of civil liberties with

Tony Blair. The story was published on the front page of that day's *Observer*. It was an illuminating article that gave Blair the chance to sound tough on crime in the run-up to the local elections. It was basically a re-run of his 'Tough on crime' speech fourteen years earlier, the argument being that civil liberties had to be compressed to protect the law-abiding majority. Having the debate as front-page news on the day of our protest was a good omen, though. I gulped uneasily at the prospect of Mark burning the Magna Carta in a Blair mask in front of the cameras, but at least there was only a small chance of being arrested now. With this much publicity the police were bound to leave us alone.

St George's Day was graced with typically English weather – light drizzle. Decked out in full cricket whites under my long coat and carrying a rucksack full of T-shirts, St George's flags and cricket equipment, I walked from Waterloo station to our meeting point, the Peace Gardens by the Imperial War Museum. It was an appropriate place to start. The museum is a wonderfully patriotic place. An enormous chunk of the Berlin Wall sits outside it beside a mind-boggling double cannon that seems to be the length of a tennis court. Inside, a Spitfire hangs gracefully in the entrance hall. Most nations would be too embarrassed to invite the Dalai Lama to open a peace garden in such close proximity to the glorification of the memory of war, but we did, and that's Britain at its contradictory best. I met Mark, Steve and another protester called Mark by his car and we were assembling our deliberately blank banners and flags bearing the cross of St George when the police put in their first appearance of the day.

A squad car pulled up beside us and the two officers inside began to laugh as they wound down their window. The WPC in the passenger seat leant over the policeman driving and said with a smirk, 'Er, this is really embarrassing, but, um, we've been told by our inspector, er, to ask you if you're, um, planning on engaging in any criminal behaviour.' They carried on laughing after that but pressed us for information about our plans, which seemed odd considering that every detail had been outlined clearly on the website for months. Steve told them we were just planning on meeting some people in the peace garden, and the police smiled, thanked us and left.

Given the rain, it was an impressive turnout with about thirty marchers by two o'clock. We assembled our banners and flags while a few Hare Krishnas served up hot food under huge umbrellas to help us on our journey to the square. One couple stood out among the cyclists, the men in drag, the people with painted faces and the lone idiot in cricket whites. They were very well dressed, very well spoken and very angry about the way our civil liberties were being eroded. The man seemed to find the colourful company slightly more awkward than his wife, but then perhaps I'm being unfair. It was equally likely that he felt awkward purely because he was among total strangers. I offered them a T-shirt each and they accepted gladly but refused to take them for free. The lady put a £10 note in my hand like my granny always used to when my parents weren't looking. They took a dim view of the police, who kept sniffing around trying to find out what we were planning. 'Look here,' the man said, 'are they trying to intimidate us or something?' I told them it was good to see them and thanked them for coming. 'Well, you've got to do something, haven't you?' said the lady. 'I mean, it's complete madness what's going on.' We spoke about why so few people seemed to be taking a stand and to her mind the reason for their reticence was clear. 'Even the ones who have noticed are too frightened, that's the problem,' she said. 'We're both retired so we've got nothing to lose. It's different if you're young. I mean, you could lose your job if you got arrested for protesting about something like this.'

I wondered whether that conversation was a prediction of the future for political protest in this country. There is a generation for whom the dream of a secure pension has become a reality, but the current economic system has peaked for the majority of people living in Britain. That's worth thinking about for a moment. I am part of the first generation that will have a lower standard of living than that of their parents, so from now on the model our society is based on, with its ever-expanding shareholder economy, will be failing the vast majority of us who live in Britain who are not already rich. However, a large number of the current retired generation have money and no longer have to work so they are perhaps the only group within society truly free enough to make a stand for what they believe in.[37] Happily, they also have the most knowledge and wisdom to share. Never mind the black panthers, it's the growing army of grey panthers that may yet hold the key to securing fairness and freedom for the people of Britain. It's time Saga stopped selling cruises and mobilized their swelling ranks. We are approaching a time when the old will outnumber the young. It's spoken of in apocalyptic terms by the government because of the threat it poses to our growing economy, but why can't we harness their knowledge and use it to our advantage? A growing militancy among the retired and soon-to-be-retired could well be on the cards as more and more people discover at the end of their working lives that building their lives around overwork and over-consumption delivered neither happiness nor security. It's a lesson the younger generation need to learn before it's too late. Before they've fallen into line and got themselves into the debt-ridden cycle of work and consumption that passes for Blake's Jerusalem these days.

It was time to go to Parliament Square. By now, four other officers had joined the original two and a police van had appeared outside the gate. As we moved off, an unmarked police car with two more uniformed officers inside began to follow us down the road. One of the cyclists was pulling a small sound system, and Bob Marley sang out through the rain 'Get up, stand up, stand up for your rights' as we set off down the road. That felt bloody brilliant, I can tell you. We doubled back a few times and dived down back streets to try to avoid the police cars, but they always kept up with us while, not for the last time that day, a helicopter buzzed around over our heads.

We made it to St Thomas's Hospital by around half-past four, which is when the police car stopped in front of us and one of the policemen called out, 'Westminster Bridge is closed to all pedestrians. There's no way you can cross there so you'll have to find another route across the river.' They looked apologetic and shook their heads. 'You just can't get across there, that's all.' This was a major blow to the plan. It would take hours to walk all the way to Lambeth Bridge and then double back to Westminster. If we couldn't get to Parliament Square by five then it would all be a complete disaster. At that point, one of the protesters came over and whispered to the group, 'That's bollocks. They're just lying. Everyone keep going.' Inside I felt a twinge of surprise, and said, without thinking, 'Surely a policeman wouldn't just blatantly lie to us all like that? The bridge must be closed if he says it is.' A few people looked at me as teachers might look at a naive child. Someone else patted my back supportively, as if recognizing that for me the penny might just have dropped. So we carried on, shouting through the rain.

As we got to the bottom of the bridge it was clear that the two officers had been lying. Pedestrians were walking both ways across the bridge. The road itself was closed, but only to traffic. As we approached, the two mendacious policemen stood in the middle of the road to block us from walking anywhere other than the pavement. So we all walked on among the pedestrians, who looked bewildered by the blank banners, while Mark began shouting, 'Freedom of speech! We demand the right to protest be reinstated! Stand up for your right to speak! Don't be silenced by the government!' Once on the bridge we were inside the exclusion zone and clearly breaking the law. I suddenly felt much less confident, and a palpable fear began to take hold as I saw the scale of the police presence surrounding the square.

I spotted Henry Porter on the sidelines halfway across the bridge. He looked surprised that I had recognized him, but came over to say hello. I asked him about the story in that day's *Observer*. 'Well, it's not every day you get an email from the Prime Minister, I must confess,' he remarked. We spoke for a moment and agreed that frightening though the legislation and the erosion of our civil liberties were, public apathy was the real source of terror. I told him about the half-hearted attempt by the police to stop us getting to Parliament Square and he shook his head in disgust. Then I turned to introduce Mark, but he had strayed off the pavement and into the road, holding one half of an enormous blank white banner. The policeman told him he couldn't walk in the road because of public safety, but other pedestrians were milling about freely in the aftermath of the marathon. Mark complained that he had the same right to walk in the road as everyone else, but the policeman – a dead ringer for the actor Ross Kemp, bizarrely – manhandled him back on to the pavement. Mark shouted at him and tried to get back on the road, but Mark being Mark, as they tangled with each other, neither giving an inch, he kept whispering 'I'm really sorry about this, mate, I didn't mean to shout at you like that.'

A few minutes later we had all made it safely on to Parliament Square where the picnickers had set up a tea and cake stand and a few banners. There were three police vans filled with bored officers and about twenty others walking around the square looking at us with disdain. I began to feel very, very nervous. Perhaps they had decided to arrest us after all. I stood there, waiting for the moment of truth, then Jeff the anarchist walked over. He had helped Sian, Dave, Esther and the other picnickers set up the table with afternoon tea and cakes (with more illegal icing). I had taken off my coat by this point to prepare for the match. Jeff grinned. 'Ah, the police have been looking for you,' he said. 'They came up earlier and asked us if we were planning on having a cricket match. They're on the lookout for protesters in cricket whites.' Later I spoke to Sian who had spent some time asking the police on the perimeter about 'what a girl had to do to get arrested' only for them to reply, 'We're too busy watching the cricket to make any arrests,' before adding, 'The state of the wicket is a disgrace. You should have a word with the groundsman.'

Dave and Esther unfurled the picnickers' enormous 'Freedom to Protest' banner and walked around the square with it while we played cricket. We were clearly staging an illegal demonstration. There were thirty of us by now, with banners, some blank and some bearing slogans, and of course there were the cakes with their revolutionary icing. If there was any doubt that a political protest was taking place it was blown away when someone in a Tony Blair mask set fire to a replica of the Magna Carta while Mark made a loud speech about the contempt the government was showing for the British people. His voice boomed across the square and was clearly audible to the police, and by now we had attracted quite a crowd. Mark continued to berate Parliament and Tony Blair for their 'blatant, unwarranted attack on our civil liberties'. It was clear to anyone with eyes and ears that we were demonstrating well within the exclusion zone and we had made no attempt to apply for permission from the police before doing so. But they still didn't budge. They made their presence felt by wandering around the square with grim faces and clipboards, but at no point did any of them tell us that what we were doing was illegal or advise us to move on. There was by this stage at least one policeman for every couple of protesters, and a second helicopter was hovering overhead, so arresting us all wouldn't have been difficult. There were plenty of vans to take us to the cells, but still they made no attempt to detain anyone. Clearly the police were not taking the Serious and Organised Crime and Police Act seriously at all.

The cricket match was a great success. Everyone joined in and the sight of people playing cricket didn't seem out of place in Parliament Square, though a few bedraggled marathon runners seemed surprised. It was all good fun, despite the fact that a guy who looked like the singer Willie Nelson seriously hogged the bat and seemed determined to hit the ball over Big Ben. Then Ed bowled him with a nice off-break that Ashley Giles could only dream of. The police, meanwhile, began to move away, leaving only a handful to keep an eye on our demonstration as it came to a close.

Around seven p.m. things began to wind down and we packed everything away before heading off for a drink in the pub. I was mildly irritated that after we'd gone to the trouble of organizing the demonstration the police had decided to ignore the law, but if I'm honest I was actually rather relieved.

You may think that we should have taken comfort in the fact that we weren't arrested. After all, surely you can't have it both ways. You can't complain that something is illegal on the one hand and then on the other complain when you don't get arrested for doing it. But surely it's unhealthy in a democracy for the police to have the power to decide which people it will allow to protest illegally by turning a blind eye to the new law and which it will refuse permission to by implementing the new law by the book. If the police do get to pick and choose which protests they allow to go ahead then they, by definition, have become politicized. If you live in a country 'controlled by political police supervising the citizen's activities' then you are living in a country that is defined by the dictionary as a 'police state'. Even if that sounds overly dramatic, it's hard to argue that it's not a very thin end of the same terrifying wedge. Personally, I don't see how it is possible to argue that giving the police the power to pick and choose like this means that they are anything but political, and that afternoon they were certainly supervising our activities.

It had been an eventful and illuminating, if not entirely successful, day. I'd hit a few boundaries in Parliament Square, and not many people can say that. My bowling was pretty impressive too. I even managed a three-wicket maiden in my first over. Watch out, Freddie. But I had completely failed in my objective to get arrested on St George's Day for playing cricket.

Towards the end of the day, Dave and his daughter Esther came over to console me. Esther, who was an old hand at this protest business despite being a seventeen-year-old slip of a thing, said, 'Never mind, Dan, maybe you'll get arrested next time,' as though being arrested was a rite of passage. I imagined them both standing outside Bow Street Magistrates Court at some point in the future cheering 'Dan lost his cherry!' like that scene from

*Goodfellas* when the teenage Henry Hill emerges into a cheering crowd of Mafiosi.

I like to think it wasn't a complete disaster, but the point of the day was to protest about the exclusion zone and try to reclaim our national day around the principles of liberty and national pride, and I'm not sure we managed it. Especially when Dave decided to burn one of our St George's flags. I was livid, gripped with rage. Not gripped enough to go over and say anything aggressive to him, mind you. Mark saw the look of horror on my face and pointed out that liberty meant being able to burn the flag of St George on St George's Day in Parliament Square if that was what you wanted to do. Which, of course, was the whole point of us being there. So perhaps it did prove my point after all, despite leaving a rather nasty taste in my mouth. A few hours later, on the train home, I realized that perhaps for the first time in my life I had indeed experienced the true taste of liberty.

The alternative St George's Day celebration Mark and I organized did get mentioned in the press, in *Vanity Fair* of all places,[38] but our tabloid and broadsheet trap had failed. A month later, when Mark and I set off on another adventure, we weren't fussed about the media after coming to the conclusion that it's enough just to keep doing things yourself if you think they have value. Validation from the press is not required if you are doing something you believe in. One day the press will catch up. So this time we just organized something lower key, although it proved to be much harder physical work.

In the meantime, things had changed in Parliament

Square. In May, the High Court decided that, like every-body else, Brian Haw should be held accountable to SOCPA's exclusion zone so he had to apply for his place opposite Westminster. He got permission, but they restricted his protest to three metres instead of running the entire width of the square. The night the police came to remove the rest of his banners was something to behold according to those who witnessed it. To prevent any unsightly disturbance, seventy-eight police officers came in the middle of the night at a cost of £28,000 to the tax-payer just to move some posters and banners. It was another example of the heavy-handed police treatment of protesters that is becoming the norm in Britain today. Brian, of course, wasn't going anywhere. He was still bark-ing at people every now and then and throwing his weight around but no-one could ever question his dedication, especially when he reached the five-year anniversary of his vigil.

It was 14 June, the day before the 791st anniversary of the signing of the Magna Carta, and Mark and I were going on our thirty-five-mile pilgrimage from Runnymede to Downing Street, where Mark would don his Blair mask and once again set fire to a copy of the Magna Carta. I arrived in Egham at ten on a cloudy and humid Wednesday morning. I walked down to the hotel that sat on the banks of the Thames and the M25, and before long Mark pulled up in his battered blue car a quarter of a mile from Magna Carta Island, our starting point. 'All right, bro?' he enquired while sliding all manner of general driving junk off the passenger seat. 'Sorry about the mess, this car's been doubling up as my home.'

I hadn't seen him for a while and he was in a slightly low mood. His application to train as a citizenship teacher had been turned down and he was feeling mildly depressed. I was far angrier about the news, though. If someone like Mark can get turned down for training to teach children about citizenship then we are well and truly fucked. I'm sorry to swear, but I have never met anyone who takes their sense of citizenship more seriously than Mark. North London's Metropolitan University should be ashamed of themselves. And as for their selection policy . . . Jesus wept. They should be stripped of *their* right to teach citizenship. Do they even know what it means?

We drove down into the hotel car park and got ourselves together. Mark had an enormous rucksack filled with his tent, clothes, a stove and all sorts of paraphernalia. Mine was packed on a somewhat smaller scale: I had a bit of fruit, some water, a spare change of clothes and a couple of thin books to read in the cells if we got arrested.

We had to arrive at Downing Street by four p.m. the following day to meet Rikki, a cameraman and reporter for Indymedia, so, straight away, we set off in high spirits along the river towards Staines. It proved to be hard going for someone who had done no training or preparation whatsoever. I was wearing a pair of old trainers because I'd decided the most comfortable shoes I owned would be the most sensible kind of footwear. I was wrong. They were full of holes and ripped to shreds from overuse.

After a few hours we had managed to wind our way to a pub called the Thames Court. My feet were already aching. One pint and a cheeseburger later we set off towards Hampton Court, the planned place for dinner.

Along the way we talked about Mark's political ideas. All his energy was being focused on an attempt to push for a new constitution. He was already planning to organize a conference to develop ideas for exactly what should be put into it. He wanted people to come and explain what mattered to them. He wasn't content with some kind of bill of rights because he wanted action for a sustainable future to be written into it and a blueprint for a new way of life to be pulled together. I admired his vision but didn't envy where a road like that could take him.

The river began to smell in the heat as we fought on towards Hampton Court. After six hours of walking our legs and feet were in agony. Eventually the palace loomed on the horizon, but my spirits had fallen so low that I was openly suggesting we get a cab back to my flat and return to Hampton by train the following morning. 'No way,' said Mark. Then he spotted something. 'Look, it's a sign!' It was nice to see coincidence lending us a hand once more (after King Arthur I'd vowed never to ignore such co-incidences again). A few hundred yards away was a pub called The Albion that welcomed us with empty sofas, luscious beer and enormous plates overflowing with bangers and mash. Big screens were showing Tunisia v. Saudi Arabia. We'd just missed Spain v. Ukraine, which was the only match I'd missed of the World Cup so far. Still, pilgrimages of political significance have to take priority over the more obscure matches of football's premier international tournament. In fact, I have to confess that the reason for our four p.m. deadline at Downing Street the following day was actually football-related: if we didn't get arrested it would mean we'd be able to watch

England's second group match against Trinidad and Tobago.

Mark then got a call from a friend of his called Mark Kemp, who was keen to join us for that night's camping and the second leg of the walk the following day. He was also a campaigner. Twelve years earlier he'd been stabbed twenty times by a paranoid schizophrenic while working as a doorman in Tooting. His attacker was found guilty of attempted murder in court one at the Old Bailey and sent to Broadmoor. Ten years later he absconded during a visit to Springfield Hospital in Tooting. Mark K only found out that his attacker had escaped back into his community when a *Daily Mirror* journalist rang him to ask how he felt about it. Ever since that day he had been campaigning for victims to be given a warning when their attackers were due for release from prison or if they escaped. He had even set up his own twenty-four-hour victim support helpline, which was his own mobile phone number.

Mark K was diagnosed with post-traumatic stress disorder after the attack, and within five minutes of his arrival at the pub it was clear to me that the events and their aftermath had left an indelible imprint on his personality. He was obsessive about how he had been let down and constantly ignored, telling his story over and over again while explaining his desire to fight for justice for victims and victims' rights. 'It's basic checks, that's all I'm asking for. Basic checks. If they'd carried out basic checks he would never have escaped and I wouldn't have had to go through this nightmare.'

To be brutally honest I was scared of him – a cruel and

cowardly thing to say, but it was how I felt at the time. Ever since Mark told me about him earlier in the day I had been expecting some kind of urban Ray Mears. Mark K sometimes wore a Kevlar anti-stab jacket, and Mark thought he occasionally carried a knife for his own protection. I felt unsettled at the prospect of camping along the Thames with someone who carried a knife and had been diagnosed a paranoid schizophrenic, but Mark patted me on the back while he was buying a round of drinks and told me not to worry. Mark K was also carrying an enormous rucksack filled with three different first-aid kits, including a stethoscope. He had more medical equipment than an ambulance. 'I know how fragile the human body is so I have everything we need in case we get into any difficulty,' he explained, which didn't do my sense of trepidation any good.

However, Mark K also had a DVD player in his rucksack so that we could watch a film in the tent, and soon proved himself to be as generous a person as I have ever met, offering to buy the drinks and to give us anything he had in his enormous bag if he thought we might want or need it. I quickly realized that he was just someone else I had met on my journey who had been let down and ignored. After chatting with him for an hour I got past my initial cowardly reaction and appreciated the fact that here was someone with more courage than I could fathom, for the catalogue of his mistreatment hadn't ended after his attacker's release. When he was at a particularly low ebb he went to a hospital to ask for help, the hospital responded by confusing him with his attacker because they were both called Mark, thought his numerous scars were evidence of self-mutilation, diagnosed Munchausen's Syndrome and decided to section him and pump him full of drugs. It beggars belief. How he was still standing I'll never know. Somehow he'd kept his sense of humour: he chuckled as he told me his story. I cursed myself for not recognizing the way my fear of the unknown had caused me to feel patronizing towards him earlier.

Mark K turned out to be something of an amateur squat finder – the Robin Hood of the squatting world, if you will. He would walk the streets looking for habitable and empty buildings before breaking in to them, fixing new locks and putting up a Section 6 (the document that tells the police that the building is being used as a home to prevent them from being able to come in and immediately evict the occupants). He would then ring anyone he knew who was homeless and give them a set of keys before going off and doing the same thing somewhere else. He was an ethical squatter, if such a thing can exist, so if anyone mistreated a building he had 'opened', by removing piping or doing anything to damage it, he would 'evict' them himself. 'I'm in the business of finding people decent homes if they are homeless, but I won't have them damaging perfectly good property,' he said. In fact, that day he was late joining us because he had removed the locks and taken down the Section 6 on a squat he had given over to two Polish immigrants because they 'drank twelve bottles of cider in one day and started trying to remove the copper pipes to sell'. Once the locks had been removed he kicked them out. It's interesting to learn about and see in action the morality of people who have been sidelined and spat out by society. I certainly didn't have a moral objection to his giving some of the Duke of Westminster's empty houses to people who had nowhere to live. One couple he gave a home to were a middle-class family with a toddler who simply couldn't afford to get their foot on the property ladder. It was the kind of story you'd read about in the Sunday supplement property pages, or see on *Tonight* with Trevor McDonald. Oh, OK. So I made that last bit up.

After a few more ales the three of us stumbled off towards Teddington after getting a tip from a woman on the next table that fishermen sometimes camped along the river there so our tents wouldn't arouse undue interest. My legs and feet ached. It took us three hours. We stopped only so that the two Marks could roll a few joints because Mark K smoked weed for self-medication. 'I'm supposed to be on morphine every day because I'm in so much pain, but I can't stand how it makes my mind feel,' he said. He pulled up his shirt to show us some of his twenty stab wounds. 'I can't eat big meals because my stomach was so badly damaged,' he added. I've never seen anything like it. (We had paused at that spot quite by chance, but as co-incidence would have it I discovered some time later that we'd actually stopped in Canbury Gardens, which is where the 'King's Stone' sits from which Kingston gets its name. On New Year's Day 1998 'Arthur Pendragon' – the former hairy, tattooed biker and Mensa member called John – went there for his coronation and became the first king in over a thousand years, since Ethelred the Unready in 978, to be pronounced king on that spot. He celebrated by jumping fully clothed into the Thames.)

Eventually we made it to Teddington via Ham, and it was like walking into a lost village in the heart of London.

I'd had no idea it was so secluded. We found a spot near Teddington Lock and the two Marks began to put up the tents. I, meanwhile, was finding the swaying bushes in the twilight terrifying and was trying my best to remember that violent crime rates are going down and statistically it was very unlikely that we would get attacked in our beds by an axe-murderer. I told myself over and over again not to worry, but it was no use. Mark K obviously saw the fear in my eyes and patted my back. 'Don't worry,' he said, 'if anyone tries anything on I'll slit their throats. I can look after myself.' I smiled nervously.

Camping and I have never really got on. Spending the night in a tent was probably more difficult for me to cope with than spending one in a police cell.

There are lots of things I hate about camping, and it would be totally out of context to start ranting about them here, but the single most irritating one, the one that makes me want to destroy every branch of Millets on the planet, is the fact that I can't stand up to put my trousers on when I'm inside a tent. Camping turns all the small but important things that make life wonderful into incomprehensible quadratic equations. The only way I've found to make it bearable is to ensure the experience is as little like camping as possible. But by the time you've bought all the gadgets that make it survivable you might as well go and stay in a five-star hotel. Every simple, normal part of life becomes agonizing torture. Drinking tea filled with sand is supposed to taste great when camping because you're in the 'great outdoors'. You soon find yourself eating over-cooked pasta with Dolmio and making orgasmic sounds of glee as the tepid slop slimes its way down your throat like an incontinent slug. But that's all beside the point. (Incidentally, Rachel and I went on a camping holiday in the South of France once. When we got home we stood outside our flat, put our tent in the wheelie-bin, poured white spirit over it and set the fucking thing on fire. Just to make absolutely sure we never even thought about going camping ever again.)

Back on the banks of the Thames, I drank as many beers as I could lay my hands on to help me sleep. Then I realized that even if I did get any sleep I'd now be getting up every hour to go to the bloody toilet. It was actually quite serene sitting there, until the aeroplanes began to roar a few hundred feet overhead every thirty seconds. It reminded me of another of my camping experiences, in a hippy commune called Findhorn in Scotland that sits next door to an American air force base. You're probably wondering what the hell I was doing there in the first place. Well, that's a whole different story too.

I woke the next morning at 5.45 with Mark shouting, 'Dan! Get up! We're in the river!' I'd had a predictably bad night's sleep, punctuated with shivering cold, and I sat up bleary-eyed. 'Look! We're in the fucking river!'

There are many bad ways to start the day, but that has to be the worst I've ever experienced. I put my glasses on and looked out of the tent. The first thing I saw was a swan floating past a few inches away. I took my glasses off, rubbed my eyes in shock, and replaced them. The front of the tent was indeed in the river. The water was about three inches deep. Then I noticed that my feet were wet and my 'sleeping' mat was marinating in the festering swamp that is the Thames.

Mark leapt out and, standing there up to his ankles in water, gestured for me to hand him everything from the tent. At this point Mark K, who had pitched his tent further away from the river, began to laugh and film our predicament with his phone. I passed everything out and stood there hunched over in disbelief. Mark looked at me and laughed. 'What are you doing? Come on, get out, I've got to move the tent!' But my legs wouldn't move. 'I'm in denial,' I said. 'I can't possibly leave this tent. I can't believe this is happening.' I sat down to consider my options. There was no way I was allowing myself to enter the Thames. 'Mark must have a knife, can't I cut myself out the back? Then I wouldn't have to get my feet any wetter than they already were.' Predictably, Mark's reaction was not what I'd hoped for. Eventually I took off my socks, rolled up my trousers and winced as I took the plunge.

Going paddling in the Thames is not something I would recommend at 5.45 in the morning. Still, it took my mind off the blisters on my feet – which would no doubt now become infected with some hideous virus – and the possibility of being arrested in about eleven hours' time. Only I could find myself camping, for the first time in years, on the banks of the Thames on the night of a spring tide. We later spotted a notice warning all river dwellers to be prepared. According to the signs, the spring tide would affect the river only as far up as Teddington Lock. Typical.

We got ourselves together, I sipped at the inevitably muck-filled cup of tepid piss that Mark was trying to pass off as tea, and then we were on our way again. I was chasing the image of a proper English breakfast and stormed off ahead. Mark and Mark K were, staggeringly, already smoking a joint. I shouted back at them, 'For God's sake, guys, we've only got ten hours to get to Downing Street!' They giggled at me and I cursed the day I'd let myself get involved with the kind of weirdos who exist only on the fringes of society. I was in a very bad mood. Like I said, I really, really hate camping.

On the way to Richmond we met a man out on a mountain bike taking his small, aggressive dog for a walk. He had a tattoo of the Union Jack on his forearm and started talking to us to find out how far we were going. He looked and sounded like Alf Garnett. We told him we were celebrating the 791st anniversary of the Magna Carta and were on our way to Downing Street, and he looked amazed. 'I bet you're the only buggers who are!' It soon emerged that he was ex-army, although he didn't divulge what rank he'd attained. He did, however, tell us that the war in Iraq was a 'fucking disgrace' and that he would have refused to go. 'I was in Malaya so I know what it's like, and I'm not saying I wouldn't go because it's hard, it's because we've got no bloody business there, that's why. It's illegal, this war.' He then told us about the large number of fat people he'd seen walking along the Thames and how stupid they looked and went on to expound his fervent views on immigration: 'Keep England for the English! Kick the lot of them out unless they're working. They can come here and work, I've got no problem with that, but none of this hands-out "give me the dole" bollocks.' Mark tried to tell him about the families with children being detained near Heathrow without a trial. He was unmoved. He then tried pointing out that there was no such thing as 'English' and asked the man if he realized that he was probably of German ancestry. He looked suspiciously back at Mark. 'Er, I've got to go now, mate. Good luck with your walk. Shoot Blair and Brown if you see them, won't you, the c**ts.' He rode on a few yards then stopped, turned his head round and shouted, 'And another thing: Fuck Europe!' before laughing and cycling off, his dog chasing after him with an enormous stick between his teeth. Unfortunately the dog opted for a narrow path that ran between two metal posts, the stick was too long to fit between them, and he was running at quite a speed when the stick hit the posts. The man returned to retrieve his stunned companion and laughed at us nervously before tottering off on his way.

From then on it was hard going until we got to Richmond, where we found ourselves a proper English breakfast. I began to feel human again, and we set off for Kew Bridge. The heat was stifling. I became paranoid about sunstroke and kept covering myself with sun cream and drinking as much water as I could get down my throat. After a while we got a bit lost and found ourselves walking between a main road and a huge wall that blocked our entrance to Kew Gardens, which led back down to the river. There was a turnstile but the entrance fee was £11.75 and that seemed a little steep when all we wanted to do was get back down to the Thames. Mark noticed a digger going through a gate a bit further on and we followed behind, hoping to nip through the gardens and get back on track.

We soon found our way to a car park where we were waylaid by an angry lady with a Kew Gardens badge who had just parked her car. 'Look here, who are you? You can't just walk in here, you know. You'll have to pay like every-one else.' She held out her arms as if she would wrestle us to the ground if we tried to walk past her. We must have looked a pretty odd sight, shorts and T-shirts, soiled after our night by (and in) the river, carrying rucksacks. Mark started chatting to her and explained that we were on a pilgrimage; we had no interest in Kew Gardens, we were just trying to find our way back to the river so that we could continue our thirty-five-mile walk. 'I don't care who you are or what you're doing, you'll have to pay like every-one else.' Mark looked amazed and turned to us. 'Let's just go in anyway,' he said. 'This is ridiculous.' The woman got even angrier. 'Look, I'll radio the office and send for the police if you walk another step. I will!' And she began to speak into her radio. 'We've got intruders, can you call the police, they're refusing to pay, get the police . . .' We were all so tired and astonished that we just stood there with open mouths. Mark tried again to explain what we were doing. 'I don't care what you're doing, you have to pay if you want to come through here,' the woman repeated. 'Everyone has to pay, there are no exceptions.'

So there you have the perfect example of the mindset that is eating like a cancer through this country. Profit is the only thing that matters. We were not people to that old lady employed by Kew Gardens, we were just £35.25, and she was damned if her employer was going to lose out. We'd lost our status as human beings and had become a small pile of £5 notes on fire instead.

She was going bright red with rage by this point. No doubt we were dirty freeloaders in her eyes. I said to the others, 'Look, let's keep walking along the road. I don't want to ruin this lady's day. She's clearly very agitated by us being here.' She breathed deeply, as if her faith in manners had been restored, said 'Thank you' and smiled at me. But then I added pointedly, 'Although she doesn't seem to be remotely concerned about the fact that she's ruining ours.'

We stumbled along the road, eventually found our way back to the river and trudged to Putney where we stopped for another pub meal. It was two o'clock by the time we finished lunch so we decided to cross Putney Bridge and walk up the King's Road before going through Green Park and on to Downing Street. It was either that or we'd have to keep walking along the river and then get a bus. I was now refusing to use any mode of transport other than our feet, but Mark K got one because he now had more blisters on his feet than toes.

Mark and I got to Downing Street at 3.15. The nerves began to kick in once again. Perhaps it was the heat, or dehydration, or even just plain old exhaustion. After all, it's not very often I walk thirty-five miles in scorching heat. Our journey had included many painful steps, but these were the ones I'd been dreading the most. Being arrested had not lost any of its ability to strike fear into me, and this was the moment of truth. There was no going back now. Everyone I'd met who had demonstrated illegally outside Downing Street had been arrested. Suddenly I didn't feel empowered or noble, I just felt plain scared.

During the half-hour we waited in the sunshine for Rikki, the cameraman and reporter from Indymedia, there were many comings and goings from Number Ten. The BBC's George Alagiah went through Security along with photographers and other members of the press. Policemen with machine guns slung over their shoulders hung around among the tourists, though they soon began to drift away over the road towards the Ministry of Defence. Prasanth appeared with his camera to take photographs of what was about to unfold. He had been in India for months filming a documentary about an old friend of his who had started an impromptu orphanage with twenty abandoned children ten years earlier and now had over two thousand children and disabled people in his care. It was so good to see him. I hugged him a little too hard. 'Good luck!' he said before letting out his trademark cackle.

Mark and I walked towards the gates of Number Ten, put our packs down and got out our props. I had the thought bubble sign Neil had given me with 'Free Speech' written inside it; Mark had a Blair mask and a copy of the Magna Carta to burn. I held up the sign to my head and Mark began to speak. The policeman on the gates of Downing Street immediately began to chunter into his radio, and within seconds three officers on motorbikes had pulled up. Mark was telling the story of the Magna Carta and how it was the anniversary of its signing. He went on to explain that it had become a symbol for a higher power than that of the state, the rule of law, and it was there to protect the people from any leader behaving with impunity. I braced myself for some kind of altercation when I heard someone else shouting. It was Mark Kemp, who had arrived just in time to handcuff himself to the gates of Downing Street. 'Justice for the victims of crime! Justice for the victims! Basic checks, that's what victims need, basic checks!' The policemen didn't know who to deal with first. But then they spotted Mark K's standard police-issue handcuffs (he'd got them from a 'friend') and headed towards him, leaving us alone.

Mark Barrett was now in full flow. A party of French schoolchildren walked over, about twenty in all. They stared at us as though we were some kind of street entertainment, along with an assortment of bemused adults. One of the children shouted to Mark, 'En Français!' So Mark began to explain what we were doing in English and French, pointing out that we could no longer say 'freedom of speech' without breaking the law, we could only think it. Someone in the crowd shouted, 'But for how long?' The crowd began to murmur. I could see the French schoolteacher standing at the back with an enormous grin on his face. His class were fascinated, and I could imagine him thinking, 'Perhaps these Rosbifs have some courage after all.' When Mark put the Blair mask on everyone began to laugh and then the burning began. The children screamed. A couple of pensioners patted me on the back and said, 'Good for you! Blair and Brown need shooting!' It was odd that so many people seemed to agree on that point.

The three police officers around Mark Kemp had by now become six. The Magna Carta was on the pavement in flames and I began to stamp it out. The schoolchildren clapped and cheered as Mark took a bow and thanked their teacher for letting the children listen. When the embers were out we picked up what was left, so as not to be arrested for littering. A few more people came over to ask what it was all about, and once again the news that protest without permission outside Parliament had been made illegal was met with shock and derision. Then the crowd dispersed, and at that point I knew we'd got away with it. I felt elated and relieved that again I had evaded arrest. I hugged Mark with adrenalin coursing through me. So what if no-one knew we had done it? So what if the media hadn't come? We had done something, and I knew then that we would carry on fighting in our own way until this raft of unjust legislation had been repealed.

Eventually Mark Kemp was given back his handcuffs and the police decided not to arrest him either. As we were all free men we set about finding somewhere to watch the football. England beat Trinidad and Tobago, but only just.

The day had an interesting postscript. We all stayed in the pub for quite some time and there we met a man called Jim who had just come out of an energy industry jolly in the House of Lords. The pubs around Whitehall always seem to be full of interesting characters. By the time he sat down with us the two Marks had headed off to a squat somewhere for a party and I was with Prasanth and two of my old schoolfriends, Hugh and Henry. Jim was clearly suffering like a man who'd been drinking all day, and after hearing about what we'd been up to earlier he suddenly became rather agitated and began to accuse us all of being members of MI5. He turned to Hugh and said, 'You definitely are. I can tell just by looking at you.' At the time Hugh was studying for a Ph.D. in the media's represent-ation of fear and was quite taken aback by the news that he could be mistaken for a member of the security services. 'You have no idea how bad the energy crisis is going to be,' Jim then added conspiratorially. The situation was utterly ridiculous, but Jim was clearly terrified about something. I told him not to worry about it, that if he thought we were genuinely working for MI5 he'd be better off changing the subject. We turned our attention to Sweden v. Paraguay, which was boring everyone in the bar.

I was intrigued to hear what Jim had to say, but a few years on the fringes of journalism has taught me that if someone wants to tell you something you have to let them do it in their own time. If they suspect you're pushing them for information they'll simply back off out of fear. He began to ask me questions about who I was and what I did. I told him about this book and he seemed interested. I could see he was becoming more and more desperate to talk about something. I added that whatever he had to say was probably nothing relevant to Britain anyway and suggested he go home for a coffee to sober up. 'Oh my God, you're joking!' he replied. I changed the subject again, but he could manage only a few more seconds before he began to open up. 'You don't have recording equipment on you, do you?' he asked. Now I was itching to know what it was he wanted to say.

He looked around, then plunged in. 'In fifty years' time the two biggest issues in Britain and the world will be the supply of energy and water. The energy industry has no answers when oil runs out. We don't know what the fuck's going to happen. Everyone's looking for places to go. The only place in Britain with any water will be Scotland, but it will be much colder than it is now because the Gulf Stream will be finished. Energy-wise, there'll be some wind power, but that will be bugger-all use. The Dordogne in France should be all right for water, and the Western Sahara and New Zealand. Everywhere else is fucked.'

I told him he sounded like a paranoid lunatic and asked why I should believe such a portent of doom. He showed me his business card to prove that he knew what he was talking about. It revealed the name of a well-known energy company, his name and his position as an expert in future energy sources. It still sounded a little dramatic so I asked him about his political leanings within the energy industry, specifically whether he was some kind of left-wing conservationist. He laughed for quite a long time after that. 'There's no politics,' he said. 'It's fact. There will be no more energy or water in Britain in fifty years, period. It's fucked. How old are you? Do you have kids?' I told him about Wilf. 'Well, you'll probably be dead so you won't give a shit, but he's fucked and so are your grand-children.'

I then asked him why he was so terrified of MI5. He looked at me as though I was mad. 'I work for the energy industry! Of course I'm paranoid about MI5!' A few weeks earlier I'd met a well-known ex-MI5 agent in Parliament Square who'd given an assessment of our secret services that didn't seem to warrant Jim's sense of agitation. This ex-spy was handing out DVDs to anyone who would take them that posed a few unsettling questions about 9/11 that had apparently been ignored by the official inquiry. It was like being doorstepped by a conspiracy-theorist Jehovah's Witness. It took a while for me to understand exactly what it was he was saying because I was too stunned by the fact that he could have gone from being a spy on the front pages of all the national newspapers to talking to a complete stranger about the 'CIA Zionist conspiracy to attack New York'.

He went on to describe a policy adopted by MI5 which he called 'deliberate incompetence': people are promoted within the secret services specifically because they are known to be useless and will therefore fail to protect us from terrorist attacks. And why should they want to do this? According to this man, it is to safeguard their future funding by government. By this point my jaw was on the floor and I'd decided he was some kind of fruitcake, but he hadn't finished. I happened to meet him the day after the report about the 7/7 bombings was released by the government. He had a few thoughts on what had been divulged about surveillance on one of the bombers. 'The reason terrorists get through is because MI5 officers are terrified of getting themselves killed,' he said. 'They just want to stay behind the safety of their desks. After all, MI5 officers don't even have powers of arrest. If they want to nick someone they have to call in Special Branch to do it for them.'

Before leaving him to his conspiracies, I told him that he'd totally shattered my image of MI5 agents as people like James Bond or the characters from *Spooks*. 'Think computer boffins with even less social life, that's your average MI5 agent,' he said. 'Those are the people supposedly safeguarding this country. Some of them are really good people who want to do everything they can to protect Britain, but they are in the minority.' So much, then, for the faceless 'experts' protecting our security.

Perhaps Jim shouldn't fear MI5 after all. But one thing was for sure: he certainly drank like someone who believed the world was fucked.

## CHAPTER 8

The laws that take away our freedom are not restricted to a thousand metres around Parliament Square. I met a man called David Mery on my journey who was accused of terrorism three weeks after the 7 July bombings. His story is a warning to us all. If you take comfort from the fact that if you don't demonstrate about anything the laws won't affect you, then think again. If you're not bothered about having an ID card because you're a law-abiding citizen who never gets into trouble with the police then think again. David wasn't protesting about anything. He was just going about his business, leaving work to go for a drink, when he discovered more than he wanted to know about the police's new powers.

He was planning to meet his girlfriend in Hanover Square, and went to get a train from Southwark underground station, carrying a small black rucksack he used as a workbag and wearing normal and unremarkable clothes. He walked through the barrier, past a policeman, and went down to the platform. A train entered the station, then suddenly police officers began to swarm around him. They handcuffed him behind his back and took away his rucksack. They told him he was being held for his own safety under the Terrorism Act, that they found his behaviour suspicious from direct observation of him and from watching him on CCTV: he didn't look at the policeman when he walked through the gate, he was wearing a jacket 'too warm for the season' (despite the day before being the coldest day in July for twenty-five years), he was carrying a rucksack and he looked at people on the platform before playing with his mobile phone. All, it seemed, were the actions of a terrorist.

David was led away from the platform, where trains were no longer stopping, to the emergency staircase. Two Bomb Squad officers walked past him and one of them jokingly called out, 'Nice laptop!' A police officer then apologized to David on behalf of the Metropolitan Police. David's handcuffs were removed and they began to hand David back his possessions. But then another officer appeared and explained angrily that this was not the required procedure, so the cuffs were put on David again. Then a police van arrived and he was told to wait in the back. Five minutes later he was arrested for suspicious behaviour and being a public nuisance. David had no idea what was going on.

He was taken to Walworth police station where Polaroid photographs of him were taken, along with his finger-prints and DNA swabs from each side of his mouth. He called his girlfriend, who was crying and kept repeating, 'I thought you were injured or had an accident. Where were you? Why didn't you call me back?' He was put in a police cell where another officer told him that his flat would now be searched under the Terrorism Act. The police agreed to call his girlfriend to warn her of their arrival, but in the end they didn't bother.

At the flat his girlfriend was questioned. David later wrote, 'They took away several mobile phones, an old IBM laptop, a Be Box tower computer (an obsolete kind of PC from the mid-1990s), a handheld GPS receiver (positioning device with maps, very useful when walking), a frequency counter (picked it up at a radio amateur junk fair because it looked interesting), a radio scanner (receives shortwave radio stations), a blue RS232C breakout box (a tool I used to use when reviewing modems for computer magazines), some cables, a computer security conference leaflet, envelopes with addresses, maps of Prague and London Heathrow, some business cards, and some photographs I took for the fifty years of the Association of Computing Machinery conference. This list is from my girlfriend's memory, or what we have noticed is missing since.' When I met David five months after the event he still did not have permission to travel to the United States, which was impacting on his job as an IT specialist, and the police had still not returned some of his possessions. He had no idea if the record of his arrest on suspicion of terrorism had been passed to any outside agencies like the CIA or Interpol. 'I just get really nervous when I fly now in case something happens to me at Immigration.'

You see, it wasn't just our politicians running around like headless chickens after the 7 July bombings, the police had got in on the act too. A week before David Mery's arrest, on Friday, 22 July, I was sitting in my office daydreaming when Rob, a designer who rented one of the desks, appeared looking flustered. He had just been caught up in a security alert at Stockwell tube station. 'I was on the train and people started shouting "Bomb!" at a bag that had smoke coming out of it in the next carriage. Then I heard loads of firecrackers, people started screaming, and everyone began running to get out of the station.' The firecrackers turned out to be the sound of gunshots: the police fired eleven rounds, six of which went into a young Brazilian man's head. The 'smoking bag' must have been the product of confused Chinese whispers.

In the report that followed a year later it was clear that the police didn't really know what they were doing that day, and their new powers to execute a shoot-to-kill policy led to tragically brutal consequences. Even the Israeli police have to be sure that explosives are present before shooting a possible suicide bomber. Jean Charles was wearing a light denim jacket and wasn't even carrying a bag. The incident proves that under pressure the police can misuse excessive powers if they are granted them by government. It is not for the police to stop and question whether or not a law is justified. They are given powers and will be judged harshly if they are found not to have used them if it turns out later that they could have saved lives, regardless of the way these laws impact on civil liberties. The more powers you give the police, the more likely they are to overreact to the 'worst-case scenario' to cover themselves rather than allow common sense to prevail – something, as we will see in a moment, that resonates strongly with anyone who attempted to protest outside the American airbase RAF Fairford during the Iraq war.

Most people were horrified at the killing of Jean Charles de Menezes but at the same time understood the pressure on the police to prevent another suicide bombing. This was the context surrounding David Mery's arrest too, so perhaps we should give the police a break. Putting to one side the moral questions that should be asked about the police adopting a shoot-to-kill policy in the first place – and the legality of keeping on a database the fingerprints, DNA and photographs of an innocent man who has never been found guilty of any crime, not to mention being able to search and remove articles from his house under terrorist legislation in the absence of intelligence or evidence of any kind that he was a terrorist – the atmosphere in London was on the verge of hysteria at the time. We were all bracing ourselves for another attack, and the police clearly were too. They were frightened and had no idea how to combat such an invisible threat. According to Andrew Gilligan in the *Evening Standard*, the police had been granted the power to shoot to kill 'entirely in secret, at a meeting of the police, MI5 and civil servants. The bodies supposed to set policing policy, Parliament and the Metropolitan Police Authority, were not even told.' There was clearly panic on the streets of Whitehall.

But while we can perhaps forgive the actions of the armed police on the scene who believed they were dealing with a genuine suicide bomber, we must have no sympathies for our government behaving in the same confused manner in the weeks and months that followed 7 July. Our

MPs act as a barrier to protect our rights and freedoms in the absence of a written constitution. It was a time for clear thinking; instead we got a catastrophic overreaction that produced reams and reams of freedom-eroding legislation. They built on the foundations of the Criminal Justice Act of 1994 with terrifying consequences.

The government's policies are supposedly just a question of opinion as to what does or does not constitute an acceptable amount of freedom in the light of the terrorist threat. As we have seen, ladders are a significantly greater threat to public safety than terrorism. And would their authoritarian policies prevent terrorism anyway? ID cards won't, according to Charles Clarke, who was Home Secretary at the time of the July bombings. This is absolutely not an ideological battle or a matter of opinion. It's about whether or not the government has proved to the public beyond reasonable doubt, through the use of evidence, that their new laws are actually necessary and will prevent terrorism. That is what it all comes down to. Is there sufficient evidence that these pieces of legislation are actually necessary to protect us, and will they work? Those are questions not one of the MPs who voted for these laws has answered in the civil liberties debate. Never mind the cost, which also has to be considered (£18 billion for ID cards, according to analysts, though the Home Office claims it will 'only' be half that amount).

Our civil rights and freedom to protest have been attacked by so many bits of legislation since Labour came to power that I risk boring you by detailing them all here. Instead I contacted Liberty, one of the UK's leading human rights and civil liberties organizations, and asked

them to help me compile a top ten list of the most un-
justified and outrageous laws currently on the statute
book. Liberty are keen to point out that a lot of the legislation in the following Acts and Orders is necessary, but
there are 'sections' tucked away in each of them that
impact severely on civil liberties with no justification. As
with the exclusion zone set out in Section 132 of SOCPA,
these sections often have little or nothing to do with the
main contents of the Acts within which they are contained. In the words of Liberty's policy director, Gareth
Crossman, 'When you become a legislation train spotter
like me you see the Government chipping away at our
freedom all the time.'

I met Gareth and Liberty's press officer, Jen Corlew,
and told them about what happened to David Mery.
Gareth leant over his coffee. 'That situation is typical of
this government's mindset when it comes to legislation,'
he said. 'They see a problem that is frightening the public
before drawing up legislation that in their view will
combat it that is as wide-reaching as they can possibly get
away with. Only to then say, "But don't worry, it won't be
misused."' On the one hand that kind of reassurance is
simply not good enough when we should have rights to
protect us. On the other, in a frightening number of cases,
it's plainly untrue.

Here, then, are the top ten Crap British Laws:

## 10. The Sex Offences Act 2003
A perfect example of the heavy-handed way in which our
government draws up new laws. Section 9 prohibits sexual
contact with a child, which is obviously justified, but when

applied with Section 13, which lists all the offences that are crimes, including if they are committed by people who themselves are under sixteen, it actually makes it a criminal offence for two teenagers to snog. So in Britain, kissing is now an offence if you're under sixteen. Fact.

Section 71 makes it an offence for anyone to have sex in a public lavatory. It may not be the most tasteful thing you could ever do, but is having sex with a consenting someone in a public toilet really a criminal offence? The absurdity of this law would be brought into focus if you decided not to have sex in the cubicle itself but outside, up against the wall of the lavatory, instead, which is perfectly fine according to the law.

If you were convicted of any of these crimes your name would be entered on the sex offenders register that everyone associates with those who have committed acts of sexual depravity on children. Not the ideal reference to get if later in life you applied for a job that involves any contact with people under sixteen.

## 9. The Children Act 2004

This piece of legislation includes unnecessary information-sharing powers brought in after the tragic death of a little girl called Victoria Climbié. Lord Laming's inquiry into Victoria's death – Social Services failed to protect her from abusive and ultimately murderous carers – described 'a catalogue of administrative, managerial and professional failure by the services charged with her safety'. According to Gareth Crossman, 'The worst possible way to introduce legislation is on the back of someone's death. There is no doubt that the information-sharing powers that already existed would have allowed information about Victoria Climbié to be shared. It's just that the staff weren't trained how to use them, they didn't have the resources they needed, and they made mistakes. In my view the new powers of information-sharing in this Act are utterly counter-productive because it means social workers are going to be recording every single thing in case something comes up that they should have spotted. Huge files will be built up on all our children and they won't be able to see the wood for the trees so the children who are actually in danger will be missed. This makes it the worst type of legislation because it totally undermines familial privacy and at the same time increases the chance of tragedies occurring. They have these wonderful justifications for recording information, "anything that might give rise to a cause for concern". Well, if you're the one who has to decide if something is a cause for concern, you may as well just say "anything". This Act creates another level of bureaucracy that staff will have to waste time wading through instead of looking out for threatened children.' Jen Corlew added, 'It's the worst-case scenario because you've got information-sharing between all the different agencies, which could lead to false conclusions. As a result of this law we're now seeing cases of children being taken away from their parents because of such false presumptions.'

## 8. The Regulation of Investigatory Powers Act 2000 Orders

Quickly dubbed a 'snooper's charter', RIPA sets the parameters for surveillance powers to monitor electronic data. It was sold as a way to combat Internet crime, and more specifically paedophiles. Fair enough, you may think, perhaps we need the security services to monitor every single thing we use the Internet for. But the Act also lists the public bodies that have access to these powers, and they include every local council and job centre in the country, the Chief Inspector of Schools, the Post Office, the Personal Investment Authority, any of Her Majesty's forces and intelligence services along with every government department, the Food Standards Agency and, bizarrely, the Egg Marketing Board – just as long as they suspect a threat to national security, are preventing or detecting crime or disorder, are in fear of something that might give rise to issues for public safety, are protecting public health, or simply '(c) . . . safeguarding the economic well-being of the United Kingdom'. We may have become blasé about CCTV cameras but at least we can see when they're filming us.

## 7. The Anti-Social Behaviour Act 2003 and the Crime and Disorder Act 1998

As we have seen, this legislation criminalizes people for being naked in their own home, howling like a wolf, putting up Christmas decorations and feeding the birds. It also creates a two-tier criminal justice system where certain people are given prison sentences for behaviour that is perfectly legal for the rest of us. Like standing on a street corner to wait for someone, or swearing.

Section 57 of the ASBA amends the definition of 'assembly' in the 1986 Public Order Act from twenty people down to two to help the government target groups of young people more effectively. According to Gareth, 'This is what the government will tend to do. They take existing legislation and amend it. How can two people possibly be considered an assembly? The 1986 Public Order Act combined with the 1994 Criminal Justice Act set the parameters for the criminalization of protest by groups of over twenty people with "trespassery assemblies". Back then everyone saw it as a way of criminalizing protest and said, "How can only twenty people be considered an assembly?" Now it's gone down to two!'

Section 30 of the ASBA introduced dispersal orders and curfew powers. The former were designed to clear kids with hoodies from street corners, while the latter are blanket powers to stop anyone under sixteen being outside after nine p.m. Liberty received lots of angry emails and letters for defending the basic right of people not to be picked up by the police simply because they are under sixteen.

## 6. The Criminal Justice Act 1994 and 2003

The Act designed to stop people having free parties in the countryside and take away the right to demonstrate back in the mid-nineties has now been amended to further reduce our right to protest. Gareth sees this as a trend that undermines our entire criminal justice system. 'If you're talking about Britain and the idea of what Britishness means in terms of our legal framework, then you've got to understand the theme that goes all the way back to the Magna Carta. It's called "the golden thread" and it's the idea of the presumption of innocence, which under this government is simply being taken away. Tony Blair is quite open about it. "The criminal justice system is reminiscent of Dickens' time" was what he said. Well, what he means is that people had some kind of process then. He sees the criminal justice system as something that is regulatory, the means by which you process people. So the perspective is, "Here are these people who we do not like for various reasons so we need to find a way to lock them up". If you read government writing on this, it's shameless. They actually say this is a process that needs updating. Apparently we need a shiny new system that gets rid of some of these time-consuming and costly trials.'

Once you've been arrested, Sections 9 and 10 of the Criminal Justice Act of 2003 start to kick in. These sections are the culmination of several changes that happened between 1999 and 2003, which have relaxed the rules on DNA retention. Previously your DNA could only be retained if you had committed a certain kind of offence, which most people feel is justified; but DNA retention has now been amended so that today *anyone* who is arrested has their DNA permanently on record. There are millions of people on the DNA database. It is estimated that up to 50,000 of them are children who have never been charged or cautioned with any criminal offence. But again the government says, 'Don't worry, you can ask to have your DNA removed.' But asking for permission for something, as we have seen with the government's exclusion zone around Parliament, is not the same as having it as an inalienable right. As if to prove the government's hollow promise, the police have since released guidelines saying that people should not, as a rule, be removed from the DNA database except in 'exceptional cases'.

According to genewatch.org, 5 per cent of British people are currently on the DNA database, which gives us the largest database of DNA in the world. Austria comes in second, but with only 1 per cent of its population. Worryingly, in conjunction with the *Observer* newspaper, genewatch revealed that stored DNA samples are being used without the consent of the people involved to study the genetics of the male Y-chromosome. One terrifying conclusion from that is that they are looking for genetic evidence for criminality. No doubt the government will rely on their new double argument, 'If you've nothing to hide then you've nothing to fear' and 'Don't worry, we won't use it for that', to make us all feel secure. Both, however, are starting to sound a little hollow.

## 5. The Terrorism Act 2006

Parts of this Act clearly have merit. For instance, before the TA 2006 it was not a criminal offence for anyone to travel to a terrorist training camp with a view to causing murder and mayhem in Britain on their return. However, it also carries the offence of the 'encouragement/ glorification' of terrorism, which makes an assumption that even Gareth, a criminal lawyer, cannot understand. 'When the government was coming out with the justification for introducing the new offence of "encouragement" of terrorism the Prime Minister went on the *Today* programme on Radio 4. He said, "You can't just have people coming over here encouraging people to go off and kill other people, it just should not be permitted." But it isn't permitted because it's an offence called "incitement to kill" that we've had since the nineteenth century, and it already carries life imprisonment! This new legislation is a totally different thing, and Blair's a barrister so you can be sure he knows that. As a lawyer I find it shameless the way the government do this. If I was listening to that and I didn't know about the existing law that already criminalizes what he's talking about then I'd think, "Yeah, damn right, they shouldn't be allowed to do that." And I'd support it. It's infuriating. The government's argument structure is to say "Proposition A: Terrorism is bad" – something that of course no-one is going to disagree with. Then they offer up "Answer B" as the way in which they think we should deal with it. Therefore, in their eyes, if you disagree with B you must also disagree with A, that terrorism is bad.'

And even the wording of the new law is unclear, as Gareth explained. 'One of the daft things about glorification/encouragement of terrorism is that no-one knows what it actually means. Despite hours and hours of parliamentary debate they still couldn't work it out. My assessment of it is a "subjective recklessness test". Now I'm a criminal lawyer so I know what a subjective recklessness test is. I'm still not sure, but that's my best guess. Now how is anyone in the world supposed to know what is or isn't a criminal offence if even a criminal lawyer is confused? And as soon as people began to point out that this term was also dependent on the definition of terrorism in the 2000 TA, the government had to start a whole new review into the definition of terrorism. The definition of it in the 2000 TA no longer worked with all the legislation they'd put in. It's so badly thought out it even criminalizes someone who escapes persecution in North Korea, comes to Britain and says, "Maybe it's a good idea to have a regime change in North Korea." '[39]

## 4. The Prevention of Terrorism Act 2005

This creates what are becoming known as 'secret courts', but that makes the false assumption by association that it is actually a 'court' with all the rights we associate with our legal process. It is no such thing. If you find yourself under one of the control orders outlined in the PTA 2005 you will be subjected to a criminal process where neither you nor your lawyer is allowed to know what evidence there is against you. And the people who do know what charges you face are not allowed to tell you. Meanwhile, you have to live under house arrest. So much for the golden thread.

## 3. The Terrorism Act 2000

The TA 2000 is at number three because of the legal term 'proscription' and the Section 44 stop and search.

The Act was brought in before 9/11 and allowed certain political organizations to be criminalized when Republican splinter groups emerged after the Good Friday Agreement. Proscription creates a special class of criminality. It is designed to make it a criminal offence for anyone to have anything to do with a terrorist group. That sounds fair enough, doesn't it? The problem with proscription is its breadth. Firstly, it's not only an offence to have anything to do with these organizations, items of clothing that support a 'proscribed' organization have also been criminalized. When this is coupled with the

Terrorism Act of 2006, which extends the grounds for proscription so that you don't have to be a violent political group, just one that encourages, promotes or glorifies terrorism, it means you could face prosecution for just going to a meeting featuring a speaker from a proscribed organization. Terrorism laws carry serious criminal punishments and they can now be broken by something as innocuous as wearing a T-shirt. Wearing a T-shirt is not equatable with someone calling for others to commit acts of terrorism; it's simply criminalizing speech you don't agree with. As Prasanth wrote on the banner he now has a criminal record for holding in Parliament Square, 'If you don't believe in freedom of expression for people you despise then you don't believe in it at all.'

Section 44 of the Terrorism Act allows the police to stop and search anyone within a designated area and detain them without suspecting that they are about to commit a crime. These designated areas were supposed to last for a month and to be used at times when a terrorist threat was most likely – during the Queen's speech, for example, or the Labour Party Conference. The police, however, have had a rolling authorization for the entire Metropolitan Police District every month since 2002. So anyone in London since that time could be stopped and searched without the police having to give any justification. Section 44 was famously used on Walter Wolfgang when he shouted 'Rubbish!' at Jack Straw during a speech on Iraq. According to Gareth, 'This government has been rightly accused of politicization of the police and nowhere is that expression more symbolic than the arrest of Walter Wolfgang for speaking up at a Labour Party Conference.'

The use of Section 44 to attack protest, however, has been far more aggressive and authoritarian than even the most ardent critics of the government could have feared. According to Home Office figures, in 2003/04 29,407 searches were made using Section 44 powers but only five arrests were made in connection with terrorism. That's a 0.02 per cent success rate. Is it possible that the police could have been using the time they wasted on Section 44s to combat terrorism more effectively? Judging by the way stop and search was used against protesters at RAF Fairford during the Iraq war, you could be forgiven for thinking that Parliament got the name of the Act wrong. The 'Anti-Protest Act' would have described it more accurately.

The campaign of harassment against demonstrators carried out by the police at RAF Fairford was so long and appalling that I'll pick out just a few highlights to prove beyond doubt that S44 stop and search has been used to stifle demonstrations and political dissent. In my view these incidents alone ask enough terrifying questions about the way the police misuse anti-terrorist powers against those who oppose the government to warrant some kind of inquiry. One protester, Charlie Lysons, who was attending his first ever demonstration because he was so outraged by the Iraq war, wrote about the way he was treated by the police afterwards. 'I now feel intimidated from carrying out lawful protest,' he said, 'and for the same reasons I do not feel like making any kind of official complaint.'[40]

Even a thirteen-year-old girl walking to her cello lesson on a cycle lane near the base was subjected to a S44 stop and search under the Terrorist Act. Another girl, Isabelle

Ellis-Cockroft, eleven years old this time, had her bike searched, again under S44. In total, 995 stop and searches were used against the protesters under S44 of the TA 2000 and Section 60 of the Criminal Justice and Public Order Act 1994. Eighty-nine of the Section 44 searches were carried out on the same twenty-six people. One woman was stopped and searched eleven times on the same day in a policy the protesters began to realize was clearly designed to demoralize them. Juliet McBride was walking on her own when she was searched by eight officers who also confiscated a tape recorder she was using to record what was going on, and refused to let her friends come to her aid. Kerstine Rogers was with her eight-year-old daughter when they were detained by police; they told her she would be searched only to release her forty-five minutes later. At RAF Welford, where other demonstrations were being held against the Iraq war, police took banners and cameras from a protester under the authority of Section 19 of the Police and Criminal Evidence Act of 1984, even though this is only legal for items found while searching premises. Juliet McBride again, who was singled out by police as one of the main protesters, was stopped while driving to the 'Flowers for Fairford' demonstration. She was held for one and a half hours while her car was searched and arrested for breaching bail conditions that were entirely made up. She was later arrested for a breach of the peace when she tried to enter one of the camps demonstrators had set up entirely legally outside the base. She wasn't charged with a criminal offence for any of these supposed acts of illegality. Unsurprisingly, not a single one of the 995 searches the protesters were subjected to resulted in any kind of terrorist conviction.

Perhaps even more shocking than any of that, though, is the tale of a bus journey from London to Fairford for that 'Flowers for Fairford' demonstration on 22 March 2003. The police were not taking any chances with the peace demonstrators: there were up to a thousand officers on duty, many of whom were in riot gear. The day before, 21 March, David Blunkett, the then Home Secretary, had stated that the Terrorism Act 2000 was not being used to prevent protests at RAF Fairford, but on the way up from London three coaches of protesters – CND members, Quakers, journalists and a samba band – were pulled off the road ten miles from Fairford into a blockade of seventy police officers, cars and vans. All the protesters were taken off the coaches in pairs, searched and filmed. Food, scarves and helmets were confiscated by the police, and after two hours of waiting the protesters were allowed back on to their coaches. They presumed they would now be allowed to attend the march, but just before they were about to move off a policeman boarded each coach and told the protesters that a senior officer had decided they might cause a breach of the peace (despite having taken away any items they considered dangerous, including a clown mask, during the two-hour search) so they would now all be escorted by the police back down to London. They were not allowed to stop at any stage of the journey, even to go to the toilet. One of the protesters later commented, 'The return journey to London was organized by the police to make us look like terrorists. A convoy of police accompanied our buses and the motorways were sealed off to the public. Even the roundabouts leading towards and away from the motorway were sealed off.'

So much, then, for living in a country where the police can't just go around harassing and detaining people simply because they don't agree with government policy.

## 2. The Serious Organised Crime and Police Act 2005

'Ironically for a democracy,' Gareth pointed out while we were discussing SOCPA, 'apart from Ministry of Defence land and some Crown land, the place in Britain where there are greatest restrictions on your right to protest is the centre of government.'

SOCPA is an interesting example of the way the government will take an Act that deals with something most people agree is a good idea, in this case the creation of a new crime-fighting agency designed to deal with drug traffickers and organized crime, only to sling in a few things that erode civil liberties for good measure in the knowledge that there won't be time for proper debate. Section 132, which outlines the protest exclusion zone, as you've probably guessed by now, is my personal favourite, but SOCPA also includes Section 110 which makes all offences arrestable. In 2004 a Criminal Justice White Paper found that the three parameters the police used when arresting someone – a non-arrestable offence, an arrestable offence and a serious arrestable offence – were too confusing to deal with. Apparently the police couldn't work out whether or not someone was breaking the law under these terms. Presumably this did not relate to obvious crimes like muggings, assault, murder, fraud, shoplifting, burglary and so on, but probably did cause problems when people were engaged in the act of protest, in which field increasingly creative methods were being deployed to get round the various bits of authoritarian legislation designed to stifle dissent. To solve this tricky conundrum, the government decided just to make *anything* an arrestable offence. Thanks to Section 110, you can now be arrested by a policeman and carted off to a police cell for walking down the road minding your own business. Or, in the case of Matthew the picnicker from chapter 2, for lying face down in the grass and not moving.

The police did add something called 'necessity' to the Act which every policeman and woman has to apply every single time he or she considers making an arrest. In human rights terms, that means in each individual situation they have to decide whether their actions will contravene Article 5 (the right to liberty) and Article 8 (the right to privacy). At the European Court of Human Rights there are hundred-page documents deliberating those kinds of things, so expecting a police officer fresh out of training school to be able to make those distinctions, without any guidance from above because their previous arresting policy, which already dealt with those issues, was scrapped for being 'too complicated', seems a little naive. Once again we have a piece of legislation that has terrifying civil liberties implications and doesn't actually do what it was supposed to do in the first place. I certainly hope you enjoyed living in a country where you couldn't just get arrested and dragged off in a police van without any justification, because you don't live in that country any more.

There are two more worrying sections squirrelled away in SOCPA, Sections 145 and 146, described as 'economic sabotage by animal rights protesters'. Now, animal rights protesters make most people squirm. Animal rights organizations are a byword for extremism and its activists are seen by many of us as hypocrites for endangering human life under the banner of saving the lives of animals. This probably explains why so few of us were concerned by a new law that was deliberately designed to target that one protest group. It would be a little dangerous, however, to jump to the conclusion that all people who want to save animals' lives are prepared to use violence. The vast majority of animal rights campaigners find such aggressive tactics counterproductive and absurd. So, assuming that these protesters are entitled to protest on behalf of their cause despite sections of their supporters being violent extremists, why is 'economic sabotage' such a dangerous piece of law?

Again, it's the breadth of the legislation. The law creates two types of offender: those who carry out criminal acts (the few extremists) and those who commit 'torts' (everyone else). Now, a 'tort' is a civil offence. A civil tort would be something like defamation or trespass. Most leaflets handed out by animal rights activists will contain lines such as 'These people are murdering animals!' It's just an opinion, they're not hurting anyone, but the fact that it is defamatory means it has now become a criminal offence. And if I'm standing outside someone's gate handing out leaflets I'm probably also trespassing on their property and committing a tort. Because any act of protest against a corporate body could be considered 'economic sabotage', I'm probably committing a criminal offence by writing this book. Again, the government said, 'Don't worry, we won't use it like that.' Well, on the one hand that's simply not good enough, and on the other they *have* used it to target people handing out leaflets, so they were lying. Any act of protest against a corporation must be an act of economic sabotage because you're trying to undermine their business.

Of course, once 'economic sabotage' is accepted as a way to tackle animal rights protest groups, you could be forgiven for expecting it to emerge in all sorts of unrelated legislation to combat other forms of protest too. A road protest could be construed as economic sabotage. Chanting outside an arms dealing convention could be economic sabotage. Demonstrating outside a high-street store that uses sweatshops could be economic sabotage. A group of thirty people standing outside Charing Cross police station blocking the road to traffic because one of their friends has just been arrested in Parliament Square for holding up a banner that said 'Freedom of Speech' could be economic sabotage too. In fact you'd be hard pressed to name any act of protest aimed at a private institution that can't be described as economic sabotage.

## 1. ID Cards

They saved the best for last. Although the ID card bill is not actually a law, the threat of it is still enough to warrant top billing in the Crap Laws top ten. Not content with making criminals out of teenagers who kiss; adding levels of bureaucracy to Social Services that will put children's lives at risk and granting huge powers that attack familial privacy; giving public bodies the right to snoop into our private lives; criminalizing and ostracizing some of the poorest, youngest and most vulnerable members of society; retaining DNA and fingerprints from people who have never been found guilty of any crime; making the wearing of a T-shirt illegal; calling anyone who campaigns against tyrants and dictators terrorists; using legislation designed to combat terrorism to intimidate, harass and threaten law-abiding citizens who oppose government policy; and giving people who hold banners in support of freedom of speech criminal records, they also expect us to trust them with every private detail of our lives.

Even if there was some kind of justification for ID cards, the government have proved beyond doubt that they cannot be trusted with the kind of information they would charge us all £90 for them to keep. But there is simply no justification for ID cards. Every one of the government's arguments is without merit. Let's take them one at a time.

*1. ID cards will prevent terrorism.* If that was the case, the men who blew up the train station in Madrid in March 2004 should not have got through (Spain has compulsory ID cards). It's also worth pointing out that every suicide bomber seeks fame with his peers. They want the opposite of anonymity. And remember, even Charles Clarke, the Home Secretary at the time of the London bombings, confirmed ID cards would not have stopped the terrorists getting through.

*2. They will cut crime.* Not in every nation that currently has them – France, Germany, Italy and Spain. There is absolutely no evidence that having an ID card will stop a robber, rapist or burglar breaking the law.

3. *The government can be trusted.* Even if so far the government's behaviour doesn't strike you as alarming, in 2006 it emerged that false information on the files of the Criminal Records Bureau had led to people erroneously being given criminal records and refused job interviews as a result. These mistakes were discovered only because the CRB has an audit so they were able to locate the errors and amend them. The National Identity database will not have an audit because it will be far too big, so you won't be able to find out what information the government has on file about you or change it if it's false.

4. *They won't be expensive.* That depends on whether you think £90 for an ID card/passport is expensive. Every time you move house you'll have to buy a new one. But the government will own it even though you have paid for it, and they'll reserve the right to remove it from you at any time. In which case you would cease to exist.

5. *They will solve our immigration problems.* That assumes our ID cards will be the first set of identity papers in history that can't be forged. If it can be made, it can be forged. Besides, all asylum seekers have been required to carry identity cards since 2000.

6. *They will stop benefit cheats.* Not the 90 per cent of benefit cheats who use their real identity but make false claims.

Gordon Brown is as much a fan of ID cards as Tony Blair and thinks that giving businesses access to the National Identity register that accompanies the ID card system would be a good way to help pay for it. According to a source close to Brown, 'There is going to be a key issue over the next ten to fifteen years about identity management right across the public and private sectors . . . It's about people coming to accept that this is not only a necessary but desirable part of modern society over the next ten years. What [the Tories] are objecting to in the political sphere is going to be absolutely commonplace in the private sphere, and saying, "it's not the British way" is just not going to work.'[41] It's interesting to note that it has become acceptable to those close to Gordon Brown for the private sphere to dictate the direction of government policy. The rest of us, it seems, just have to accept that it is 'desirable' because our elected representatives are so spineless when it comes to standing up to private interests.

I spoke to my dad about ID cards and he told me an interesting story from when he lived in Jersey in the 1970s about sharing personal information with the state. At the time the States of Jersey were undertaking a census and the old woman my dad lodged with when he first arrived on the island refused flatly to fill in a census form. He asked her why she was making such a fuss, and she gave an interesting reply: 'When the Nazis arrived during the war the first place the soldiers went was the town hall. A few days later they rounded up everyone listed as Jewish on the public records and sent them to concentration camps. I never saw some of my friends ever again. I might trust this government but how do I know if I can trust an unknown government of the future?' Putting aside the hyperbole for a moment, it is worth considering what her *experience* under German occupation had told her rather than what her, or anyone else's, *opinion* might be. You may trust the government to have that kind of information about you now, but what about a government of the future of which you have no knowledge? Once you've given up that kind of information you will never get your privacy back.

Of course there is one argument for having a voluntary ID card and that would be to give people better access to benefits or public services, but there is no justification in making that kind of card mandatory. So why is the government so determined to make us all carry an ID card? Because it's not financially attractive for a private company to run the ID card system *unless* it is a mandatory policy. The only way the government could get companies to tender for the contract is if we are *all* made to have one. Hence the argument about terrorism and crime – it's their only hope of persuading us that ID cards are necessary. They unquestionably are not.

Before my meeting with Liberty's policy director Gareth Crossman ended, I asked him if there was anything he wanted me to record about the law for Albion that he felt was being ignored. Once again, asking that question caused the kind of eruption of intelligent passion and outrage I had now become accustomed to. 'Back in 2002,' he began, 'the Prime Minister's Performance and Innovation Unit came up with a document called "Strategies for reassurance: public concerns about privacy and data-sharing in Government"[42] which said it wanted a world that had changed from one where information was only shared if there was a need to do so to a world where it was all shared unless there was a reason not to do so. And this is why we get the "nothing to hide, nothing to fear" argument from politicians whenever they do something that takes our freedom away. But this is a seismic shift in the way things have always been in Britain historically. If you combine that with the way in which this government has taken all the best things about what the British legal system is – how we presume people are innocent, how we give people fair trials, how we don't pass laws to stop things unless there's a need to do so – and they've turned all that on its head, it's created a country where we all live in fear, where laws are passed not because we need them but because it's a greater means of social control, where we collect information on people not because we need it but because it might be needed at some random point in the future. It threatens everything about what it is to be British. I think there's a quote from the mid to late nineteenth century which said something along the lines of "a gentleman of this nation can go from birth to death never needing to prove his identity to the government". Now of course that's not going to reflect modern-day life, but it's this idea that people's individuality is something sacred. Well, it's simply not any more.'

Speaking as someone who has spent months trying to get his head round government legislation, which is written in the kind of absurd language few of us can ever hope to understand, I recognize that Liberty is trying to occupy the void Parliament is supposed to fill by acting as a barrier of conscience between our civil rights and a

I FOUGHT THE LAW

government that seems increasingly determined to undermine our freedom and our legal system at the same time.
They are a membership organization and rely on sub-
scriptions to fund their work. They have a website,
www.liberty-human-rights.org.uk.

The worst of the laws in our top ten are the result of
the government's response to terrorism. The threat of
terrorism has brought about an unprecedented attack on
our civil liberties from those who are supposed to protect
us. The ones added in the aftermath of 9/11 and 7/7 have
created an atmosphere of fear that even Osama Bin Laden
could only have dreamt of. Of course the government is
privy to secret information and that could perhaps explain
the hysteria of their policies, but we are not allowed to
know about this 'evidence'. After the laughable dossier
that was misused to justify the Iraq war we must be
extremely cynical about claims of a 'secret threat'.

In fact, 'state secrets' are rarely kept for our protection
at all, according to the American linguist and political
activist Noam Chomsky, whose books are quoted so often
in humanities circles that only the works of Shakespeare
and the Bible rival him. 'I spend a lot of time looking at
declassified government documents,' he wrote. 'You take a
look at secret documents from the United States or, to the
extent that I know about them, other countries. If they are
protecting secrets, who are they keeping them from?
Mostly the domestic population. A very small proportion
of these internal documents have anything to do with
security, no matter how broadly you interpret it. They
primarily have to do with ensuring that the major enemy –
namely, the domestic population – is kept in the dark

about the actions of the powerful. And that's because people in power, whether it's business power or government power or doctrinal power, are afraid that people do care, and therefore you have to . . . consciously manipulate their attitudes and beliefs.'[43]

One thing is certain: we have definitely not had a reaction from our leaders that our enemies wanted the least. Terrorists have achieved more through the hysterical reactions of our elected representatives than they ever did with their bombs. When a policeman can arrest a Charlie Chaplin impersonator for holding a sign that says 'Not Aloud' outside Downing Street because of the 'terrorist threat', it's clear the government is playing into the terrorists' hands. When the act of protest can be criminalized in Britain because of something statistically less dangerous to the public than putting up some shelves, you have to start believing in magic. How did they manage to convince us that it was all so necessary? There has been little actual convincing when you think about it; they've just fanned the flames of our paranoia. Not to mention the fact that they haven't proved their policies are a realistic way of combating terrorism even if it *was* as great a threat to our well-being as they claim.

The government always cites public safety when questions arise about their response to terrorism, so it is surprising that they have refused to have an inquiry into the 7 July bombings. It's almost as if they don't want to know why a British citizen felt compelled to become a suicide bomber. Shezad Tanweer, one of the terrorists who blew himself up on 7 July, explained his motives on a video callously released on the first anniversary of the bombings. He said that Britain 'deserved to be attacked' because it elected a government that 'continues to oppress our mothers, children, brothers and sisters in Palestine, Afghanistan, Iraq and Chechnya'. Regardless of his despicable behaviour, it is surely sensible to stop for a second and assess what he's going on about if we want to understand why we have become a target. Just because his desire was to create a way of life reminiscent of feudalism or one that in our eyes is 'evil' doesn't mean that we should assume by default that we are progressive or 'good'.

Robert Pape, Professor of Political Studies at the University of Chicago, published a study of 462 suicide bombers in August 2006 that gives an even greater insight into what makes someone prepared to blow up themselves and slaughter innocent members of the public. Its findings completely contradict the government's insistence that terrorists are all fanatical Muslims who want to destroy 'our way of life'.

> Previous analyses of suicide terrorism have not had the bencfit of a complete survey of all suicide terrorist attacks worldwide. The lack of complete data, together with the fact that many such attacks, including all those against Americans, have been committed by Muslims, has led many in the US to assume that Islamic fundamentalism must be the underlying main cause. This, in turn, has fuelled a belief that anti-American terrorism can be stopped only by wholesale transformation of Muslim societies, which helped create public support of the invasion of Iraq.
>
> But study of the phenomenon of suicide terrorism

shows that the presumed connection to Islamic fundamentalism is misleading.

There is not the close connection between suicide
terrorism and Islamic fundamentalism that many people
think. Rather, what nearly all suicide terrorist campaigns
have in common is a specific secular and strategic goal: to
compel democracies to withdraw military forces from
territory that the terrorists consider to be their homeland.

Religion is rarely the root cause, although it is often
used as a tool by terrorist organizations in recruiting and
in other efforts in service of the broader strategic
objective. Most often, it is a response to foreign
occupation.

Understanding that suicide terrorism is not a product
of Islamic fundamentalism has important implications for
how the US and its allies should conduct the war on
terrorism. Spreading democracy across the Persian Gulf
is not likely to be a panacea as long as foreign troops
remain on the Arabian peninsula. The obvious solution
might well be simply to abandon the region altogether.
Isolationism, however, is not possible; America needs a
new strategy that pursues its vital interest in oil but does
not stimulate the rise of a new generation of suicide
terrorists.'[44]

Rather like their approach with ASBOs, the government has reacted to terrorism in a heavy-handed way and
made little or no attempt to tackle the causes of the
problem. Of course it's obvious why they can't: their
economic policy is incompatible with dealing with grind-
ing poverty and our dependence on cheap oil. So instead,

all we got from our leaders was defiance. In a statement after the attacks on London, Tony Blair, flanked by George Bush, said of the terrorists, 'They should not and they must not succeed. When they try to intimidate us, we will not be intimidated. When they seek to change our country or our way of life, we will not be changed.'

When you look at the anti-terror legislation and how it has actually been used by the police, it is clear that the bombers have achieved far more than they could possibly have hoped for in terms of undermining 'our way of life'. The dreadful irony is that their greatest successes have come from our own Parliament's overreaction to their behaviour.

## CHAPTER 9

It was 3 July and England had just been dumped out of the World Cup on penalties. Again. Meanwhile, amid the gloom of defeat, the nation was being overwhelmed by global warming. The south was taking a battering from a heatwave while the north sank temporarily under flash floods.

I was fighting my way across London on the tube during rush hour, which was a strange experience for a workshy layabout like me. I was wearing a suit and tie though, which helped me fit in with the sullen faces packed on to the Northern Line train. A few days earlier my great-uncle Fred had passed away at the age of eighty-eight and I was on my way to his funeral at the family home in Lincolnshire. 'The family home' sounds absurdly grand – I don't mean it in a Jane Austen way. It was just a very proud and ordinary house filled with wonderful memories. My great-grandparents, a gamekeeper and his wife, moved into it in the late nineteenth century and raised all ten of their children there, at least one of whom had lived in the house ever since. It wasn't a very large house, with only three upstairs bedrooms, a small kitchen downstairs and a lounge, along with an outside toilet that had long since fallen out of use and a caravan in the garden that Fred and his wife Joan used as a sweet shop for the children of the village. But, as I said, it was a house overflowing with memories for the children, grandchildren and great-grandchildren who visited it throughout their lives. The Newton family had been part of the community of Springthorpe for over 125 years. I wondered whether it would survive the loss of someone like Fred.

King's Cross station was filled with men in suits and ties clutching copies of the *Financial Times* when I arrived shortly before nine. I guiltily bought a McDonald's breakfast, a bottle of water and, largely out of curiosity, my own copy of the *FT* before finding my place on the train.

I once read somewhere that the only newspaper that tells you the truth is the *Financial Times*. Apparently, normal people like you and me don't actually need to know the truth of what is going on in the world, which is why we buy all the other newspapers with supplements that tell us what problems we have and what we need to buy in order to cure them. The people with power and money, on the other hand, who have to know the truth to ensure that they keep hold of their money and power, quietly buy the *FT*.

I scanned a few of the headlines of that day's edition. INCOMING CBI CHIEF SAYS BLAIR UNCERTAINTY IS BAD FOR BUSINESS; FURORE OVER SECOND HOMES IS MISPLACED,

SAYS MINISTER; BNFL EXPECTED TO REPORT RETURN TO PROFITS; COMPETITIVENESS 'SUFFERS FROM BAD GREEN LEGISLATION'; BUPA PREFERRED IN HEALTH DEAL; AL-QAEDA THREAT TO UK MAY BE GROWING, SAYS COMMONS PANEL; and THE CAR INDUSTRY NEEDS CARBON TRADING. I read each article in turn and got the distinct impression that because Richard Lambert, the new head of the CBI, said that business wanted him to go, Tony Blair would be replaced by Gordon Brown sooner rather than later. That because business didn't approve, the proposed increase in taxation on second homes would not materialize after all. That because it was becoming more profitable, nuclear energy would soon become the 'answer' to our looming energy crisis and that any meaningful 'green legislation' would begin to disappear from government policy altogether. That BUPA would begin the process of privatizing the NHS, the hysteria around terrorism in Britain would be whipped up again as the anniversary of the 7 July bombings approached, and carbon trading would soon be adopted by all major political parties. It was like a corporate Christmas list to anyone with political ambitions. The *FT* doesn't just tell you the truth. I'm willing to bet that because of the power held by business interests in modern Britain it also tells you the direction of future political policy, whichever party happens to be in government.

An hour and a half later my dad's cousin Tony and his wife Cilla picked me up from Retford station as the GNER service for Leeds pulled away behind me. My granny was the one child who had moved far away from the family home. She couldn't have gone much further than

Chichester on the south coast, but this meant that my immediate family and I weren't as close to that side of the family as the generations that had remained nearby. Which is a roundabout way of explaining that this was the first time I'd met Tony and Cilla. I knew nothing about them at all, other than that they were generous enough to come and pick me up from the station and drop me back after the funeral. 'Don't be silly, you're family,' Tony said when I thanked him profusely. In their eyes that alone seemed to entitle me to their limitless kindness and hospitality.

We arrived in Springthorpe half an hour later, turned left towards the church, and then I saw the house opposite the churchyard in the middle of the village. It was probably the first time in almost twenty years that I'd been there. I got out of the car and was immediately overwhelmed with images and feelings. I could see my brother Gareth trying to play tennis on the grass; I could hear my great-aunt Joan calling 'Yorkshire puddings!' and see the most glorious smile on her face when we both ran into the kitchen. 'It's an old tradition, you know,' she said as she took off her oven gloves and swept me on to a chair while my granny chuckled in the background. 'In Springthorpe we have Yorkshire puddings with raspberry vinegar as a starter before we eat roast beef and more Yorkshire puddings for lunch!'

I walked through the little kitchen into the lounge and found Joan, in a black jumper with a single set of pearls around her neck, sitting in a deep trance. She got to her feet and briefly confused me with my dad while a tear like a rivet welded itself to her face. My memory immediately pulled Uncle Fred out from behind the curtains he'd just closed to get a better view of the cricket. Joan looked up at me, her eyes full of sadness, but proud of her grief, while Fred sat my nine-year-old self down patiently and tried to explain why 'Cricket is the greatest game in the world!'

There was something in that house that even now I can't put my finger on. Perhaps it was just the heat, or perhaps it was a sense of something else that is lost today. A sense of place and 'being' through all the seasons and the generations of your family's life. Cousins and aunties, friends and neighbours began to appear in the room looking nervous and embarrassed at the long-lost faces, but soon their memories began to collect around them too and Great-Uncle Fred came alive on the deep green carpet. Someone said, 'I remember this room as Auntie Gert's bedroom before it became the lounge'; others nodded and smiled with their eyes. Another of my dad's cousins, Zena, the kind of explosion of fun and laughter every family desperately needs, remembered being told as a child to go to the toilet before leaving to visit Grandma so she wouldn't have to use the one outside. I introduced myself to her and Cousin Maureen as little Dan and they both nearly fainted. When we arrived none of us really knew what to say to each other, but our memories soon jostled together, pulling and shaking us all back into life. It was almost as if a house really can work its way into your genes.

Tony took me out for a walk around the village and told me a story about my great-uncle Irvine, who was sent out by his mother to the shop every week with a penny to collect her 'medicine' (which turned out to be a little bottle of gin) and another penny for him, which he always spent on cigarettes. He began drinking half the gin and smoking four cigarettes behind a haystack every time he went, filling the bottle back up with water afterwards on his way home. 'There's plenty water in Springthorpe,' he always used to say. And so Great-Uncle Irvine developed a taste for gin and cigarettes from the tender age of seven. He lived to be well over eighty.

The church bells began to ring. One of them was obviously cracked and it clunked each time it fell, but the muffled sound was oddly appropriate. The little church was rarely used now, despite once being the hub of the community. My great-grandfather was the churchwarden when he was alive and his sons and daughters had played their part in keeping it, and the community, going, but now both were falling into disrepair. The family were bringing the little church back to life on this day of sadness, though. My second cousin Pauline, who was keeping another family tradition alive as a member of the cloth, was preparing to lead part of the service.

I walked at the back as we all made our way round to the entrance of the church. Tony pointed out the broken guttering on one side and said, 'When I came to see Fred last week we talked about that needing to be fixed.' The churchyard was completely overgrown with daisies and tall grass. It wasn't just Uncle Fred that had died. There was nothing of the village left. The shop and the post office had gone, the school was long closed, even the pond had been filled in. Apparently the pub owners thought it was a waste of land and extended their car park over it, but now even the pub had closed down. There were white rocks that marked where the pond had been, like a mouth of small white gravestones being sucked back into the earth. Once there was a space in this country for places like Springthorpe, but today small communities are not profitable so they are deemed to have no value and are just left to wither and die.

After the service we went back to the house, drank cups of tea and talked about all the other brothers and sisters who had long since passed away. All of those ten children were gone now apart from my beloved granny, who hadn't been able to come because of her health. I felt a twinge of panic and wanted to be with her, to listen endlessly to the stories of her life and her memories of our country, a country that was now changing even faster than when she was a nurse during the Second World War.

There's something about death that pushes into focus how much of our lives we waste, how many minutes, hours, days and years we spend asleep in offices and factories, in meetings and seminars. Perhaps we need the sense of importance our careers give us, but I doubt whether anyone has ever lain on their deathbed and wished they'd spent more time at work. Of course many will bang on the table and talk about the need for careers to keep the wolf from the door, or say that it isn't greed that takes our time from us but necessity. Most of us work full-time, five days a week, forty-eight weeks a year, from the age of eighteen to sixty-five (and probably well beyond for my generation) because we would all starve and live in penury otherwise. Well, stand back for a moment and ask yourself if that is a good enough life for the economic status Britain holds in the world. What's the point of being one of the largest economies if none of us even gets to control our own time? According to the Office of National Statistics, the average amount of time working parents spend with their children each day is nineteen minutes. *Nineteen minutes!* They do get to spend another sixteen minutes with their kids, but they're usually doing something else like housework at the time. The same study found that 50 per cent of mothers only want to work part-time so they can actually spend some time with their children. Why doesn't the government do what it can to facilitate that instead of suggesting that schools stay open longer to offer free childcare so that parents can spend even more time in the office?[45] No wonder the rates of family breakdown are skyrocketing. It's clear to anyone with a pulse that the single biggest threat to the break-up of family life is our culture of overwork, but no politician or political party is ever likely to terrify the business community by telling you that.

Uncle Fred was an ordinary man who lived a long and happy life. No-one spoke of his work over those cups of tea in that old room we had all played in as children. No-one talked about the professional status he acquired. Perhaps I'm being naive and simplistic again, but life and death are unavoidably simple. If life seems too precious to be spent fighting your way through the rush hour or queuing up to buy the latest high-definition television set, then that's because it is. If it seems too wonderful to be wasted on targets and league tables and all the other corporate infrastructure that binds us together in fear in the Britain of today, then that's because it is. People often talk about trying to find a work–life balance. Well, as my friend Gwyn once wrote in one of his brilliant cartoons, one day you'll find it – when you breathe your final breath.

On the train home I went back to the *FT* and read an interview with Richard Lambert, who had just been announced as the new head of the Confederation of British Industry. He was wonderfully forthcoming about the role he sees for business in modern Britain. I was feeling a little strained and reflective, but as I read I began to realize that the simple and obvious common sense of life and death has no place in the eternal world of work and business. According to Mr Lambert, corporate interests that prize short-term profits above everything else pose no risk to human beings or their communities despite the reality of our daily lives staring us all in the face. 'A healthy society needs a healthy business sector and vice versa,' he said. 'There is no moat or castle wall between them.'

It would be nice if that were true. There is certainly a big moat between society and business when it comes to tax. Oceans of water, in fact, between us and the Channel Islands, the Cayman Islands and all the other tax havens into which the large corporations pour their profits so they don't have to pay tax on the money they make here in Britain. It certainly feels like there's a moat between us when I'm trying to cancel my mobile phone subscription for half an hour on the phone to someone in India, or trying to claw back the £25 the bank took out of my account for going 3p overdrawn. Lambert also revealed that 'Politicians find it easier to deal with business than to tackle voters – especially when they are under attack.' I had long suspected that to be the case, so it was nice to hear from the horse's mouth that our politicians prefer to deal with businessmen than the people who actually vote them into government. Also, according to Mr Lambert, it appears that taxing global corporations that make billions of pounds of profit in Britain isn't a good idea (again, that's the ones who don't farm them out to offshore accounts and pay no tax at all, like the entrepreneur Phillip Green, who according to the BBC's *Money Programme* avoided a £280 million tax bill by doing just that). 'A tax on business is a tax on everybody,' he said. 'We need to get across the idea that we're all in this together.' Oh, bless him. He struck me as absurd as the teenage anarchist I'd met on the first day of my journey back at the YMCA who wanted us to overturn the state. Both were so caught up in their extremist ideologies that they had completely lost touch with the reality of people's everyday lives. Can even the supporters of the CBI read this stuff with a straight face?

According to the *FT*, the channels of communication within government were well greased by Lambert's predecessor, the parasitic pachyderm Sir Digby Jones. Lambert, the paper stated, 'has inherited . . . an organisation whose voice is now a powerful one in Whitehall', leaving him to set the role of the CBI and their members in Britain's future. 'We're here to champion the conditions under which business can flourish and attack barriers to its growth,' Lambert explained. 'Our members are always quick off the mark and it is because we are such a broad church that we can have an enormous impact on policy.' 'Attack barriers to its growth' is an interesting choice of words when you consider that the 'barriers' he's talking about are people. People like Dorothy, and communities like the one she was fighting to protect in Derby. (Dorothy, incidentally, became the target of a hate campaign a few weeks after Mark and I visited her. Bottles and stones were thrown at her night after night, then she started to receive death threats. She could handle all that, but it was the promise of a violent sexual assault if she remained up there one blustery night that finally persuaded her to come down. She was terrified and contacted the police, who told her she would have to give up her protest for her own safety. Derby will get its casino built on a flood plain after all, and Adam from the pub, the man with the black eye, will no longer be able to take his son to their favourite place by the river to feed the ducks. I can't imagine he'll take the time to write to the council or his MP to complain about it, though.) Lambert claimed that the CBI has 'an enormous impact on policy'. One would hope that voters have an equal impact, but people like Dorothy can't afford to employ a lobbying firm to fight things like the Riverlights development. Of course we're not supposed to need to employ a lobbying firm because we have MPs to represent us.

I flicked through to the sports section and found a particularly curious story with the headline NATIONAL HYSTERIA THAT COULD DESTABILISE BRITAIN. Its central argument, that overt nationalism during the World Cup could lead to a break-up of the United Kingdom, which would in turn be a very bad thing for business, seemed out of place among the other articles. After the confidence and bravado emanating from the rest of the paper I couldn't help but detect a distinct whiff of fear here. It was a message of corporate doom that seemed to imply power had not yet shifted completely into the hands of the money markets and shareholders of corporate Britain. The final paragraph read, 'As football gets ever more significant, and the political and cultural implications of devolution sink in, this has the potential to destabilise the country in ways we cannot yet grasp. This might not bother Steve McClaren, Eriksson's successor. It should worry Gordon Brown, the next manager of the UK.' Perhaps this is what Orwell meant when he wrote, 'One day Patriotism and Intelligence will come together.' This sleeping giant of Patriotism, shackled to football, cricket and the Queen, has a different role to play in our lives. It should really be what we rally around to celebrate our sense of national and community pride. No wonder taking power back to a community level, the policy with which Sergeant Gary Brown has had such success in Spilsby, is so feared by the corporate behemoths. Decentralizing power into local communities might improve people's lives but there's no money in it, so the very idea terrifies them.

If that is what the business community fears then I have news for the CBI and Richard Lambert, Gordon Brown, David Cameron and anyone else seeking to control Britain's future political agenda. There *is* a moat between the 'experts' who govern us and we amateurs who just want to lead happy lives. No-one with a brain, even those who support the CBI's interests, believes for a second that 'we are all in this together'. Try and get away with saying that in the Bransholme Estate in Hull or in Cumbernauld, or to the families of those who've committed suicide because they were in so much debt. Or the rest of us, for that matter: the people who want their children to go to university but who now can't afford the fees; the ones paying off those car loans; the ones dutifully buying all those DVDs. Or my stepgrandfather, who worked hard and paid tax throughout his life and saved every penny he could lay his hands on only to be told that because he's got assets of more than £20,000 he'll have to sell his house to pay the £800 a week his new nursing home will cost. If he wants a room with an ensuite bathroom it'll cost him £1,000 a week. Thank God we have such a powerful economy that shareholders can make tidy profits from our pensioners when they come to the end of their lives. Thank goodness the free market has devised such an effective way of taxing the elderly and moving money from their bank accounts into the pockets of shareholders rather than their families or the state. Thank God for the market answering all our problems, and making every decision we face come down, somewhere along the line, to the mindset of a tedious desk job with its obsession with ever-expanding profits. That's sure to give us all a great quality of life. If we *are* all in this together, when are the rest of us going to get a bite of Britain's enormous economic fruit? All I can see us sharing equally is Britain's mountain of debt.

Of course the only argument required to shoot down these ideas is to say that I'm being 'anti-business' or 'lazy', both of which are becoming akin to the cry of 'Witch!' in the sixteenth century. I'm harking back to a time that never existed, and it's absurd to hold back the tide of 'progress'. It's as though anyone who dares to suggest that we may be getting the balance wrong is being absurdly simplistic, or is some kind of raving communist. But business existed in Britain's communities for decades happily without destroying our towns. The independent shop sector has taken a hammering from the ever-powerful supermarkets. There is evidence for that which no-one can argue with. How many independent greengrocers and fishmongers do you have on your high street? How many supermarkets do you have in your town? Once we were a nation of shopkeepers, but not any more. The shareholders of all these supermarkets live all over the world, so the money from our communities is not even guaranteed to remain in Britain, let alone the local area. And we wonder where the fruits of our economy have gone. Is it socialism to argue that this is unfair and wrong? Or anarchism? Or, if David Cameron is anything to go by, conservatism perhaps? Or is it none of those political ideologies and just simple common sense to suggest that if things are allowed to continue the way they are going then Britain and the vast majority of its people are in for an uncertain and impoverished future?

Perhaps a sense of national pride might help us answer these questions, whichever political standpoint we adopt. Maybe that is the true role of nationalism. If we could get past the lazy interpretation of it as mindless thuggery, and reject the idea that there is something to be ashamed of in having a shared sense of belonging and pride in our nation and what it stands for, then we might be prepared to fight for it and for ourselves. Of course our economy would not grow at such an impressive rate if we were radical enough actually to put the health of Britain and the people who live here ahead of those seeking ever-increasing profits, but those of us who are not members of the CBI would all probably be better off financially.

If we can prove that commercial interests left unchecked are undermining our sense of community and personal happiness and turning Britain into a homogenized American outpost, then where do we go to make our voices heard? What if, like Dorothy's opinion of Derby council, our MPs are of the view that 'the interests of the community and the economy are the same thing'? A look at the register of MPs' interests does little to challenge this assumption. If you are prepared to wade through it, you will begin to realize just how many of our MPs have their fingers in the great business pie. None of these details reveals anything illegal, and there is no suggestion that any of these MPs have broken any rules. I would suggest, however, that if there is a distinction between the interests of those who live in Britain and those people who want to make money here, then our MPs should not have any outside interests if they are to behave with impartiality on behalf of the electorate that employs them.

Of course, in their defence, one could argue that if we want our high-flyers to enter Parliament we have to allow them to generate the kinds of salaries they could command in the world of business, otherwise we wouldn't benefit from their expertise. We must expect them to have well-paid directorships to make up the difference. Personally, I think politics should be seen as a vocation like teaching or nursing. I don't think we do want to poach these supposed high-flyers from the business world. I think that anyone seeking to be elected as an MP should have some knowledge of the nation they are about to serve through having journeyed around it and experienced what the reality of life is for the whole country, not just their constituency. To me, that seems more relevant to the role of MP than having a background in business. But, MPs might argue, they have uncertain careers and can only secure a four- or five-year contract, leaving them open to the perils of unemployment beyond that term. Well, that's what the world of work has become for the rest of us these days thanks to the ever-expanding economy so I don't see why they should be exempt. Living in the real world might make our MPs seem more relevant to us than they do now, with their ten weeks off over the summer and being allowed to vote on their own pay rises. We need to attract people who see being an MP as something valuable for its own sake rather than a way to generate influence and power and pick up a few tasty directorships once they've retired.

Now there are MPs who do see their roles as a vocation. I don't know of any offhand, but the law of averages states that there must be some. No doubt they are also the ones who put their constituents ahead of their own careers, which more or less guarantees that they will be kept well clear of important posts in the Cabinet where such a sense of privilege is elbowed out of the way by a desperation not to hinder progress up the greasy political ladder. If we did do something as drastic as ban MPs with directorships then the House of Commons would have eighty-seven empty seats, according to the List of Members' Interests.

Conservative MP Tony Baldry comes top of the list with fifteen directorships including Angle Gate Ltd, a property developer in the UK; Red Eagle Resources, a firm that invests in agriculture and natural resources in Sierra Leone; Invicta Africa Ltd, a venture capitalist investing in Africa; Carbon Registry Services Ltd, a company that consults on carbon trading strategy; Symphony Global Ltd, which promotes business development between the UK and Eastern Europe; Black Rock Oil and Gas, which specializes in oil and gas exploration in the UK and abroad; Battlebridge Capital, an investment fund; Tiresias Ltd, which invests in Gulf States; and Saudi Arabia and Westminster Oil Ltd, another oil exploration firm. It's a wonder that he has any time left to represent his constituents.

As we know, MPs have a tremendous workload. They attend debates in Parliament, they have to spend time in their constituencies, and if they are ministers they have even more things to worry about. How, then, do they find the time for any extra jobs? We've seen that it's illegal for a company with shareholders to spend money that will not increase that company's share price, so these companies must be getting something out of these eighty-seven MPs. Is it too outlandish to suggest that it is simply having close contact with an MP, with all the prestige and influence that implies, that some of these companies are actually paying for?

Which leads us into the murky world of lobbying. The Association of Professional Political Consultants doesn't seem to like the word 'lobbyist' because it explains too well exactly what it is that they do. They'd much rather be thought of as 'political consultants' because then you're scratching your chin to determine exactly what services they really offer. The association's 'rule' number seven seems particularly optimistic. 'Save for entertainment and token business mementoes, political consultants must not offer or give, or cause a client to offer or give, any financial or other incentive to any person in public life, whether elected, appointed or co-opted, that could be construed in any way as a bribe or solicitation of favour.'[46] Well, we wouldn't want any solicitations of favour in the world of lobbying, now would we? That would be awful. It's clear, then, that all their clients pay them to ensure that they *don't* get any special treatment from government; strict impartiality is what they are after.

Now who's being naive? Of course our political parties get loaded money from businesses. They used to be called donations, but then people started asking too many questions about links between money and government policy, especially when Labour decided to make motor racing exempt from the ban on cigarette manufacturers sponsoring sporting events after Bernie Ecclestone happened to donate a cool million to the party. All those lofty ideals about being up front with the public about where their money was coming from turned out to be untenable under the pressures of actually being in power so they were soon in need of a loophole. Thankfully they had written one into their proposals: there was no mention of 'loans' when it came to disclosing who was giving you money.

The Committee for Standards in Public Life announced new rules for party funding in 2001, which included one to ensure that every donation over £5,000 was disclosed. Lord Neil, who chaired the committee, commented at the time, 'Many members of the public believe that the policies of the major political parties have been influenced by large donors, while ignorance about the sources of funding has fostered suspicion.' It seems laughably quaint to say this today, but giving money to a political party is supposed to be an act of pure altruism.

In July 2006, Labour's chief fundraiser Lord Levy was arrested because of the cash for peerages scandal, and in November the Metropolitan Police sent letters to every member of the Cabinet in the run-up to the 2005 General Election with a view to learning what they knew about loans and nominations for peerages. Tony Blair has done his usual trick of fronting out the crisis by revealing how far his standards have slipped since becoming Prime Minister. 'There are places in the House of Lords reserved for party nominees,' he reasoned. So why not just hand them out to the highest bidders? The four party supporters in question are: Sir David Garrard, who gave a £2.3 million loan and who also ploughed £2 million into one of Labour's new business academies (where a large injection of cash gives you a say in what gets taught in the college. According to Cindy Denise, a parent of two children at a new city academy in Doncaster bankrolled by Christian philanthropist Sir Peter Vardy, children at the school are disciplined if they don't carry the Bible around with them on specific days, while Emmanuel College in Gateshead, another of Sir Peter's schools, has been accused repeatedly of teaching creationism alongside science); Sir Gulam Noon, known as the Curry King, who loaned Labour £250,000 and got nominated for a peerage (Noon told the BBC that Lord Levy told him not to worry about mentioning the loan to the Lords Appointments

Commission); Barry Townsley, who lent Labour £1 million and also gave £1.5 million to another of these new academies, but got turned down for a peerage by the Lords Appointments Commission; and Chai Patel, the chief executive of the Priory Group, who lent Labour £1.5 million but also got rejected by the panel. Incidentally, the day Lord Levy was arrested he was supposed to be meeting Phillip Green, with his fresh knighthood, to discuss funding for the city academies programme.

There does seem to be a lot of circumstantial evidence suggesting that the securing of financial backing for the new specialist schools and academies involved promises of peerages from the government. It certainly seemed that way to Des Smith, who used to advise the government on their specialist schools programme. He told a court in East London that there was a 'well-established link' between backers of the programme and peerages, as he tried to get dispensation from a drink-driving charge that was caused by the stress he said his involvement in the scandal had caused. Then John Prescott managed to get himself into a tricky situation with a secretary, a cowboy hat, a pair of leather boots and a man who wanted to open a super-casino in the Millennium Dome. It certainly seems as though business and government are becoming entwined in ways that seemed at the very least unlikely back in 1997, when Labour joyously poked the Tories with the 'sleaze' stick. My favourite quote during Prescott's troubles came from the man Prescott's secretary was going to marry. When told that his fiancée had slept with the Deputy Prime Minister he is said to have replied, 'I feel sick.' Well, quite.

We were promised by Labour a new dawn of

transparency and accountability back in 1997. Sadly, that doesn't seem to have emerged. It's not just Labour who have been made to look stupid, though.[47] The Liberal Democrats' largest donor, Michael Brown, gave £2.4 million to the party before the last election but has just entered a guilty plea in a civil case against HSBC for perjury and deception. He faces the prospect of a jail term. And God knows who gave the Tories their million-pound loans. These financial angels were promised anonymity so we will never discover if any of them, as is suspected, were not even British citizens, which would be against the law.

There is, of course, no hard evidence that companies donate or lend money to political parties in exchange for peerages, favourable legislation or a reduction in the effectiveness of proposed legislation that might harm their businesses – apart, that is, from the rectangular bit of paper on which they write out a number followed by lots of zeros that gets handed over to their preferred political party. We all know favours are being traded, but because there is no 'smoking gun' evidence we all act as though it isn't happening. But we don't have to find the smoking gun of corruption or even uncover seedy loans to notice corporate interests getting a little too chummy with our government. You just have to keep an eye on ministers once they've left office and see what jobs they move on to.

By coincidence, many of these ministers seem to go and work for companies that were given large government contracts. EDS, for example, the company that provides the computer system that pays RAF crews, chose Michael Dugher to be their chief lobbyist. Before taking up this new position, Dugher was the then Minister of Defence Geoff Hoon's special adviser and his chief responsibility was 'procurement'. At the time he was working for the government in that role, EDS was chosen to run the payroll system and given the £2 billion 'information infrastructure' programme for the MoD. Lord Robertson, the former Defence Secretary and NATO Secretary General, now enjoys a directorship with the Smiths Group, which makes parts for warplanes. According to the *Guardian*, he isn't alone. 'More than a third of the 92 ex-ministers who resigned or were sacked since May 1997 are enjoying nice little earners'[48] in the private sector. There is nothing wrong with Mr Dugher working for EDS or Lord Robertson going to the Smiths Group under current rules, but it might be nice in future if no MP was allowed to work in any capacity for a firm that was given lucrative contracts while they were in office. It just doesn't look good.

This glance at our MPs' interests and party funding may not prove any wrongdoing, but it does show that there is no clear water between our politicians and business interests. It is clear to me after my journey around Britain that the short-term interests of the business world are not the same as the long-term interests of the communities in which they operate. But it's becoming impossible to question any aspect of the globalized economy without coming across as some kind of Marxist dinosaur. So how did we get to the stage where it is suicide for political parties *not* to have some financial contact with business interests?

The reason our politicians are in bed with big business

is fear. Our politicians are only desperate to keep the economy growing nicely because we want them to. That's why New Labour promised to stick to the Tories' spending plans when they came into power all those years ago, and that's why David Cameron and George Osborne parroted out the 'economic stability before tax cuts' line at the Tory Conference in October 2006. It was to reassure us that they wouldn't screw up the economy. But why are we so desperate to have a thriving economy if things aren't working in our daily lives? If we're all in debt, if we work so hard that we only get to spend an average of nineteen minutes every day with our children, and if we're all so stressed out from overworking and over-consuming that the number of anti-depressants being prescribed by the NHS has gone up by a bewildering 33 per cent in the last six years alone to 29.4 million? Why are we so terrified of upsetting the economists and brokers of the Square Mile? Why do we want the huge companies listed on the FTSE 100 to get larger? Why are we reassured when these corporations make bigger profits, whatever price our communities, or we as consumers, increasingly have to pay?

The only reason I can find that explains why we're all so desperate to carry on pushing the economy forward is because our lives literally depend on it. That's why the government keeps telling us to save more and more money for our future in stock-market pension plans. You see, the working mindset doesn't stop when we retire. Indeed, that's when it actually gets into its stride. But having a pension fund and being a shareholder means taking your share of the blame for a supermarket giant destroying your community; for the Riverlights development, for the road-building programme of the eighties and nineties; for places like Springthorpe being laid to waste; for all the crap towns up and down the country; and for all the decisions the politicians have made to keep our economy moving whatever and whoever it crushes in its path.

It all comes down to our relationship with work, or in this case what my friend Matthew DeAbaitua calls 'the secular afterlife'. If you live in a country with low taxation where everyone spends most of their time working and people who need help from the state are described as layabouts and spongers by the press while corporate spongers who take vast profits out of the country but don't bother paying any tax get rewarded with knighthoods, then things will continue to break down. Of course retirement was a good idea when people had jobs for life and we didn't live as long as we do today. It was the carrot that went with the stick of work. If you put in long hours while you're young you need the prospect of a comfortable retirement to keep you from going mad. But there are no jobs for life now, apart from MPs' directorships perhaps, and some people who have paid into their pension plans for decades are discovering when they are ready to retire that all their money has vanished. I'm thirty so I find myself being bombarded with adverts from the government screaming at me to get a pension – although not as many as I get from banks screaming for me to get into debt, which shows precisely the problem. That is the catch 22 of our economic nightmare. We have to keep the economy going at a relentless pace, by overworking and over-consuming and getting into ludicrous debt and turning a blind eye to greed and global atrocities, because that is the only way we can keep the stock market afloat, which in turn we hope will keep us in work and keep our economy thriving, which we pray will eventually help us retire with a healthy pension. The minute you tie your future prosperity to the stock exchange the very idea of living in a sustainable way becomes akin to a turkey voting for Christmas. Why would you do something to threaten the economy if your future prosperity relied on it, especially if you've been paying into that stock market for decades? So we all keep going, hoping it could be us when it comes to the lottery but that it isn't us when it comes to the companies we work for going bust before we get to retire.

I don't have a pension. I don't believe in the secular afterlife. I think it's time our relationship with work moved into the twenty-first century. There's no point in saving for retirement if you have debts, anyway. My dad, who is a bank manager, told me that. Unless you are being offered a guaranteed interest rate for your pension that is higher than the rate borrowers are charging for your debt, of course, and that would be, for obvious reasons, impossible for any business to sustain. But still the government pleads with us to save for retirement. They're even considering making us do it by force.

But the answer lies in the opposite direction. There is a conspiracy of silence about the future. Sooner or later those of us under thirty-five will have to accept that retirement simply won't exist for us. We'll all be working till we drop. You simply can't earn enough money to spend the way we do in Britain to keep the economy expanding and still be able to save enough to retire on. If you stop to think about that for a moment then your attitude to work will begin to falter. If at the start of our working lives we were all told that we would have to work until we dropped dead, then work, and our demands of it, would radically change. If all of us under thirty-five are going to have to work for that long then we're all going to want to do something for a living that we enjoy. A business model of an ever-expanding profit won't be realistic for a workforce that wants to work less, to have a greater say in how their lives are organized, and to see their children for more than nineteen minutes a day. If that didn't happen, life would simply become too miserable. It'd become one long tread-mill of work. Getting a job when you're over sixty is hard enough now; how easy do you think it's going to be if our slavish acceptance of a constantly expanding economy continues for another twenty years? If we don't start to challenge the current work ethic soon, things will get much, much worse. Life will become nothing but work, if you're lucky enough to find it, and poverty if you can't.

Of course some people will have retired with excellent pensions by then. MPs, for example, and no doubt the members of the CBI. Perhaps they'll move to Dubai with all our retired footballers. They won't want to be in the crime-ravaged Britain of the future where gangs of 'extremist' pensioners march on Downing Street every week to protest about poverty. Perhaps by then those of us without pensions who have the nerve to complain about it will start being described as 'terrorists', our actions having been deemed 'economic sabotage' that threatens the profitability of Britain.

It may sound odd for someone who considers full-time

work to be the main source of life's problems to say that a hopeful future entails working for ever, but that is the reality, however unpalatable it may be. In which case, as I said, work will have to change or our society will continue to fall apart. The answer to this problem is the same as that for all the other great issues that loom over our politicians, which none of them want to discuss: sustainability. Some people – mainly men and women with beards, mind you – have been calling for it to save our climate for years. Sustainability may in fact be our only hope for any kind of future, especially when you start looking into energy security.

You see, how we work, why our civil liberties are being eroded and the 'war on terror' all boil down to the same thing.

Energy.

## CHAPTER 10

Most of us know that in a few hundred years' time climate change will really kick in and oil will run out. We don't really want to think about what life will be like then because it reminds us that all of us and everyone we know will be long dead. I think we all realize that life is going to be something of a struggle in the years to come, but we'll be well out of it.

Or so we think.

When it comes to our over-consumption of energy we are all behaving like a drunk in the bar at Douglas Adams' *Restaurant at the End of the Universe*, ordering more drinks than we can get down our throats because we assume we won't be alive to experience the horror of our hangover. But some of us may live to feel that hangover. That couple of hundred years has been shrunk to anything between ten and fifty by the ever-expanding global economy, according to those who have been looking at the future of our energy supplies. For those of us who are thirty and under, that means we will live to experience the energy hangover of our overworking, over-consuming age.

The evidence for it is all around us if you stop and think about it. Newspapers and TV stations are falling over themselves to write and make programmes about the emerging markets of China and India and the new economic order that looms on the horizon. With this economic order the role of energy will become more and more important as the new powerhouse economies compete with the current major economic powers for the only resource that can help them expand economically and generate more global power – cheap energy. The problem is that these changes are occurring at a time when the amount of oil in the world is plummeting. 'Peak oil' was supposedly way off in the distant future. Now some people are beginning to think it could even have been in the past.

The Iraq war perhaps gave us a window of opportunity to change the way we live, but many people think the government wasn't honest with us about why we went to war so the moment was lost. We all know it was about oil; it's become something of a cliché to talk about the non-existent 'WMDs'. Some have even started labelling Blair and Bush as 'war criminals', which is a trifle unfair really when they were only doing their jobs as CEOs of Britain and the US respectively. Once everyone was agreed that the war was about oil, most people thought the trail of blame came to a halt with a bunch of fat American men wallowing in money, but in reality the oil trail went way beyond George Bush's pals. I'm afraid there is no conspiracy theory here. The person at the end of the oil trail is you.

Even the most fervent petrol guzzler will now openly admit that our days of oil are numbered. After meeting Jim the energy man in the pub in Whitehall I started to read everything I could lay my hands on about oil and energy in general. It turns out that he was slightly hopeful when it comes to our energy supplies. The most wildly optimistic estimates for how long our oil supply will be able to keep our constantly expanding global economy afloat are around eighty years; the extreme pessimists say oil production has already plateaued and will certainly have declined by 2010. The hopeful middle ground is somewhere between twenty and fifty years, depending on the growth in demand from China and India in the years to come, and we all know how fast their economies are expanding. It's obvious to everyone that our current global economy will continue to expand only if we can maintain a steady flow of cheap energy into the market. You can't have out-of-season food or exotic fruits flown into your local supermarket for a couple of quid if the price of oil shoots up, or it runs out completely; you can't keep getting T-shirts for three quid in Oxford Street if you can't afford the oil required to get them here from the sweatshops of South-East Asia; and you can forget about flying to Europe for the price of a king-size Mars bar too. If our supply of cheap oil ends then every aspect of life as we know it will change completely. It literally becomes a matter of national security. I was told by a well-placed government source that during the oil blockade demonstrations of September 2000, Britain was twenty-four hours away from a state of national emergency. That blockade prevented petrol getting out into the country for a paltry seven days. Back then a barrel of crude oil was $35 and petrol prices in Britain were 80p a gallon. Recently a barrel of oil was over twice that price and petrol nudged over the pound-a-gallon mark. If we could barely cope with an oil shortage for a week then how are we going to cope with an energy-rationed future?

Everything our lives are built on is threatened without a steady supply of cheap energy. We may not like the fact that our leaders decided to go out and secure control of the country with the second largest oil reserves after Saudi Arabia by military force in order to stabilize our future economies, but we were the ones who demanded they do it by living the way we do. Tony and George just knew we wouldn't be able to handle the truth so they decided to assuage our collective guilt by calling the war 'Operation Freedom' and talking about spreading 'democracy'. It would be nice if politicians were honest with us occasionally, wouldn't it? Especially when it comes to a declaration of war. The prospect of a national emergency caused by running out of energy may have left us slightly less squeamish about liberating the Iraqi oil fields, especially if we thought about how taking no action would affect our future. You can see why it made sense to Tony and George though; after all, Britain and America have been behaving like this for years. We don't need that Iraqi oil right now, but it was prudent to make sure we got control of it before our competitors' emerging economies and growing wealth gave them enough clout to beat us to it at some point in the future. At the very least, if our leaders had told us this latest energy war was for our own good some people might still have decided to oppose the war and use the mobiliz- ation of public opinion to force the government to make us less reliant on such unstable parts of the world. Perhaps it could even have been the catalyst that made us start to question our slavish acceptance of the ever-expanding economy and prepare ourselves for a more sustainable and peaceful future.

The future looks bleak whatever we do now. Global warming seems inevitable. Even if America voted in the most energy-conscious president imaginable it would not be enough to halt climate change. China has so much coal it makes no economic sense for them to use anything else to power their growing nation, and coal is the most polluting hydrocarbon energy resource on earth. If oil becomes more expensive they may well switch over to it completely for everything apart from transportation. The carbon dioxide emissions that will cause will seal our fate as far as climate change is concerned. That isn't to say we should give up, but all we can do is try our best to limit the consequences.

The reality is that we are simply running out of choices. We can no longer carry on as we are with our heads in the sand, working too hard and consuming too much and taking as much Prozac as we can lay our hands on until we run out of cheap energy or die of stress-related heart disease, whichever comes first. As I said, no-one knows for sure the timeframe for this, but it will certainly not happen suddenly. We won't wake up one morning and suddenly find we've run out of oil. It is said that if you put frogs in boiling water they jump out, but if you put them in a pan of cold water and slowly bring up the heat you can boil them alive. That is the position we find ourselves in. When oil prices start rising we should consider ourselves warned. Unless we act, by the time big changes in our cheap energy supply do occur we will be too late to do anything meaningful about it.

When our cheap energy supply looks to be coming to a close, things will really begin to change globally. According to Paul Roberts in *The End of Oil,* 'moving to a gas (Liquid Natural Gas) economy is probably the only feasible way for the world to delay the effects of a changing climate while we figure out how to revamp our energy economy . . . converting to this "bridge" fuel will be slow, painful and quite costly'. America will go out looking to secure their energy future, but this time it won't be Iraq they'll go after. The balance of power will have shifted away from the Middle Eastern OPEC countries to those with LNG, and the two nations that control half the world's natural gas reserves are Iran and Russia. America and Britain won't be the only ones getting twitchy about their energy supplies either. Natural gas is the next best fuel to oil in terms of being able to exploit the existing oil industry infrastructure like petrol stations and cars; other fuels, like hydrogen, would require trillions of pounds of investment in brand-new delivery systems that any company hoping to increase its share price in the short term could never justify spending. So China and India will no doubt start thinking of natural gas too. Ninety per cent of the transportation the global economy relies on uses oil, and despite it being costly, it is nevertheless possible to convert lorries and cars from oil-based petrol to a liquid natural gas-based equivalent. Even if transportation began to use electric power, that electricity has to be found from somewhere, and today LNG is used extensively in the production of electricity too. So it seems highly likely that every major global economic power with an energy crisis will begin to start flexing its muscles in the near future under huge pressure from their domestic populations to keep their economies, shares and pension pots growing, and LNG is what they'll go out looking for.

In fact it's already happening. We get 25 per cent of our domestic energy from LNG today and prices are already rising, so if oil dries up we'll no doubt be using a lot more of it in the future. This will leave us more reliant on places like Russia and Iran for our economic stability. By the way, Russia, the USA, China, the UK and India all have nuclear weapons but Iran does not, so you can perhaps understand why it is so desperate to acquire them. With that much at stake, and with each electorate (where there is such a thing) no doubt voting in right-wing governments of the kind you get in such economically uncertain times, you could be forgiven for getting rather nervous about the prospect of a large-scale energy war between nations armed with nuclear weapons. This scenario is not limited to the quest to get hold of LNG either; a very similar battle will take place much sooner over the remaining supplies of oil in the Middle East. The US imports 70 per cent of its crude today and that figure is set to rise sharply unless Americans can reduce their appetite for energy. Nowhere else in the world is oil as plentiful, cheap and accessible as it is in the Middle East. If you look at the number of American military bases in

the Gulf and the Caspian basin you can see how advanced
the military build-up has already become. China is following suit. Russia and India are becoming nervous. No large
economy of the future can afford to be jostled out of the
way by American demand if it hopes to be a player. The
current unrest in the Middle East may well be seen as a
trifling squabble compared with the energy war that could
potentially kick off. We may look back at the invasion of
Iraq and see it as just the first in a whole series of energy
wars. That may sound alarmist, but it's hardly as though
world powers with huge military forces have ever been
scared to declare war to secure cheap energy supplies and
increase their economic power. It's a while since we've had
three major global powers, let alone four (the USA,
Russia, China and India).

This scenario also gives us the one guaranteed way to
increase the likelihood of global terrorism. To maintain
their global dominance, despite their own dwindling cheap
energy reserves, the USA is pushing forward with its
policy to militarize space.[49] As you can imagine, all other
nations with nuclear weapons are rather nervous about
America being able to attack them at twenty minutes'
notice from the heavens. Thanks to US policy, these
countries are making more and more nuclear weapons in
an attempt to safeguard their own positions. There's only
one way to make it more likely that terrorists will get hold
of WMDs and that's if the countries that harbour them
build more and more. In the future the terrorist threat may
become far more compelling than it is today. Massive
nuclear proliferation also makes mistake firings more
likely, especially in the relatively inexperienced fledgling

nuclear nations. The looming energy crisis certainly has the potential to create the kind of global unrest we don't want to imagine. And thanks to the 'war on terror' all of this is much more likely to happen now than it was before George Bush and Tony Blair decided to attack Iraq. (Incidentally, on 3 October 2006 Environment Minister Ian Pearson revealed at a summit of the world's twenty most polluting nations how serious the British government is when it comes to energy independence. He pledged £500 million to increase investment in renewable energy sources over the next five or six years. A few weeks later it emerged that the Iraq war had so far cost the UK taxpayer £4.5 billion and the projected cost of the 2012 London Olympics had risen to £9 billion: a bill that included a £400 million payment to the developer to ensure the building programme doesn't 'over-run'.)

Then there's the possible future water crisis. In August 2006 a report was published predicting the return of cholera to London, a mass migration from Africa that could lead to civil unrest all over Europe and economic meltdown in China – by 2015. All thanks to a global shortage of clean water. This report did not come from Greenpeace, Friends of the Earth or any of the other environmental pressure groups that are sometimes criticized for trying to shock the public into paying attention. The people who bankrolled this report had motives that are far more credible than mere ethical principles. It was funded by two hundred of the world's largest food, oil, water and chemical companies including Coca Cola, Shell and Procter and Gamble, who are becoming rather concerned about how the planet's dwindling fresh water supplies might damage their future profits. The International Water Management Institute confirmed that global demand for water has increased by six times in the last hundred years and will double again by 2050. Meanwhile, 2 billion people around the world are living in areas where the water table is already falling rapidly and rivers are drying up. This problem is particularly pressing for agriculture because global food demand is set to increase by 50 per cent by 2025. To make matters worse, analysts are predicting lower rainfall over the next twenty years because of the effects of climate change.[50]

But perhaps there's nothing to worry about. Perhaps the world's politicians have everything in hand and are already preparing to switch over to the new energy economy (not to mention an alternative water supply) but they just haven't told us. When it comes to ending our dependence on cheap oil, the one major stumbling block these politicians face is that a more sustainable way of living would mean opposing large corporate interests that want to make as much money as possible from oil while they still can. To maintain short-term profits, every last drop of money must be squeezed from the cheap oil economy. OPEC countries are lobbying governments to oppose anything that might damage the profitability of oil in the short term – such as preparations for a new energy economy. This is from *The End of Oil* again: 'The Saudis . . . have gone so far as to file complaints with the World Trade Organization claiming that European programs to cut $CO_2$ emissions unfairly constrain the Saudi oil trade. "We are against any policy that unfairly discriminates against oil," one top Saudi oil official told me bluntly. "We want to keep oil the fuel of choice."' Given the power corporate interests have in Whitehall, we can be forgiven for being pessimistic about our leaders having the courage to lead us into a more sustainable and peaceful future.

In my view, whether our leaders manage the transition or not will have no impact on the way our lives will have to change in the end. All they can control is how smoothly this transition occurs. When we move over to a new energy economy we will be forced to move away from the ever-expanding economy with its working mindset; we will have to start thinking about our use of energy and listen to a simple, sustainable, common-sense mindset instead. The one bonus of living in a sustainable way is that it will actually give us lives based around living rather than the ones we currently have which are based around overworking and over-consuming.

When the price of oil begins its inevitable rise transportation will increasingly become a luxury few will be able to afford on a daily basis. That doesn't mean we won't be able to afford to use cars or heat our homes, but we will have to start paying a realistic price for our energy use. Where energy is concerned, the two basic factors are supply and demand. With increased prices, demand will hopefully begin to reach more sustainable levels. The electricity meter will probably move out of some dark corner of your home and be put on the wall by your kitchen clock instead so you can keep an eye on what you're spending. The car will be taken out only a few times a month on special occasions. To save money, people will begin to think more about energy efficiency and adopt a more responsible attitude towards an issue we have been complacent about for far too long. There are even suggestions that in the future taxation could move away from your income and become entirely based on your use of energy instead. Whichever way you look at it, things are set to radically change.

This new world isn't something to fear, providing we force our government to take action to prepare for it now. But that involves hard choices the large energy companies won't like. Britain is unusual for having nuclear energy in private hands, which is the primary reason why we should be highly suspicious of it as the answer to the situation we face. Any expert will tell you that nuclear power is absurdly expensive. In every country where it is used extensively it has massive public subsidies. According to one energy expert I spoke to, nuclear is at best 'a sticking plaster on the broken leg of our energy crisis'. It does have one thing going for it in the eyes of private industry though: it's very profitable, whereas other renewable options are less so. But the government has to start thinking beyond the needs of shareholders.

We do have one energy resource we can rely on, one we can guarantee will always be there, come what may, twelve months, six years, eighty years from now, and it's wind. Some people don't like the idea of having wind farms all around our coastline or in picturesque parts of the country, but they simply have not grasped the seriousness of our predicament, or they think they will be dead when disaster strikes so they don't care. Once you've bought wind turbines and the infrastructure they require, your only costs are maintenance. You don't have to decommission a wind turbine, or worry about terrorists flying planes into them to cause a national catastrophe.

The biggest danger nuclear power poses to our future energy security is the effect putting so much public faith in it will have on our renewable energy options. People in the City will not invest substantial amounts of money in any alternative energy resource unless the government safeguards their profits, so all the money the government has for our future energy security will go to nuclear if that is the choice they make. Wind and other renewable resources desperately need that subsidy in order to develop because while we still have relatively cheap oil they will never be competitive. As the oil crisis bites they will become so, but only if they are already in place. Any large-scale transition from one energy resource to another will be hugely difficult to perform; one without long-term planning would spell economic and political disaster. If, however, the transition to wind was given the funding and time it required we could combine the extensive use of wind power with a smaller amount of LNG and then we would be far more self-sufficient than we are today, which would make us more secure and less reliant on countries like Russia and Iran for our energy. If you accept that we have no choice but to change the way we live then you have to have an alternative energy source that is effective but, above all, secure. There's no use lurching from one energy crisis to another when we can solve the problem once and for all now. We have our own wind, and it's free. We don't have, or are rapidly running out of, our own oil and gas.

Perhaps the biggest fear when it comes to living sustainably, though, is the notion that we will be forced to regress into a black-and-white world where rationing blights our daily lives. The truth will be the opposite. Everything will improve if our attitude to energy begins to change. We will not be staring at an apocalyptic vision if we have the courage to win the energy battle by doing what is necessary now and stop allowing ourselves to be hamstrung by a fear of change and the desire of those with stocks-and-shares portfolios to stick with the status quo. If transportation costs skyrocket and you can't get around the country as freely as you used to, then the 'break-up' of family life may start to reverse as families relocate nearer to each other than they are today in order to see each other more easily. The social benefits of that are incalculable. Massive out-of-town shopping malls and supermarkets will find it hard to survive if the costs of their products increase and people begin to tighten their belts. Enormous corporations rely on the low production costs of overseas goods to drive prices down and eliminate any opposition that can't compete with the sheer scale of their buying power. If we begin to source more locally produced food and clothes, because they'll be cheaper than foreign imports on account of not having to be moved around the globe to get here, not only will local entrepreneurs begin to thrive but our high streets will probably start to shed their ubiquitous branding and become more individual too. And in that kind of environment people will have a much more realistic chance of changing the way they work. People will become far more entrepreneurial. We might even become a nation of shopkeepers again. If the big corporations begin to collapse, our economy won't fall apart even if the stock market does because people will fill the gaps with their own small-scale, high-quality operations. It's still business, but it's the kind of business that builds communities and retains profits in the local area.

Even in our current economic situation, my small family has found that an 'idle' life based on two part-time wages provides enough money to live on very comfortably if you don't have debt and you don't gorge yourself on buying things you don't need. We don't wear rags, eat lentils, forgo deodorant or act all smug and self-satisfied, we just buy things we can afford instead of things we can't (see Appendix: The Seven Steps to the Idle Life for more information). But there is no blueprint or 'expert' who can tell you how things will have to change for you and your family. You'll have to work out how you can live in a different way by looking at your own circumstances and thinking about it yourself. Of course, some people's jobs are so badly paid that they can barely survive on two full-time salaries let alone one, but that is something the government needs to sort out with their friends in the boardrooms and tax havens of the world rather than evidence of the supposed impracticality of living in a more sustainable way.

When I was young I listened to stories from my grand-parents and great uncles and aunts about the sacrifices their generation was prepared to make during the wars to safeguard their children's future. Sacrifice isn't a word you hear very often today. As I write this, my eighteen-month-old son Wilf is sitting on the other side of our kitchen table gradually falling asleep while eating his lunch. He's just starting to drink out of a normal cup and I'm very,

very excited about that. Life to him is all about enquiry and wonder. He has no conception of the state of the world he lives in but he trusts Rachel and me to look out for him and protect him. He's not even aware that he expects that of us. He takes it for granted, and so he should. His generation should also be able to take for granted that we will look after this country for them. It's time we took the responsibility our grandparents and great-grandparents were prepared to take for us in the battle we are facing.

If we don't start thinking about our way of life soon our children will be left in the kind of nightmare we can barely imagine. The good news, if you can call it that, is that whichever way you look at it we are soon going to be *forced* into living in a more sustainable and self-sufficient way. I don't mean we'll all be living like Richard Briers in *The Good Life*, although that will appeal to some, but as a nation we will all have to pull together to find a new way of life for the future. And it could be a very bright future: a highly advanced technological country running on clean, renewable energy where family and community ties are gradually being restored and where the economy is based on small-scale businesses that feed their profits back into the communities in which they operate. Now, lots of people will start throwing in practical questions like, 'Who's going to pay for schools and hospitals in this small-scale utopian future?' I don't have the answer to that because I don't know what the future holds. The question for them to answer, though, is what their alternative is, because our current way of life will be far from viable. If we're going to get the opportunity to reorganize things then let's start designing the future we want now rather than allowing our fear to push us into the unknown completely unprepared.

It would certainly make sense to set up a few test-case 'future communities' with the kinds of parameters imposed on them we could expect in an expensive energy future. We could try to model what the future is likely to hold in terms of energy supplies and pricing, and ban large corporations so that new small-business initiatives could grow and give us some idea of how viable part-time, energy-conscious working communities could be. I'm certain there would be no shortage of volunteers to go and live in a place with values like those. If these communities flourished we could roll out more, gradually, in time for our energy transition. If they didn't work we'd have time to go back to the drawing board and come up with some different ideas.

None of this changes the global implications of an energy crisis, but you can only change the way you live and hope others follow your example. If we were seen to be doing something radical, others would take notice. After all, Britain started the world off on the road of shareholders and an ever-expanding economy with the Industrial Revolution so perhaps it's also our responsibility to lead the world out of this mess. It would be better to assume that role in the world than the one we currently hold. Success would inspire others, and who knows where that could lead.

If things do become more decentralized then power will have to become decentralized in many ways too. To make that happen we will need to find a political party committed to giving power away the moment it gets into office, and that, we have to accept, is not hugely likely. To persuade our leaders that they need to take a different approach to the way government and this country is politically organized will require the kind of sea-change in political opinion that eradicated slavery in the days of Empire, and apartheid in 1990s South Africa. The way we waste our time and energy today will one day be viewed with as much disdain. It won't be easy, and it will require a great deal of public protest and unprecedented demonstrations of public support if it is to have any hope of success. The simple fact is that we could be talking about preparing for a different way of life in thirty years' time. Every person in any position of political or corporate power is over fifty, so we have to persuade them to act against their own interests, whether it's their company's share price or the lifespan of their careers, for the sake of a future they will probably not live to see. Clearly it will take something extraordinary for that to occur.

Worryingly, as we have seen, our civil liberties are now in a perilous state, giving us less and less control over the political process and removing our ability to question or complain without fear of arrest. If the energy crisis does take hold of the world in the way Jim the energy expert, Paul Roberts, author of *The End of Oil*, and many other experts and amateurs I've spoken to seem to think, then we will have least control over our lives at a time when we'll be most in need of it.

Of course I'm no expert. One thing is certain, though: a period of economic instability is not very far off. The stock market cannot keep rising, as it has historically, if our cheap energy supplies begin to drain away, and then trusting one's long-term financial security to the stock exchange will not make economic sense. Those over forty who still believe in retirement on account of the amount of money they have already saved in pension plans will have to find somewhere else to invest their money, but that will involve a fight with the government too. It's impossible to believe that the wholesale withdrawal of the money currently in the nation's pension funds will not impact severely on the profitability of the stock market, and the government simply won't allow that to happen. If we could unshackle ourselves from the stock exchange, however, we would be less dependent on a financial system that fails us and tears our communities apart.

If the prices of daily goods begin to rise because of increased transportation costs and a stock market fall causes the economy to falter as we all start tightening our belts, then we'll be in a situation called 'stagflation' where costs and unemployment rise while incomes fall. At that point debt will become the biggest problem in all our lives. Bankruptcies will snowball and business leaders will start to lobby the government to tighten restrictions as more and more people decide that in a future of no cheap energy and decentralized power things like credit ratings – and all other aspects of our global economic structure, like insurance – seem rather pointless, and they default on all their loans. If faith in our economic system falls away to any large degree then life is likely to get rather unstable.

If things were to get that unstable then civil rights might well suddenly become far more valuable than they seem to be to us today. Those in the future who recall Maya Evans being arrested for reading out the names of dead soldiers by the Cenotaph may also recall the words of Winston Churchill with horror: 'If you will not fight for the right when you can easily win without bloodshed, if you will not fight when your victory will be sure and not so costly, you may come to the moment when you will have to fight with all the odds against you and only a precarious chance for survival. There may be a worse case. You may have to fight when there is no chance of victory, because it is better to perish than to live as slaves.'[51] After all, if the government is capable of going to war without telling its population the truth, what other decisions might it make 'for our own good' in a time of real crisis? In a country in the grip of that scenario, having to carry an ID card may begin to feel a little more oppressive than it would today. The police would certainly want to use every form of control in their armoury to maintain public order, even if the public want them to do the opposite. All of a sudden a constitution to safeguard basic principles of freedom of expression, protest, privacy, and no detention without trial becomes something we all actually need to rely on again, for the first time since 1215. We certainly owe it to future generations, who may rely on these civil liberties, not to allow those in power to take them from us today. The fact that we are in a position to have high standards at all makes us even more obliged not to allow them to be arbitrarily removed.

The people in power and the members of the CBI stalking the corridors in Whitehall will laugh heartily at this and say how preposterous it is to suggest there will be such a crisis and how 'unrealistic' it is to live in such a radical (i.e. fulfilling) way. They'll be quite content to carry on as they are, like King Canute commanding the tide not to come in. But it isn't written in stone that things have to be the way they are. There is no law of humanity that says our current way of life is the only way of doing things. Just because no-one else has had the time to come up with any workable alternatives doesn't mean they don't exist.

But what do I know? Perhaps this is pure fantasy. Perhaps I'm wrong, all the research I've done is nonsense and all the people I've met are just lunatics on the fringes of society. Perhaps the reason their voices are not being recorded is because they don't know what they are talking about. The energy crisis doesn't exist and everything will actually be fine as long as we all keep our heads down and keep doing what we're told. Maybe there's nothing to fear if we're happy to play along and be spoon-fed, and we don't do anything that might rock the great economic boat. Well, all I can say is, why don't you look into these subjects yourself and make up your own mind?

This journey has simply been my attempt to make sense of the country I see around me with my own eyes rather than the one the adverts, the politicians and the media keep telling us all is out there. The conclusions I've drawn are childlike in their simplicity, but that doesn't make them any less true. We do not live in a very sensible way. It isn't sustainable, it causes wars, it means we don't get to see our children grow up, and it doesn't even seem to make us very happy. The reason we all seem to live in this way, regardless of those depressing facts, is because our sense of fear is wildly out of proportion to the threats we actually face, and this false fear takes our attention away from the things we really *should* be afraid of. Like the fact that anyone who actively questions this way of life is portrayed as a workshy lunatic, or a violent criminal, and faces arrest merely for having the temerity to complain, when in reality these people are doing the most to uphold what this country is supposed to stand for. We are now facing a crisis in the near future that will undermine the very edifice we all seem to be so miserable living on, and are seemingly so powerless to change, and that, to my mind, is the kind of opportunity you can only dream of.

In the year since I started writing this book I lost count of the number of times I got off the train at Charing Cross station, skirted around the bottom of Trafalgar Square and made my way down Whitehall to Parliament Square. As that year drew to a close the scaffolding that had surrounded Nelson's Column for much of that time came down, leaving a brighter, cleaner statue for the tourists to admire. Nelson is someone we could certainly all learn from today. During the celebrations marking the two hundredth anniversary of the battle of Trafalgar, I read that Nelson didn't beat the French because he had better men, better ships or better guns; he prevailed because the French were too afraid of losing to do what was necessary to win. Nelson had no such qualms. He knew what had to be done to achieve victory and he had the courage to do it with conviction. Two centuries later the people of Britain are still proud of the actions he took with his men.

We are faced with a similar dilemma in the way we live today. What is the stronger sense within us? Is it our fear of the failure that may result from change or our conviction to do what is necessary to win? After meeting a few of the people taking a stand all over Britain, the patriot inside me tells me this nation has the courage to do what is required, but I have little faith in the willingness of those who lead us to share that conviction if business interests see the necessary change as a threat to their power and influence.

So it will come down to the people of this country changing things for themselves, and the question then becomes, do we have the stomach for the fight? Especially in a time when civil liberties have been eroded to an unprecedented level. Whether or not you feel that is a fight for you will depend on whether the country I found is the one you see with your eyes. Critics may argue that I'm accusing others of preaching fear to push an agenda, only to do the same thing myself. The difference, I would argue, is that my argument and my evidence rely on how life in Britain seems to be to everyone who lives here. Don't take my word for it, trust your own judgment. How do things seem to be going for you? Are you in control of your time? Are you happy with the amount of time you get to spend with your kids? Even if you're financially well off, are you confident your children will be? Do you value freedom of speech? Are you in more debt than you can afford? Do you roll your eyes every time a politician is interviewed on TV? Do your energy bills keep rising? Do you think Britain's once high standards seem to have slipped? Is your local hospital/school/ swimming pool/environment/town centre/university/ playground under threat because of some government or private initiative that doesn't make any sense to your local community? Does someone getting arrested for reading out dead soldiers' names at the Cenotaph alarm you? Do you want a government that is prepared to go to war on an illegal basis to know every detail about your life through a microchip in a plastic card? Does your job make you feel so sick and bored that you drink yourself into a coma sometimes just to escape? Is four weeks off out of fifty-two a good enough return for the short amount of time you have to savour being alive? Do you think we are steering the right course for the people of Britain's future? Do you think the interests of our communities and the economy are the same thing?

You could always start by coming down to Downing Street or Parliament Square next Sunday for afternoon tea to let our leaders know what really matters to you. You won't be the only one asking these kinds of questions if you do. And don't worry about getting arrested. My middle-class force field seems to be working overtime; I can't seem to get nicked however hard I try. So just stick close to me. I'll be the idiot dressed in white who's trying to organize a game of cricket.

# Epilogue

It's impossible for me to write about Britain and not mention two of our greatest writers: George Orwell, who wrote about Britain in *Why I Write* in 1946, and Gavin Hills, who wrote about Britain forty-nine years later in *The Face*. I'm convinced that Gavin would have proved himself to be Orwell's heir, if only he hadn't run out of time.

In 1946, Orwell wrote:

We are a nation of flower-lovers, but also a nation of stamp collectors, pigeon-fanciers, amateur carpenters, coupon snippers, darts-players, crossword puzzle fans. All the culture that is most truly native centres round things which even when they are communal are not official – the pub, the football match, the back garden, the fireside and the 'nice cup of tea'. The liberty of the individual is still believed in, almost as in the nineteenth century. But this has nothing to do with economic liberty, the right to exploit others for profit. It is the liberty to have a home of your own, to do what you like in your spare time, to choose your own amusements instead of having them chosen for you from above . . .

Nearly half a century later, Gavin's sentiments remained much the same:

It's the simple things we want, the same things people have wanted for years: social and economic justice; not having to worry if you're sick, old or down on your luck; a roof over your head; a good education for all; peace; a right to diversity, fun and freedom. We want this for our-selves, for our country and for our world. Simple desires yet hideously complex to achieve. We can start by trying to claim our country, and find the power that enables us to find the answers to make changes for the better. The alter-native is increasing alienation and descent into a disparate land of paranoid people. When we don't give a toss about our fellow countrymen, we don't give a toss when hospitals get closed, when gangs rob cabbies, when Nazis bash Pakis, or when the rights of thousands are dismissed as expendable. The simple realization that most of us will never make enough money to do anything other than skin up and buy trainers should be enough to force us to dream of a golden future. One day, this nation will be ours. Let's think what we want, then see what we get. We are not alone, we are many.

We are Robin Hood, Twiglets, Linford Christie, King Arthur, KLF, William Blake, Echobelly, Marmite, Oasis,

George Orwell, Irn-Bru, Johnny Rotten, Boudicca and Vimto. We are joy-riders, hooligans, dealers and drunks. We are those who struggle to get a life and those who enjoy themselves despite. We've glimpsed Jerusalem, squinting through half-closed eyes, scrambling messily on a Sunday morn. We must wake from our fantasies, revive our visions and stake a claim on the future. Then ours shall be a golden nation. A land of real hope and glory. Well, it would be a laugh anyway.[52]

Sadly for us, George Orwell and Gavin Hills are no longer with us, and however relevant their ideas and opinions may seem today the government is right about one thing: the world and the country we are now living in has changed.

Whether Britain, or Albion for that matter, is a place for the protest exclusion zone outlined in the Serious and Organised Crime and Police Act; a place for ID cards; a place where an eighty-two-year-old can be arrested for saying 'Rubbish' at a party conference; a place where casinos get built on flood plains; a place where every town looks the same; a place where an eleven-year-old girl can have her bike searched because of a 'terrorist threat'; or a place where you can be arrested for reading out the names of soldiers who have died in a war – this is now up to those of us living in Britain today.

Which leaves two simple questions. Does Britain mean anything today? And if it does, what are you prepared to do to protect it?

As far as my journey is concerned, I think the people closest to me think I lost the plot slightly. As it happens, I think I lost the plot too, but as plots go it wasn't a difficult one to lose. I discovered a much better plot than the old one, anyway. I'd rather be part of a plot where people actually do what they believe in than talk in loud voices and in the columns of newspapers to make themselves feel clever. I'd rather be part of a plot where King Arthur actually exists, fighting in his own way, laughing at himself and bravely standing up against the tyranny he sees threatening his land, this land of Albion. I'd rather be part of a plot where a sense of the wonder of being alive drives you to savour every second of your life rather than one where overwork and over-consumption force us to sell so much of our time, the only thing of true value we all have. I'd rather be part of a plot that's based on the truth of human thought and love rather than business ethics and fear.

I certainly found snatches of Albion among the brave and passionate people fighting to ensure there is some corner of this country that remains forever England, and I've certainly seen a glimpse of it in our future. It's time we all considered losing the plot, this plot in which we are all trapped but which none of us chose, if this country is ever to mean something of value again.

# Appendix

## The Seven Steps to the Idle Life
(taken from *Idler 35: The War on Work Issue*, Spring 2005)

As a dedicated man of the sloth I am always promoting the merits of an Idler life to anyone who will listen. But whether it's in the pub, on late-night radio phone-ins or on dodgy cable TV shows, the response is always the same: 'Well, it's all right for you to be an Idler, but the rest of us can't afford it. Some of us have to work for a living.' This argument will resonate with some, but it's important to point out that the *Idler* magazine isn't a network of smug, independently wealthy parasites. There's nothing unusual about any of us, but we all do have one thing in common: at some time or other, we've all taken a leap into the unknown to pursue a different kind of life. So if you can't face spending another day doing a pointless job you hate; if you loathe the fact that you only get four weeks a year actually to 'live' and spend the other forty-eight staring at a clock wishing your life away; if you want a different, more idle life and you don't know how to get one, or don't think you can afford one, here's a seven-step guide.

## Step One – Give Up Ever Wanting to be Rich

In the words of that apostle of the amateur creed, poet/painter/musician Billy Childish, 'If they've got what you want then they've got you.' So if you can stop wanting what they've got then you've cracked the hardest part of becoming an Idler and a life of freedom is yours for the taking. Not wanting to be rich is the single most immediate and liberating act you will ever make in your life. Of course, some Idlers become rich accidentally as a result of following their natural instincts, but being rich is never their goal, just a stone that gets into their shoe somewhere along the journey.

## Step Two – Rid Yourself of Debt

Mortgage, literally translated, means 'death grip' – such is the patronizing and bloated nature of the lender/borrower relationship. But western society is built on foundations of overwork and over-consumption so a life without debt is becoming increasingly difficult to attain. The mortgage is probably the only kind of debt we can no longer live without and still remain self-sufficient, but all other kinds of debt are completely avoidable.

The cycle of debt is what traps most people in a job and a life they hate. The harder they work the more miserable and stressed they become.

So they go to the shops at the weekend and buy themselves something nice because they've had a tough week. Even if they don't have enough money they can still buy whatever they want with a criminally usurious credit or store card. But when their statement appears they get that gnawing feeling of dread in the middle of their stomachs as they realize the mountain their debt has become. So they work even harder. They take all the overtime they can get to pay for everything they've bought to make them feel less stressed, which makes them more miserable. They work so hard, in fact, that the rest of the time they're totally exhausted. They're either arguing with the person they love, becoming strangers to their children or drowning their sorrows in the pub. And by this point, because they're in so much debt, they couldn't live a different life even if they wanted to. Those spiralling monthly payments have trapped them in a crap job and they have a house that's full of crap they don't need.

Ridding yourself of debt will give you the opportunity to live a different kind of life, but it can take time, years even, to clear. Bear in mind, though, that even if it takes you ten years it's a much more sensible thing to pursue than a career.

## Step Three – Don't Buy Useless Crap You Don't Need

Everyone buys useless crap they don't need and won't use to compensate for the misery of their forty-eight-week-a-year job that destroys their soul and dignity. Take responsibility for your own happiness and stop trying to fill the hole in your life with grot. This doesn't entail wearing rags, growing a beard and patronizing anyone who wears Nike trainers. Just bear in mind that the more you buy, the more you'll have to work to pay for it. Remember, the rule is, no credit. If you can't afford it, you can't have it.

## Step Four – Ditch Your Pension

The pension is one of society's safety nets that doesn't actually make anyone feel safe. 'Work hard, be miserable now and save just enough money so you can stay alive in penury when you're old and grey,' say those who advocate pensions. Er, no thanks. But this is the fate that awaits those of us who've helped make the UK the fourth largest economy in the world. Pensions aren't safe. Invest your money in yourself and your own happiness now instead of in a pension plan that will probably vanish some time in the future.

Pensions are also the justification for corporate greed. Chief executives bleat about 'the needs of shareholders' to warrant their savage pursuit of a rising share value. Nothing is allowed to get in the way of increasing a company's share price, even at the cost of decimating any sense of community in our towns and villages across the country. Gross, unnecessary warehouse-style shopping malls are built, village banks are closed and arms are sold to dictators. So if you want to do your bit for the planet, remove any money you have in the stock exchange. This simple act will improve your life and, indirectly, the lives of other Idlers all over the world.

## Step Five – Work Part-time

Once you've given up wanting to be rich, you've got yourself out of debt and you've stopped buying useless crap you don't need, you'll need much less money to live on than before. So now you can quit your full-time job and get a part-time one instead.

Part-time jobs are becoming more and more popular

with businesses because they remove a company's legal obligation to give you the benefits associated with full-time work – sick pay and so on. But that's OK because the happier you are the healthier you are, and the less you work the happier you will become, so you won't need these so-called benefits.

At this point, as you while away the hours reading and sunbathing in the park, you may find yourself feeling guilty that you don't have a full-time job. This is hardly surprising. Since primary school you have been brain-washed into thinking that hard work is virtuous. Well, it bloody well isn't. As the late Jeffrey Bernard once said, 'If there was anything virtuous about hard work the Duke of Westminster would dig his own fucking garden, wouldn't he?' Ignore the guilt, enjoy your new spare time and have a lie-in. If you start feeling that you're no longer a pro-ductive member of society then log on to the *Idler* chat board at www.idler.co.uk/forum and we'll all talk you out of your panic attack.

If going part-time is a daunting prospect then work four days a week to start with and gradually wean yourself off your addiction to work. A three day-a-week job is popular with many Idlers now; four days off, three days on is a far more civilized way of living than the criminal two days off, five days on that our greedy western world depends on.

### Step Six – Do That Thing You've Always Dreamt of Doing

Once you've worked through the guilt of no longer being 'a productive member of society' (i.e. you've stopped working and consuming more than you need in order to be happy), you'll find time on your hands to pursue the things you've always wanted to do. Far from being an unrealistic goal, this is precisely where your future security lies.

The Idler's ultimate goal is to earn a living doing something so enjoyable that it can scarcely be called work at all. And when the way you earn a living is something you love doing, the idea of retirement becomes ludicrous, so you won't need a pension either. It will take time, but eventually you will work out how to earn money doing whatever it is you want to do with your life. Later, you will earn enough to cut down the hours of your part-time job until eventually you'll be able to quit the world of the crap job completely.

This is the Idler's life, seeking happiness, not success, and wisdom rather than cleverness. As *Idler* subscriber and TV supremo John Lloyd put it, 'People are obsessed with cleverness when it is wisdom that counts, and anyone can be wise.' With wisdom comes the acceptance of truth, personal happiness and the creative, self-directed life so many of us crave.

## Step Seven – Take the Test

Read this passage from *Wind, Sand and Stars* by Antoine de Saint-Exupéry. If you can read it without shuddering then you've made it. If you can't, there's still time. There's always time.

> Old bureaucrat, my companion here present, no man ever opened an escape route for you, and you are not to blame. You built peace for yourself by blocking up every chink of

light, as termites do. You rolled yourself into your ball of bourgeois security, your routines, the stifling rituals of your provincial existence; you built your humble rampart against winds, tides and stars. You have no wish to ponder great questions; you had enough trouble suppressing awareness of your human condition. You do not dwell on a wandering planet, you ask yourself no unanswerable questions . . .

No man ever grasped you by the shoulder while there was still time. Now the clay that formed you has dried and hardened, and no man could now awaken in you the dormant musician, the poet or the astronomer who perhaps once dwelt within you.

# Acknowledgements

My journey into the heart of Albion wouldn't have lasted very long without the time and guidance of many kind and generous people. First and foremost Mark Barrett, whose enthusiasm and passion for civil and community rights puts most of us to shame. If I hadn't stumbled into such an eye-opening friendship with Mark you simply wouldn't have this book in your hands.

Prasanth Visweswaran always brought a vast amount of fun and humour to every nerve-racking situation we found ourselves in, and it was his idea that our democracy was the gold standard to which other nations aspired that pushed me into the subject of reclaiming patriotism from the bigots who've done so much to tarnish our sense of national pride.

The Parliament Square picnics every Sunday gave me a base where all sorts of connections were made. I met a huge number of selfless and passionate people there, all of whose stories deserve to be told. It is perhaps unfair to mention some and not others, but these are the people I saw most regularly and who made most of an impression on me: Dave and Esther, Danny, Sian (aka Mary Poppins), Matthew, Rikki (the tireless contributor to Indymedia), Marianne the Texan (who was in Richard Linklater's film *Slacker* – now how cool is that?), Mark Kemp, Sam and Alex (who came up with the idea of holding a slumber party on Parliament Square on the first anniversary of SOCPA and spent the night in sleeping bags and Wee Willie Winkie hats because 'Democracy Is Sleeping'), Jeff the anarchist (whose encyclopaedic knowledge of all things authoritarian is something to behold), Mark, Ed, Jamie, John Mark, Katie and Alan (who came along for the cricket match) and Steve (also there that day, who was violently arrested a few days later for holding a banner outside Downing Street bearing the Orwell quote, 'In a time of universal deceit telling the truth is a revolutionary act'). I was also full of admiration for Barbara, whom I never met properly but who, at the time of writing, has the record for the most number of SOCPA arrests. And then of course there's Brian Haw, who will no doubt take a few moments away from his vigil to come and punch me in the face if he ever decides to read this book.

John Nicholson will one day get the credit he deserves for a lifetime spent researching the largely ignored parts of our history. Why no-one pays him vast sums of money just to get him to talk about some of our unrecorded history and film him doing it so we can all listen in is a mystery to me.

I'd also like to thank Dorothy Skrytek, Paula Fentiman,

Mick and Adam in Derby; Honor Gibbs, for putting me on to Ian Nairn; the readers of the *Idler*, who actually wrote the *Crap Towns* books; Sergeant Gary Brown in Spilsby; Stuart Craft; Neil Goodwin, aka Charlie Chaplin; Billy Childish; Jim the energy man; Gareth and Jen at Liberty; and all the other people whose names I have changed or omitted because they felt telling the truth about their jobs might put their livelihoods at risk.

Over the last year I've had lots of help and encouragement from my *Idler* pals, Tom Hodgkinson, Gavin Pretor-Pinney and Clare Pollard. And from friends and family: Colin Charde, Henry Littlechild, Ben Hassett, Kevin Parr, Hugh Breton, Ian Vince, my parents, stepparents, Granny, and brothers Gareth, Ben, Nick, Richard and Kit. I'd like to say a special thank you to my mate and agent Simon Benham who actually gave me the idea for this book in the first place, and to John Lloyd and Chris Yates – my most philosophically astute friends – for so many uplifting and inspiring conversations.

At Bantam Press, my editor, Brenda Kimber, never ran out of patience with me even when she discovered that the book she had persuaded Transworld to pay for would not be forthcoming and I handed in this one instead. I also want to mention Jonny Mendelsson who did such a great job with the cover and Daniel Balado the copy editor, who corrected my numerous grammatical mistakes.

Finally, I would like to thank Rachel for her patience, support, kindness and good humour. It's hard living in a tiny flat with someone trying to write a book on the kitchen table, especially with a toddler charging about. Wilf will be very glad that the ordeal is over too, having registered his disgust over the last twelve months by punching my computer and stuffing coins into it whenever my back was turned. But it could have been worse for them both, I suppose. I could have decided to do something *really* stupid, like write a book about driving across England in a milkfloat with my friend Ian. Now that really *would* be an adventure. If I could get Prasanth to come with us and film it we could call it *Three Men in a Float* . . .

# Notes

1. 'While allowing directors to give consideration to the interests of others, [the law] compel[s] them to find some reasonable relationship to the long-term interests of shareholders when so doing.' American Bar Association, Committee on Corporate Laws, 'Other Constituencies' Statutes: Potential for Confusion', *The Business Lawyer* 45 (1990): 2261, as cited in G. Smith, 'The Shareholder Primacy Norm', *The Journal of Corporation Law*, Volume 23, Number 2, Winter 1998.
2. 'A corporation is the property of its stockholders . . . Its interests are the interests of its stockholders. Now, beyond that, should it spend the stockholders' money for purposes which it regards as socially responsible but which it cannot connect to its bottom line? The answer I would say is no.' From Joel Bakan, *The Corporation* (Free Press, 2004), p. 34.

3. 'If I walk from Waterloo station across the river to the palace with "Bollocks to Blair" on my lapel, I will be caught by this statutory instrument. The whole thing is utterly absurd, and until the Government tell us what they mean by "demonstration", which is not defined in the Act or in the statutory instrument, they must face the ridicule that they richly deserve . . .'
www.publications.parliament.uk/pa/cm20050/
cmstand/deleg2/st051012/51012s01.htm
4. *Hansard*, 3 November 2004, column 386.
www.publications.parliament.uk/pa/cm200304/
cmhansrd/vo041103/debtext/41103-27.htm#41103-27spnew10
5. *Evening Standard*, 24 November 2004.
6. 1 July 2005, www.news.bbc.co.uk/1/hi/england/london/4640007.stm
7. 17 June 2005, www.guardian.co.uk/humanrights/story/0,,1508594,00.html
8. 23 July 2005, www.news.bbc.co.uk/1/hi/england/london/4710019.stm
9. *Hansard*, 8 December 2005, column 995.
www.publications.parliament.uk/pa/cm200506/
cmhansrd/cm051208/debtext/51208-06.htm#51208-06spnew4
10. CNN, 8 January 2003. www.edition.cnn.com/2003/WORLD/europe/01/08/uk.ricin0720/index.html
11. From Adam Curtis, *The Power of Nightmares*, BBC 2, 18 January 2004
12. *Horizon*, BBC 2, 13 July 2006.
13. Office of National Statistics. Cancer, suicide, flu and asthma deaths from 2000, MRSA deaths from 2003.

14. 18 March 2001, www.news.bbc.co.uk/1/hi/uk/ 1227441.stm

15. A survey carried out by the *Guardian* and Reward Technology Forum found that the salaries of directors of Britain's FTSE 100 companies rose by an average of 28 per cent, or 25.5 per cent above inflation, in the 2005 financial year. Average earnings rose by 3.7 per cent, or 1.2 per cent above inflation, for the same period.

16. In July 2006, the Healthcare Commission found that at least forty-one patients died in Stoke Mandeville Hospital because the hospital's chief executives were more concerned with waiting-list targets than with keeping the hospital clean. Inspectors found 'dirty wards, dirty toilets and commodes, bedding and equipment lying on floors, faeces on bed rails, pubic hair in baths, mould and cobwebs in showers'. Anna Walker, the commission's chief executive, said there had been 'serious failings on the part of senior managers who did not follow advice on stopping the spread of [superbug] infection', and that the hospital trust's board 'mistakenly prioritised other objectives such as the achievement of government targets, the control of finances and the reconfiguration of services'.

17. In November 2006 the homeless charity Shelter published the findings of a report in which they found that 1.6 million children in Britain are living in 'Bad Housing': homes that are unfit, overcrowded or temporary accommodation. They discovered that children living in 'Bad Housing' are almost twice as

likely as other children to leave school with no
GCSEs, twice as likely to have been excluded from
school, suffer poor health and be persistently bullied.
They are five times as likely to have nowhere quiet to
do homework, and more likely than other children
to run away from home at least once in their lifetime.

18. 1 May 2001, www.guardian.co.uk/mayday/story/
0,7369,481222,00.html
19. 2 May 2001, www.guardian.co.uk/comment/story/
0,,481636,00.html
20. *Hansard*, 19 May 2004, column 242WH.
www.publications.parliament.uk/pa/cm200304/
cmhansrd/vo040519/halltext/40519h01.htm#40519
h01spnew1
21. *Hansard*, 7 February 2005 (Sir Patrick Cormack
column 1300, Glenda Jackson column 1301).
www.publications.parliament.uk/pa/cm200405/
cmhansrd/vo050207/debtext/50207-41.htm#50207-
41spnew0
22. Sixty serious injuries in 2004 (and 2006) as opposed
to zero serious injuries in 2004, Office of National
Statistics.
23. 7 April 2002, www.number-10.gov.uk/output/
Page1712.asp
24. Reprinted in *Idler* 25, Winter 1999.
25. A medieval peasant worked fewer hours than the
average American does today (www.timeday.org/).
26. *Idler* 35, *War on Work*, May 2005.
27. www.pm.gov.uk/output/Page4644.asp
28. From ASBO watch at www.statewatch.org
29. 11 September 1996.

30. Joseph Rowntree Foundation report, 'Parenting and children's resilience in disadvantaged communities', by Peter Seaman, Katrina Turner, Malcolm Hill, Anne Stafford and Moira Walker.
www.jrf.org.uk/knowledge/findings/socialpolicy/0096.asp

31. Dr Phoenix, 'Youth justice: tough on punishment, soft on the causes of crime', Bath University, research funded by the Economic and Social Research Council.
www.bath.ac.uk/news/articles/releases/youthjustice300306.html

32. *Oxford Student*, February 2004.
www.oxfordstudent.com/ht2004wk6/Feature/the other oxford

33. *Idler* 25, *Man's Ruin*, Winter 1999.

34. Arthur Pendragon and Christopher James Stone, *The Trials of Arthur – The Life and Times of a Modern-Day King* (Element, 2003).

35. B. Bryant and M. Denton-Thompson, *Twyford Down: Roads, Campaigning and Environmental Law* (E&FN Spon, 1996).

36. *TLS*, 21 February 1997.
www.monbiot.com/archives/1997/02/21/multi-issue-politics/

37. 'Those aged over 50 now have accumulated assets estimated at £500bn. They own four-fifths of the nation's wealth.' *Guardian Unlimited*, 21 May 2006.

38. 'In the shadow of Winston Churchill's statue opposite the House of Commons, a rather odd ritual has developed on Sunday afternoons. A small group of people – mostly young and dressed outlandishly –

hold a tea party on the grass of Parliament Square. A woman looking very much like Mary Poppins passes plates of frosted cakes and cookies, while other members of the party flourish blank placards or, as they did on the afternoon I was there, attempt a game of cricket.' Henry Porter, *Vanity Fair*, July 2006.

39. In order to understand what a subjective recklessness test is, you first need to know what objective reckless-ness is. Here are Gareth's definitions of both: 'Objective recklessness' is when a person does not give his mind to what is likely to happen, although a reasonable person would realize that some harm would follow from his act. If a person does something which is harmful without giving his mind to the consequences, and a reasonable person would have realized it would cause harm, that is 'objective recklessness'. 'Subjective recklessness' is where a person realizes the consequences of his act yet goes on to carry out that act, although he may not intend that those consequences follow.

40. www.liberty-human-rights.org.uk/publications/pdfs/casualty-of-war-final.pdf

41. *Observer*, 6 August 2006. www.guardian.co.uk/idcards/story/0,,1838364,00.html

42. www.strategy.gov.uk/downloads/su/privacy/papers/perri6.pdf

43. Noam Chomsky, *Imperial Ambitions* (Penguin, 2005), p. 103.

44. From Robert Pape, *Dying to Win: Why Suicide*

*Terrorists Do It.* http://observer.guardian.co.uk/
comment/story/0,,1838199,00.html

45. 'By the end of the next Parliament every parent with
children in primary school will be offered the
guarantee of affordable school-based childcare from 8
to 6, from breakfast clubs in the morning to after-
school clubs in the evening – and not just during term
time but all the year round.' Tony Blair, 10 November
2004. www.pm.gov.uk/output/Page6561.asp

46. www.appc.org.uk/homepage.html

47. In November 2006 it emerged that the Labour Party
were £35.5 million in the red.

48. 25 June 2004, www.guardian.co.uk/comment/story/
0,,1246893,00.html

49. 'Without fanfare, the White House Office of Science
and Technology Policy (OSTP) rolled out the
National Space Policy on October 6 [2006] . . . the
Bush policy supports use of space nuclear power
systems to "enable or significantly enhance space
exploration or operational capabilities". The document adds that utilization of nuclear power systems
"shall be consistent with U.S. National and homeland
security, and foreign policy interests, and take into
account the potential risks" . . . the Bush space policy
is designed to "ensure that space capabilities are available in time to further U.S. national security, homeland
security, and foreign policy objectives." Moreover, a
fundamental goal of the policy is to "enable unhin-
dered U.S. operations in and through space to defend
our interests there." ' www.usatoday.com/tech/
science/space/2006–10–09-bush-space-policy_x.htm

50. www.wbcsd.ch/plugins/DocSearch/details.
    asp?type=DocDet&ObjectId=MjExMTM
51. Winston Churchill, *The Second World War, Volume 1: The Gathering Storm* (Cassell, 1950).
52. From 'Apathy in the UK', first printed in *The Face* in 1995. The full version is available in *Bliss To Be Alive: The Collected Writings of Gavin Hills*, ed. Sheryl Garratt (Penguin, 2000).